The Republic of Paradise

"A Fairytale of the Heavens
And a Myth of the Gods"

BY KEVIN CAVEY

Back Cover - (Top) An Oil Painting; The three persons of the Trinity and Miriam
looking down on creation, depicted by the fictional George Kuhn.

Back Cover - An Oil Painting; The Mandala showing the Triangles of the Trinity in
the act of creation! It was provided by the fictional Professors Eldron and Kuhn.

Order this book online at www.trafford.com
or email orders@trafford.com

Most Trafford titles are also available at major online book retailers.

Print information available on the last page.

ISBN: 978-1-4251-8781-1 (sc)
ISBN: 978-1-4251-8782-8 (e)

Trafford rev. 11/20/2023

 www.trafford.com

North America & international
toll-free: 844-688-6899 (USA & Canada)
fax: 812 355 4082

A Thought!

Scripture says; the Holy Spirit is oft' referred to as Rauch, the Paraclete or Wisdom, but an entity that was also seen as feminine in nature!

Proverbs 9.1

Wisdom builded her house, she hath hewn out her seven pillars.

Corinthians 1. 12

"The Son is like a single body, which has many parts; it is still one body, even though it is made up of different parts. In the same way, all of us, whether Jews or Gentiles, whether slaves or free, have been baptized into the one body by the same Spirit, and we have all been given the one Spirit to drink."

The Author

The Author was born Dublin 1941. His grandmother on his Father's side came from Ohio. In 1969 he married Anne Marie Kelly a college sweet heart and was blessed with a son name Paul and two daughters Carolyn and Georgina. In 1962 he graduated from The Dublin Hotel School and then worked in Switzerland's Hotel St Gotthard, also his Father's Famed Royal Starlight Hotel in Bray.

He was a competitive swimmer and in 1964 he managed to visit the Hawaiian Islands and by 1965 introduced surfing to his country by forming the island's first surf club. In 1966 he represented Ireland in the World Surfing C/Ships San Diego California. In 1967 both he and his club staged the first Irish Surfing Championships in Tramore Co Waterford. He then became first President of the newly formed Irish Surfing Association. In 1972 he was one of the organisers of the first ever European Surfing C/ships to be held in Lahinch Co Clare.

In 1974 he and his family moved to Canada where he joined Calgary's Four Seasons Hotel, and later Western International, as it was then known. He also studied Architecture in the University of Calgary and later became a Canadian Citizen. In 1981 they returned to Ireland where he studied Philosophy, Theology, Personnel Management and Graphic Art.

Finally he became Catering Officer to Beaumont Hospital Dublin. On retirement in May of 2006 he joined the Shelborne Renaissance Hotel in Dublin. He has now become a second level Surf Instructor and also Skis, Hikes, Oil paints reads Physics, Cosmology and the study of Amphibious Warfare.

Acknowledgements

The production of this book was achieved because of the continuous devotion of my wife Ann, and family who encouraged, and kept the home fires burning while I worked at what often seemed to be a wasteful fantasy!

To close friends who contributed so generously – Fergus Slevin for the cover design, Phil Tricket who kept the IT in order, Lisa Westerman for Computer Graphics and Jurek and Alex Delimata for invaluable advice.

Some places in mind while the book was being written- Baltimore, Barlycove, Crookhaven, and Castle Freak all of which are in West Cork. St Brigid's Church in Clarendon St and Trinity College Dublin, Cape Canaveral Florida, and of course - The Cosmos!

To Bray Library which as far back as 1961 was able to produced some startling books on Albert Einstein's Theory of Relativity. Also to George Lunin for donating his treasured copy of the 'Phenomenon of Man' by Pierre Thillard de Chardin.

Finally to the good Lord who has promised forgiveness and that he will eventually raise us up body and soul to Paradise and to the Holy Ghost fathers in St Mary's and Blackrock Colleges, who diligently assist him in this daunting task!

PREFACE

Discourse cannot describe the full meaning of the Theory of Trinitivity without becoming weighed down with detail. To solve this difficulty the far reaching scenario becomes a Novel, a Myth and a Fairytale, all bound up in one great adventure!

This Cosmogony simply sees the Metaphysical Trinity relative to each and every facet of life - from the micro cosmos to the extremities of reality. Its matrix is conveyed by the four forces of nature, each one representing part of that unity - and of course one other - the living universe - waiting to be born! The management and deliverance of this is performed by the AMGOD or Trinity in the act of Creation.

Do believe this story, because you will have a treasure for life, a minds eye panorama and a road map to the future! Despite this feast of mental gymnastics one will not be deflected from one's own personal exploration of cosmic consciousness. Nor be deflected from the good practice of being at one with one's neighbours and being an active and charitable citizen in one's native land!

Scripture says, "I will build a new heaven and a new earth." Therefore let us board the good ship Callisto meet its passengers and crew, enjoy the odyssey that is in store and above all let there be hope!

Chapter 1

Larry Coughlin looked down on a city of splendid white buildings, as flight 1073 from Houston approached Miami International Airport. He was impressed by the modern architecture and old Spanish style properties set amongst boulevards of waving Palms and sparkling waterways. The plane arched over Biscayne Bay and Indian Creek River and then made its approach. Once landed, he gathered his kit and alighting into a Floridian world of brilliant sunshine and balmy temperatures. After claiming his baggage he secured a trolley and wheeled it to where he located a stop marked NASA. This was the designated place where he would wait with for special transportation. There were others also waiting and judging from their business like looks, they had the same purpose in mind.

Larry stood helpless as the baking Florida sunshine sapped away his energy. He was laden with bags that were filled with science notes, and a laptop computer. As the yellow school bus arrived, he diligently shuffled into line. They were all bound for Coco beach and the NASA's Special Space Exploration Centre. Larry was ready for an important mission and was therefore appropriately decked out in a grey green polo shirt with a flight insignia stitched on the pocket. Not only was he a physicist, but he was also a qualified pilot. He was a tall 'hombre', quite tanned, wearing a blond crew cut and sporting ray bans, all quite in keeping with the sort of adventurer he really was!

Though in his late twenties, he was still a child at heart - sad to be leaving home. Despite this yearning it was too late to turn back! He had crossed the Rubicon and that is why he and other scientists were scheduled to begin their trip from a space platform now orbiting earth. The station had been assembled over the past ten years, becoming a floating launch pad for future outward journeys to God knows where! The space trip would be the second in a series of ten, and was therefore considered to be of immense importance and also because it was the first trip ever planned to venture beyond the range of human communications!

Despite the arrival of their transport and the mounting excitement, Larry was still feeling fatigued from a long journey that had been thwarted with delays. His friend Hiroshi was already on the bus, he hoped, having got on at Coral Gables. Sure enough he saw a familiar smiling face in the window and as luck had it, there was a free space beside him, which Larry took immediately.

"How yeh bin Larry?" He grunted, and yawned. Then without waiting for an answer, he remedied his tiredness by falling blissfully asleep - his Japanese eyes looking like creases on his pale face.

Hiroshi's life's plan had taken him to study in Ireland, where he had stayed with Larry's family while attending college. Larry often wondered if his sister Jill had a crush on him – they would have made a nice couple and their children would be oh, so cute! With that Larry also drifted into slumber, just where he also should be at that time. He dreamed he was waving goodbye to his Dad, Mom, little Amy and Jill. Then he awakened with a jolt! This was not a dream; it was a nightmare because he might never see them again!

An intercom squeaked into life the voice of the driver said in a slow drawl,

"Prepare to get off! Please do not leave any belongings behind. Thank you."

Twenty eager men and women scrambled to their feet and began to collect their baggage, much of which was marked with labels from around the world. As well as astronauts and physicists, there were scientists and military personnel from a host of countries, all eager to fly their banner where no human has ever been before. With that Hiroshi awakened, and bounced to his feet amazingly full of pep,

"Larry great you made it. Here we go, after three long years here we go!"

Larry looked at his watch and noted that they had been sleeping for well over an hour. He brushed his hand across his forehead and laughed. Hiroshi's enthusiasm amused him. Though Hiroshi was tallish, Larry was a head higher, so he politely pulled both their bags from the rack above. Just then he was addressed by a fellow with an American accent, not unusual in Florida!

"Excuse me, could you also pull that one down for me?"

Larry looked around. There was a dark haired man with a swarthy Italian American look and bearing a pleasant smile. He was pointing to a large bag. Larry tugged at one which was obviously his, as it was marked University of Tampa.

"Thanks so much, my names Richard Opelli, conceptual physics department in the University of Tampa and this guy,"

He said pointing to a big fellow beside him, who finished the sentence,

"I'm Don Travis, your pneumatologist (1) and Padre to the trip, what's yours?"

"Larry Coughlin, flight coordinator and speculative physicist with the mission, with the task of investigating gravitational anomalies, pleased to meet you!"

Then as if embarrassed by his flamboyant introduction he added,

"Don, excuse the mouthful, but I know that your science is much more valuable than mine particularly on a trip such as this!"

Everyone chuckled and Larry then said still looking at Richard,

"Opelli, why you must know my old Jewish professor called George Kuhn from your University. He told me in our last mail to look out for you!"

Richard's face lit up,

"Yes I know him very well as we often work together. Then you must be Larry Coughlin from the Irish Section!"

"Yep, that's me and by the way, meet my colleague Hiroshi Meguro mathematician and artist from Japan another astrophysicist."

Richard said,

"Now just call me Rich and Larry your accent sounds like somewhere between the States or Canada, is that usual?"

"Yeh, Rich, got grandparents from Ohio, and I lived in Canada!"

Still talking the four moved towards the door. The group was brought into a trim three story building where another ten physicists who had come earlier, were patiently waiting. Officials then checked off their names and they were given lockers where they could leave their surplus gear. They were asked to shower in medicated hot water before donning their newly issued clothing for the trip. An hour later they clambered on board small buses, and were driven through an underground tunnel to a launch pad which lay at least a quarter mile away.

The ship that would bring them up to the platform was sitting on a high plinth. It looked tall but quite heavy around the base and a bit ungainly. It must have stood about fifty feet high and had large jet motors mounted all around its midriff. It was attached to a gantry and also to an array of support machines and tanks of liquid fuel. Larry thought it looked a bit obese, and hoped it would be able to get off the ground!

The group were delivered to the upper level of the plinth and ushered through a large orange coloured door with 'Short Haul Transport' written in neat letters. As there were also supplies being wheeled through the same entrance, one item caught Larry's attention. It looked like a birdcage – strange he thought! The group entered the ship and were told it could manage the equivalent weight of up to fifty people and their equipment. It had a large payload as its fuel was derived from pure oxygen and nuclear fission. It gathered oxygen as it went and then as the oxygen thins, the nuclear power kicks in, and it all balances out in the end. These transporters were basically freight elevators, and not suitable for distant flights. Larry was told that it was the commercial sector that had developed the idea, all because vacations in space were gaining in popularity. They also added that it was designed on the principal of a scram jet.

They were issued flight suits and head gear and were seated in a low ceilinged chamber with star patterns, much like being in a Planetarium. There were small windows around walls specially to allow a sense of location for the travellers. After belting in and being instructed on what to expect, it was time to go! The instructors left the chamber and the door was locked. Then there was a count down and at zero there was a swish and a burst of extreme G force, as they were taken aloft.

After about thirty minutes of flight. Larry glimpsed a bright star appearing, it was undoubtedly the space platform. Beside it was a shining spec and that was undoubtedly the good ship Callisto, the ship that would take them into deep space! As they neared the platform it appeared as big and circular and was dull grey in colour. However it went almost unnoticed as people chatting excitedly about the magnificent golden coloured craft that awaited them! Hiroshi said to Larry,

"Look it's a pretty ship, no jagged edges and very gentle curves, its quite aerodynamic."

Larry was very much in agreement and noticed a nose antenna that protruded quite far in front. The rear was wide and had several windows yet its propulsion would come from large circular outlets across the lower side of the stern. There was a turret on top with a laser like object, which Larry knew, could be used for many purposes!

Richard exclaimed,

"What a beauty!"

Just then another announcement,

"Thank you for being so patient, we are now approaching the Space Platform and will disembark almost immediately as your ship the Callisto has been fully prepared for departure by its crew of cadets. As most of you know it is the property of EUSARUSS –European, United States and Russia agency. Your ReferenceNumber is now UM – 171. Please indicate that on all correspondences or S-mails. From here on your Captain Dave Mc Cluskey USAF and Laura Bingley UK Space, will take over. Have a safe trip!"

With a hiss the SHT interlocked with the entrance to the platform. The group flowed into a lobby. It was like being in an airport. There were lots of onlookers watching their arrival. Quite a few were dressed in white and Larry reckoned they must be the cadets. Others were in polo shirts and some wore light khakis. The group were ushered to an assembly area and offered tea, coffee and sandwiches, earth style. It seemed there were a host of nationalities on board as a server smiled and said "Spasibo," when Larry handed back his empty cup. Along the wall there was a series of photos of the earlier flight crew, he wondered would their photo also be taken!

Then seven officials entered the room. They consisted of six men and a woman, who paraded to a raised area and turned to face the group. A tall man of about forty spoke. He was dressed in beige 'suntans' like a naval officer.

"Let me begin by congratulating the thirty of you on the tenacity, determination and interest that has delivered you here today. To my right find physicists Casper Mantz German Aerospace Centre, Cologne and Jean Moreau from the French Institute of Aerospace Technology. He will coordinate the whole science section and space medical admin. You probably know of him already. Next is Ernst Sprungli from Zurich, our atomic energy engineer who is permanently attached to the Callisto - it is his baby!"

Ernst gave a broad grin. Then he pointed to a tall Afro American,

This fellow is Major Benson Tuscaloosa, and he is our crew master - refer to him as Ben or Chief, but above all do as he says!"

Ben was about thirty and looked like he could manage any crisis. He just smiled and raised a finger. Dave continued, sweeping his hand in the direction of a tall thin fellow in a blue jump suite,

"This is Ivan Kozma, from the Russian Institute of Applied Physics, both he and Mantz have been working on this project for quite a few years."

Then he went on,

"Also beside me here is Laura Bingley my vice Captain, and between us we will be available 24/7 and by the way, I'm David Mc Cluskey your Captain from Spokane, just call me Dave or Skipper!"

There was a round of applause mainly from the Cadet's. Then Dave concluded,

"Thank you for that, and I want to add that your ship is the Callisto UMEX (Ultimate Manned Expedition) 171 /10,000 series. It is named after one of Jupiter's Moons and is driven by eleven Electromagnetic Atomic fired power packs produced at CERN (2) who contracted to Oerlikon of Switzerland."

Ernst gave another smile. Dave continued,

"This is the Callisto's second trip, the previous was by way of testing the ships performance and readiness, but this time it's to be the real mc coy! If you look behind you will see many of the crew who were on that maiden voyage."

People looked around at a group of about twenty cadets and crew who responded by nodding.

"Now as this is a proud moment, please gather in the main arrivals area for a photo, and then you may make your last communications with home, there after, the flight team will take you on board the Callisto."

As Hiroshi turned, someone dug him with an elbow, but did not apologise. Hiroshi turned just in time to see a lanky fellow disappear in the crowd. Maybe he does not like Japanese Hiroshi thought, shrugged and followed Larry to the main hall.

"Hello, Pat. Can you hear me? It's Rich. We are up on the platform and leaving soon. This is the last call so remember it when I say, I dearly love you Pat!"

Pat was standing at a sliding door watching her children splashing in the pool with tears in her eyes and a phone to her ear. They had a very nice Florida home and she only wished Richard could be her to enjoy it.

"Rich, Oh Richard, it is great to hear from you. God Bless keep safe, Claire, Madeline come and say hallo to Dad."

Richard sadly let down the phone and then tapped a message on the s-mail as a follow up. Then he moved away and made room for someone else.

The Cadets began to escort the people into the ship as they returned from the communications centre. Hiroshi was still on the phone, so Larry lost in contemplation followed behind some others as they and headed in. Then a voice said,

"Sir, this way please,"

Larry looked in disbelief. There in front of him was what he reckoned to be just about the most beautiful female ever! She was undoubtedly a cadet, but with a difference. She had dark brown eyes and delightful Spanish features, and spoke with a slight accent. Her hair was of medium length and was silky black. She was very business like yet smiling. Her golden service badge and Lieutenants bar glinted as she beckoned him with a clip board, to follow along with the others. Larry became instantly alert, all tiredness was suddenly gone and the boredom that had haunted him earlier had disappeared. He quickened his step and caught up with the snowy white figure striding down the corridor - her charisma had taken him over! As they walked through the ship she pointed out various aspects while explaining at length,

"This ship has a gravity equaliser like the stabilisers on a liner. In the ebb and flow, it will keep the deck steady, so normal gravitation attraction can work!"

Then for all to hear she commented,

"The command area is called the main concourse. Your people and some cadets will be seated theatre fashion in the centre of the ship, and with a limited view through the front window expanse. The complete area is ringed with a stepped up area where computer controllers have a better view of where the ship is going and can observe all that is happening at the Captain's console in front. The navigator stands at the console which is combined with an in depth space visor; know as the EM/SPEC – Electromagnetic Spectrometer. Sometimes it is called the 'Maggie' for short. This great machine can see things that the naked eye cannot perceive. Almost all our deep space navigation will rely on that machine!"

She swept around letting her eyes meet with Larry's. Larry recoiled and shifted his gaze with shyness. He was not prepared to mix emotions with the mission but what now could he do? Whether she liked him or not did not matter, he was already a victim! Then they travelled past a small galley with busy cooks. Soon after, they visited the sick bay, a study a library and an oratory for ecenimical gatherings. Next she took them down a flight of steps to the escape and emergency area. There parked in a large hold, were several modules that could take a dozen people each and to be used in dire emergency or for critical repair work.

Then she glided into a wide dormitory area, where she turned into an enclosed section and said,

"This is the sleeping quarters where you become separated. Ladies to the right, gents you are to the left. I'll take the Ladies first."

She lifted her clipboard and led the ladies through. During this time Larry made acquaintances with the other guys one of whom said,

"Ain't she sweet!"

Larry pretended not to notice what he said. Then she returned and began to check off the names to allocate their accommodation. Pulling back a curtain she pointed to a bed like object with a Perspex cover.

"Now let me explain. This is what we call a 'Hybo'. It's the short for hibernation box. One can either take a short nap or have a Rip Van Winkle which ever you like! All you have to do is open the cover lay down, close the cover, set the alarm and proposed temperature required. In about a minute you will be in dream land with Aristotle, Plato or Pluto!"

Then she allocated the Hybos and showed everyone that their radiation protection, RP suits were stored under each unit. These will be worn almost continuously as the trip evolves. As Larry was the last on her list it allowed him snatch a few private moments with the fetching lieutenant. While the others were examining their new billets, he seized the opportunity and said in his most manly voice,

"May I please ask your name?"

She pointed to her nametag, but it was not there!

"Oh," she said, "Sorry I forgot to wear my name tag. Gee no one would have known who I was. I'm Everina Spazola from Albuquerque."

Then she added,

"Rather than have you guess, my age is twenty-three!"

She smiled and asked Larry some searching questions about himself. He was delighted by her interest and also by her informality, particularly after such a stiff introduction. He therefore responded readily,

"I'm Larry Coughlin Physicist with the Iropean Space Commission (3) twenty-eight years and still a dreamer. But again what about you? Were you on the last mission? Will you be on this, or are you staying on the Platform?"

His heart seemed to miss a beat. She smiled again and said,

"Yep, this is my first mission. You know I'm a Cadet and this is my life's ambition, I would die rather than miss this trip!"

Then she turned and said as she departed,

"Nice meeting you Larry, I will see you around; there will be no doubt about that!"

Then she was gone!

---

(1) Pneumatologist, one who studies spiritual beings.

(2) CERN – European Laboratory for Practical Physics, Geneva Switzerland.

(3) Iropean Space Commission- Envisaged, Ireland segment, specialising in comet samples and analysis for the European Space Commission.

Chapter 2

The main concourse became the scene of intense activity. Dave was still dressed like he was commanding a battleship in the Pacific, while Laura was decked out in conservative style white blouse and navy pants. Ernst in blue denims was down in the engine room doing a last minute check on the atomic power packs. The computer banks were alive with dancing lights. Everina and several other cadets were engaged in collecting information from the banks and delivering it to Lionel Marsh the navigator for input in the EM/SPEC. He was the person who would have to bear responsibility for the ships progress - a very responsible job indeed. He had told Everina that he was from Surrey and she had been quite taken by him, but now that she had seen Larry her feelings had altered. Never the less, Lionel was one hell of a guy and he had a level of excellence that she would eventually like to achieve.

Larry and Hiroshi were unpacking the equipment needed for their trip, and Richard was taking part in a pre-departure brief in the Captain's quarters. Punctually at the arranged time the flight management team emerged – all quite ready to go. Dave therefore took position close to the Navigator at the EM/SPEC. Laura began issuing standard instructions before departure,

"All personnel must fasten safety belts. Navigation and engine crew note, departure will be at 0.700. Major Benson, please inform all personnel to secure loose objects."

Larry and Hiroshi went to their designated seats close to the computer banks. Everina was already seated and buckled in place, and was talking to another female cadet. She turned as Larry sit down. Her friend looked at Larry and said something to Everina – they both smiled. Hiroshi saw this and nudged Larry,

"What's up with you and that Lieutenant? I think you have something goin' for her?" and he chuckled.

Larry said in a whisper,

"It's just a one way street, don't know what she thinks?"

Hiroshi whispered back,

"That's my boy Larry, no boredom on this trip but don't let her get in the way of your work! Never know you might meet an even nicer martian girl!"

Then he thought of another matter, and pulled a piece of parchment from his pocket and handed it to Larry.

"Larry this was addressed to both of us. It had been sent by Professor William Eldron, do you remember meeting him at the Trinity College Space and Creation Simulation? He had been your Dad's lecturer years beforehand."

Larry nodded and Hiroshi carried on,

"Eldron said in a note that it had been passed to him by a Professor George Kuhn the physicist from Tampa University. Wasn't he the guy you mentioned to Richard? Well he said, old George had been vague about its meaning, but it had originally been drawn by a Chinese Student. What do you make of it?"

It was an oriental Mandala, (see back cover) and its title was simply, 'Creation'. It was marked with various shadings from green to blue through maroon, gold and then a rainbow. There were two large triangles, and the top one was connected to a horseshoe shaped Omega. There were no markings as a guide to unlocking its secrets, so one would have to guess the meaning!

Larry looked with curiosity and said.

"Yep, you're correct, that is the same picture that we saw in the Trinity College Simulation. I remember Eldron had promised to send it on to us. You know my old man was working on a theory like that but he called his the Theory of Trinitivity!"

Hiroshi put on a knowledgeable expression and said,

"Yeh, Lar, I know that, I remember it. We can have another look at it after we take off?"

Then the final countdown began, and with a shudder, the power packs fired and they began to move forward very slowly. Dave gave an order and the ship began to turn. Then at a given moment the velocity increased. Not only did it increase, but it roared like mad, and everyone was squeezed back into their seats. Larry felt like his whole life was passing in front of his eyes. Once again he saw his family and then he imagined he was riding his surfboard on a transparent wave but that it crashed on the shore and then went speeding over land finally pitching him on the shingle! Throughout the ordeal the navigator could be heard diligently reading out co ordinates till he finally said,

"Peak velocity is now149, 000 k per second and stabilizing."

The acceleration stopped. The imaginary stones cutting at Larry's body became soft like sponge. He felt a new calm and began to recover. People let out sighs of relief, and the sound of the engines reduced. Then Laura announced,

"As you were and you may release their seat belts."

Larry lumbered to a standing position, and shook hands with various other personnel as a tribute to their survival thus far! Hiroshi followed, as they went down to the rest area where they enthusiastically spread out the Mandala for further inspection. Hiroshi pointed to a small triangle marked in green and said,

"Larry I have seen a lot of Mandala's in my school days; many as you know are of Japanese origin."

He pointed again at the centre of the picture and said,

"That is defiantly the universe. It has tiny stars marked within it!"

Larry studied the picture but had always being a bit unconvinced with his Dad's work. So he reacted cautiously saying,

"Then my tall little friend, what the heck are those two triangles doing around it, when there is no proof that anything exists beyond the threshold of light?"

Hiroshi shrugged and said,

"Look they are the forces of nature electro magnetic, Strong Nuclear and Gravitational, and they are shown here as being outside the threshold of light, that you mention, so surely you can agree there is a possibility they are effecting everything within the universe?"

"Okay Hiroshi your right maybe we should show it to Mantz and of course Ivan Kozma when things settle down a bit!"

Chapter 3

Richard now in a buoyant mood and bearing a smile, He had discovered a calendar in his Hybo. And was bursting to explain its meaning,

"Did you ever hear the saying, never in a month of Sundays? Well in space, as you may have learned, but may have forgotten – we have four Sundays per month, and indeed four of everything else. This space Calendar was devised by EUSARUSS and is quite simple!"

He continued,

"There are thirteen months of four weeks each - twenty eight days per month. Mondays are always the First, Eight, Fifteenth and Twenty Second. It all amounts to 364 days per year. This leaves one day short per annum, and therefore every seven years an extra week is added to the new month so it will have five weeks instead of four, during that year only. The extra month is called 'Newzember' and it follows December. This means the New Year is usually four weeks later than Christmas, giving everyone a breather!"

Larry laughed at this but then discovered one of Richards calendars also attached to his Hybo. So he accepted the new innovation and diligently marked it off one day at a time knowing that Mondays would always start a month and Sundays would finish it.

"Okay" said Larry,

"Hope you guys also remember that we have been trained to working with a decimal clock; a hundred minutes per every hour, not sixty. I find it much better for paper work calculations, any comments!"

The only comment was Hiroshi who added that it was his Japanese mathematicians who said that zero was not nothingness but a bubble that raised the magnitude of numbers – two zeros thus 9 becomes 900. Therefore 9 is the highest number existing! For example any nine sequences of numerals generate a pattern such as $(1) \times 8 + 1 = 9$ then increase it to $(12) \times 8 + 2 = 98$ and so on seven more times till finally you end up with $(1 \text{ to } 9) \times 8 + 9 = (987654321)$. Almost artistic and there are countless other combinations demonstrating the totality of nine but maybe later! Also three by three is nine and there are said to be three persons in the Trinity, isn't that right?"

Larry nodded three times in jest.

Chapter 4

It was time to turn in. Larry's first experience was memorable. It was just a normal night's sleep that lasted eight hours. Feeling full of curiosity - he had climbed inside and set the controls for a wake up call for 6.75 a.m. No sooner had he laid back his head, than sleep took over. It began by his drifting into an imaginary oceanic encounter on a visit to his family summer home at Trahmahon Beach in West Cork.

His Dad, Daniel known as Dan was with him. Dan was watching through the lens a camera from the cliffs above the beach. Waves were beginning to arrive, just as it had been forecast by a naval internet wham report. Larry entered the deep water channel beside the cliffs to his left. This was where a tiny river flowed into the bay causing a rip that would carry him out through the incoming surge. He therefore paddled out encouraged by the push from the current. As he went he pondered the immensity of the ocean ahead!

"Could waves be alive?" he wondered!

"Could they read your mind and do they have feelings?"

Larry was right in his questioning the phenomena, because the approaching waves were all but living beings. They were the result of a giant earthquake in the Azores. They were a family ranging from small to large, the largest of course being the most dangerous of all!

As Larry paddled out over the approaching walls - they seemed to be growing taller by the minute. This meant that as he was now committed, and could not stop because he could get hit by a breaking section and perhaps thrown back to shore.

Fear began to grip him as he realised that he was now much further out than intended and that he was now meeting a sea of larger proportions than intended. He gulped for air – more air!

It was then that his Dad shouted from the cliffs,

"Larry, Larry look outside, giant walls,"

His voice was carried in the wind and Larry did not hear it. Just then the first of the Tsunami like set broke on the outer banks where wave rarely occur. Their roar alerted Larry to the predicament. Maybe his fantasies were correct and this was a family of waves! If that were true then he would firstly meet the smaller ones and finally meet the biggest of the set – the Bull wave, and he would call it Gasper!

Gasper was travelling at thirty-five miles per hour and had already swallowed up many smaller waves; thus possessing their energy. There was a small surface bug up ahead and he intended to devour it also. The bug was of course Larry, who was a blemish on the seascape.

Then with incredible effort he managed to paddle up and over each of the sodden family as they wobbled trustingly towards him. Then finally the bull arrived! This was the largest darkest wave he had ever seen. It stood towering over thirty feet above him - he had no choice. If he did not ride it, it would land on top of him and crush his bones. Just then a sea gull swooped bye and quaked. It was the loneliest and empty sounding wail he had ever heard. It seemed to herald approaching doom. Larry thought about the writer, "James Joyce's quotation - three quarks for muster mark."(1)

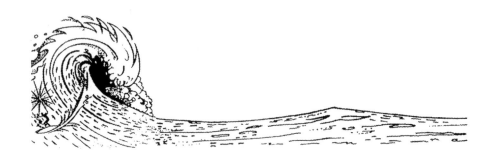

Gasper. Was it a dream?

Now very cold and facing the immensity of the wave, Larry thought,

"I badly need a tow in behind a jet ski pull to catch this monster, and even at that my board is to short and light."

Then he said with resignation,

"Lord, please, you tow me on to this it's all your design!"

With a mighty effort he paddled furiously towards shore, as the awesome wave began to overtake him. Still thrashing furiously he was drawn up Gasper's boiling face, hovered for a split second, and then began to rocket downwards. He jumped to his feet crouching low as he took the consequences of the decent.

The acceleration was immense; his board hit large ripples on the wave causing it to bounce under his feet. Larry recoiled as the updraft sent spray that felt like needles to hit his face. Now he had a choice of riding to his left where there was a fast curling tube or right where it humped up in a great standing shoulder because of the river!

Despite the challenge he retained control and snatched the safest route swinging hard to his right, and driving across a new forming crest. Before him was a continuous wall of water that looked like a moving precipice of green ice. As he did so, there was an enormous shudder - the wave behind him began to peel. He pivoted high on the great shoulder and for a fleeting moment, saw his Dad on the cliff and some others below on the beach, scurrying back from the shore.

"This one must be big," he thought!

Then as in the final moments he began to carve with his board, radically climbing and dropping and tearing the remainder of the wave into shreds. Gasper groaned as the fins tore lines in his watery face. Once more he reached out his powdery paw in an effort to swat the bug - but failed! Larry had by now planed off the shoulder and into the river just in time to hear an enormous roar as the shattered remains of the wave hit the shore line. Gasper knew that he had run the course, done his best and this was to be his demise. Despite that he had reached his goal, his nirvana just as the other members of his family had done moments before. Then he was gone and all that remained was a mass of foam blowing in the wind.

Larry's surf ride had taken him almost to the beach and so with a few more strokes he was there, back on dry land. He was greeted by shouts of approval from his Dad who held up the camera for him to see and shouted,

"I got yah. Idiot, I got yah!"

Larry raised a shaking hand in appreciation and then walked across the beach and gazed down on all that remained of the vanquished. He felt humbled by the great experience and admired the energy and might of the once proud Gasper, now nothing but a mass of bubbles on the sand. Perhaps it was a dream or maybe it was real, but to his surprise, he saw hundreds of eyes looking at him helplessly from within the foam. His ears were filled with the sound of a wailing ocean. Then feeling horror stricken, he shuddered and awakened with a jolt!

Meanwhile, Hiroshi had also been asleep. He had dreamed about his lovely Island home in Japan. He heard chimes in the wind and he dreamed that he was home again in Hokkaido with his family Meguro. From his home he could see Mount Yotei looming above his beloved town. His Mother Nasko had prepared tea and Mochi-gashi cakes; he was invited to eat them but in the dream never did. Then he found himself happily playing with his little brother Jinkichi for what felt like hours. Suddenly he heard more chimes but this time they were different it was his wake up call.

Larry arose, washed, and still feeling upset by the dream, headed for the galley. Once there he poured himself a coffee. Then he took a Danish pastry from inside a display case and squatted beside Hiroshi.

"Gee, Hiroshi there isn't much space in here, its all outside the ship - did you have a good sleep?"

They both agreed that the Hybos were a success. Just then Richard arrived.

"Hi you guys, may I join you?" He took orange juice and toast and said in a low voice,

"There are a couple of strange people on this trip.

He turned his eyes in the direction a fellow who was out in the main concourse intent on computer work.

"See that fellow in the navy shirt." Hiroshi interrupted,

"Rich, he is the guy who did me in the ribs!"

"Shush," said Larry,

"Want him to hear you?" Richard continued,

"His name is Hamish Cauldron and he has associates called Raphael and a woman called Dalia something or other - I got the info from Benson's human resources log. They are here on a project called Lamda Exclusive. It is related to repulsion and the Anti-matter content that lies beyond the Oort Cloud – An area at the extremity of the solar system were comets evolve."

"Humm" said Larry, "That overlaps with some of the work I'm doing!"

---

(1) Quotation by James Joyce; "Three quarks to a munster mark." Also quoted in physics to illustrate the colour force in nature.

Chapter 5

Larry sat looking at his work but while now quite awake was not able to concentrate properly. He was preparing some spectrometer reports for the Captain but it was an uphill push! Something was on his mind. He began to think of about the Trinity College Assimilation that they had discussed as it was beginning to have a bearing on their trip. It all happened when he and Hiroshi were in the final year of their masters in physics in Trinity College Dublin.

That was two years ago. As best he remembered at the time; Jill his sister was back in town glowing with a suntan from working in Australia. She intended visiting Larry in the University, because they were working on an interesting experiment and had invited their Dad. The university was running a computer simulation about the origin of the universe and where the energy for that first split second originated! The latest large Hadron collider experiment in CERN had smashed Protons and lead ions head on to release energy but it was not enough and another approach was needed. The kernel of this system has already been running for twenty-two weeks assembling bits of information all the way back to before the first 10^{32} seconds of time, and then to the first hundredth of a second or less after this moment or Big Bang as most people call it!

Larry was quite excited and as Jill and Dan arrived he burst into a scientific explanation of what was about to occur,

"The system employs the assumption that time and space, form a lattice of points, just like a dot to dot! We have persuaded them to include in their quantum dynamics, Dad's speed of light to the power of three - you know $2.69 \text{mx} 10^{25}$ 900,000 kilometers per second!"

Jill looked puzzled. Larry reacted with a look of disappointment therefore saying,

"The object of the exercise, you silly goose, is to get an overview of the construction of the cosmos, galactic filaments and hopefully dark matter.

The extravaganza is computer linked with a worldwide network so all participants can observe the progress."

Jill nodded at last and then said,

"Dad, I'd prefer you to explained it."

Dan quickly said,

"You know from your biology, that it all begins with the atom - the concept introduced to the world by the ancient Greek Democritus during the 5th centaury B.C. The atom has a nucleus of elementary particles, the proton and the neutron with electrons orbiting around them. Now there may be an important link with space through the medium of the forces of nature! Just to list them they are Gravity, Strong Nuclear, Electromagnetic and Weak."

Then he hastened so as to finish,

"First here's the connection at micro level. The Neutron has interaction with Gravitation, the Proton, to the strong nuclear and the electron with electromagnetism. The fourth force is the weak, and its influence is tiny but it acts on the strong nuclear and the electromagnetic. It also can split large atoms into smaller and is associated with radio activity. Now today's assimilation will be at macro level in an attempt to show what lies behind that Big Bang."

Jill interrupted,

"Dad, I know most of that already and also that the electron is the force that permits the covalent bond which in turn holds molecule together - hence life! The electron is a sort of wizard of ozz!"

Dan just went on,

"Correct. An earlier assimilation but smaller version of this same experiment (1) looked just at the universe and showed condensed galaxies in chains and filaments stretching about at random. Like the chaotic Carina Nebula there seemed no pattern, rhyme nor reason for its topography. In fact it looked like the result of hot lead hitting cold water. Everything curled or stretched in grotesque shapes."

Jill said,

"I remember you showing me the effect of an egg leaking albumin into the boiling water. Isn't that much the same?"

He agreed and said that nevertheless the question begs science to answer whether the myriad of galaxies were organised in some meaningful way. However my theory describes what that meaningful way is about!

Amongst the audience were senior lecturers from various science faculties, and members of the press. Interestingly enough there were also some renowned neurologists from the nearby Royal College of Surgeons. The screen was the largest that had ever been installed in the University and measured 30 ft across and 25 ft in height and was connected to a bank of computers by cables. Several of the physics team were poised and ready at a set of keyboards. People were subdued and the scene took on an expectant air. Larry had just drunk his second coffee and as he crunched up the cup and discarded it. The screen suddenly became alive, filling with snow like patterns, and every now and then series of numerals.

The crowd gave grunts of satisfaction. Then an oriental fellow spoke and introduced himself as Steve and then tapped in some messages on a keyboard, and said,

"We now expect to see pictures from just before the embryonic universe formed, let's call it 'Egg-spansion'. He paused and continued,

"As an added touch of excitement we will increase the speed of light to the power of three! This is because we are attempting to get behind that first moment. We have been advised by Tampa University to do it this way!"

Larry looked at Hiroshi and said in a low voice,

"George Kuhn, I'll bet he is responsible, I have read about him and he is a sort of an Einstein re visited."

At that moment the screen turned jet black. Then text appeared at the foot of the screen,

"Z – 00 2l. T = Zero. Negative- vacuum - 040210."

It all began with an enormous Omega (Ω) sign. Out of this object's lower section poured golden lines that slowly twisted as if governed by some empirical law. They immediately turned in on themselves to form large hoops which in turn formed a transparent cylinder in the shape of the traditional 'horn of plenty'. It extended in a curve down the left of the screen while all the time it was full of swirling motion.

This simplistic beauty caught everyone by surprise. The blunt end of this amazing torus had become filled with smaller tubes each rotating independently. Larry thought it resembled the fractal called the 'Vague Attractor of Kolmogorova' (2) and he was not far wrong!

Then two tiny sections emerged one at a time and began to unfold. The first was a dark midnight blue triangle and the second and the one that remained attached to the Omega shape was maroon. It was attached by a line or a winding optic tunnel of sorts. To the alarm of the audience there was a flash of light and the emergence of a tiny green object which took its place in an enclosure at the base of the blue triangle. Was this to be the universe?

"*002-xzi - Forces of nature x³, plus red light anti-colour * o-b-h*"
Steve spoke to the audience in excited tones,

"This is quite different than we had anticipated! At best we must assume that we have witnessed what happened before the first moment - that is before that green dot arrived. The flash must have illustrated that moment! Evidently there is a benevolent system at work using the forces of nature as a medium. The flash would have delivered the coded information to all parts of an embryo telling what sort of a universe it should turn out to be! This is not unlike the action of stem cells in the human body! After all, the void itself is really a recent occurrence and is literally one enormous collapsed section of gravity in which all information is trapped. The universe is the custodian of this information and by the use of its own intelligence hopefully can self develop. Now let's look at this new born universe!"

He moved a gyro lever in a semi circle and typed in the expansion factor that he had already mentioned. The text responded,

"*Command - Hubbell constant 100 km /per/mps x 3 - command effect.*" (3)

The effect was dazzling. The green dot increased and took on a fractal like shape. The crowd gasped again and Steve said,

"This shape is much like a 'Mandelbrot' from the well known 'Juliet Set' (4). This is no miniature but an immense fractal. I have a hunch The University of Rome (5) with Lucian Pietronero and his team, will be celebrating this discovery. Please not only do we have a fractal shaped cosmos but it is also saddle shaped as a result of the curvature of the torus"
Some more statistics appeared,

"*Point, z o, towards infinity, mapping z − z² + command effect c³*
(6) *Guv = 8mG (Tuv+Pvac Guv).*

One of the professors was invited to comment,

"That equation is both the 'Mandelbrot' expression at a higher magnitude and the equation for repulsion combined. The problem is that all this speculation puts us beyond the threshold of light, and theoretically beyond existence, and therefore begs the question, how then can light reach us? One scenario might that light is not ours! It is generated from a hyper dimension and not belonging to our state. When we observe, it is like looking at people in a passing bus – we just borrow their light. In other words, light and imagery, is always perceived 'second hand', thus giving us a sense of impermanency!"

Then one of the International link people spoke,

"Good morning, pardon afternoon, this is Bill Ivers at Princeton, as far as we are concerned this is 'fan-damn-tastic' we've never seen the like! This simulations shows a bounded universe, flat and curved but benefiting from a sort of turbo charging perhaps of dark energy from somewhere beyond. You know this will cause a stir in the astrophysics community, as it's the closest we have to experimentation on a 'Brane Theory' (7). The question still remains where about of all this dark matter? Also what is the constant for repulsion while being off set by incoming energy?

There was an immediate outburst of chatter from around the laboratory, with some people leaving the room in haste. Some began using mobile phones while others crowded around Steve and the organizers. Dan and Jill made their way over to Larry and Hiroshi.

"Jill you look a little bewildered," said Larry.

"Dad you look like a man on a mission. What did you think of the exercise?"

Dan smiled and said,

"15 million light years-3 degrees Kelvin, that wasn't a bad trip at all!"

Jill again chirped up,

"Hello brother, thanks for ignoring me, and hi Hiroshi. Now as far as I'm concerned, the whole thing looked biological. Remember we are all entitled to take our own meaning, like I might see it as a living molecule, while a surgeon might envisage a brain, an obstetrician an embryo, a mathematician will see fractals, an agnostic will see it as a random fluctuation, and a cleric will see it as divine!"

Hiroshi noticed that in the midst of all the spectacular science he had suddenly felt an attraction to Jill. She looked so pretty, sun tanned and cheerfully dressed in bright gear. He also liked her funny chatter and noticed that in her company his pulse rate seemed to increase!

The show concluded but then there was a peculiar occurrence. The blackness of the screen began to swirl and there was a sound of thumping like an approaching locomotive. This continued for several minutes and then faded away and was followed by some illegible, erratic and chaotic text. It reflected the discord that was perhaps indigenous to the void or maybe its inhabitant! Then there was a deadly silence, and the screen went blank. From the back of the room several people applauded. Steve then concluded,

"Please excuse our deliverance of such a controversial ending. Believe you me there will be re-runs with an intense study done to ascertain the validity of our assimilation. Thank you each and everyone for being here, safe home." Then one of the audience jumped up and said out loud,

"We have been treated like kids in this exercise, it's a disgrace!"

Another said sarcastically,

"I agree - and also thanks' a lot for the Play Station demonstration!"

Others were a bit more mannerly and began to talk in depth about what they had seen. Dan who should have been vocal was the quietest of all. He was stunned mainly be his own successful prophecy, but also because he knew he would not get any credit for his work. He also knew that though today's activities had been so demonstrative, it might be years before the findings will be tested and accepted. As a coincidence a white haired man approached. Dan exclaimed,

"Mr. Eldron, my lecturer, from years gone by, how are you? I haven't seen you in a long time!"

Eldron smiled and shook hands saying,

"Dan are you anything to do with this ballyhoo? It looks just like what you would be up to - Trinitivity and all that, not my style as you probably know. Anyhow in spite of everything, it's a jolly sound hypothesis, and one that has potential to supply us with a decent theory of everything. Of course that is after the corners have been knocked off it, and some real testing performed. Look, I will be writing it up and I'll give it good press."

With that he said,

"Must go now are these your family, fine bunch indeed, cheerio. Oh by the way I'll be sending you and your friends a copy of a Mandala that I procured from a Japanese student of mine – it matches what we have just seen – I know you'll like it. Cheerio!"

Later while passing the College Library Dan said that it had been built in 1753 by the cities Surveyor General, Colonel Thomas Burgh who incorporated a curtain of arcades that separate the building from the ground because it was because was built on marshy ground at that time.

There was a recital at the time and the strains of Mozart's Lacrimosa filtered through the ancient wall of the college. They stopped for a moment and listened to ebb and flow of the orchestra and the sound of fine young voices chanting into the night. Dan said how he appreciated having been a student in such a fine institution.

Larry snapped out of his day dream. He had to get back to work. That simulation is the reason Hiroshi was so concerned about the Mandala. He was correct and we will have to show it to Mantz right away.

---

(1) Refference to Richard Gott and Mark Dickinson and Adrian Melott and The Omega Point by John Gribbin..

(2) TheVague Attractor (of Kolmogorov); A Hamiltonian Mathematical construction also known as KAM and is a mathematical iteration that depicts a torus of concentric sheaths of quasiperiodic motion. A cross section of this consists of a series of smaller sections replicating the outer shell.

(3) Hubble's discovery of universal expansion is calculated using the Hubble Constant for universal expansion.

(4) Mandelbrote man; A mathematical accumulation of chaotic points that resemble a human figure.

(5) Lucian Pietronero New Scientist 1999 concertinas while as indicated, gravity bores straight through. The theory has been developed by people such as; Lev Kofman the University of Toronto, and to Savas Dimopoulos and Nemanja Kaloper of Stanfort

(6) GUV Equation for Repulsion; Einstein held that the properties of space had their own energy. It has not yet been proven but is once again a popular theory amongst physicists.

(7) Brane Theory, is a spatially mathematical concept in the string theory.

Chapter 6

While the skipper was in his office someone knocked on his door.

"Come on in!"

A tall officer stepped in and saluted. It was Benson.

"Come in Ben and have a seat."

"Sir, just as you asked I have brought the fitness reports."

He held up a small disc and handed it to Dave.

"Sir when you go through them you will see the names marked Q1. These are the questionable people, and I don't know how they passed our scrutiny. Basically I don't trust the intentions of some of the group from the central European zone."

Laura who was also present turned from her desk and excused herself saying,

"Dave, I think Officer Benson is correct in his concern, as I also have felt uneasy about them. Two of them, have been based in the states for a long time and seem to have picked up some bad habits. They have expertise in dark matter analysis which is most valuable. I guess that is how they qualified!"

Dave said he would look at the report and in the interim, perhaps Laura would ask EUSARUS to run a fresh profile on the people in question - that is before we are out of range!" Laura nodded in agreement. Then he added,

"Also we will have to include Jean Moreau and Ivan Cozma in our discussions." Then he turned to Benson and said,

"Ben thanks for that, just keep them in your sights till we will let you know what's happening!"

The Callisto travelled past Mars and they observed a new communications station that was being built on Phobos but now yet ready for use. Soon after that they had Jupiter clearly in sight. Because of their distance from earth unfortunately the ship had passed its limit for S-mailing purposes, but maybe not yet for radio communications. A sense of isolation began to creep over the crew, resulting in people having long faces, yawning and becoming irritable with one another. Despite this drawback, in general they had settled down to the tasks on hand, and adapted to their daily routines. As Jupiter grew larger quite a few of the team were in hibernation, and therefore missed the spectacle. One of Jupiter's moons called Io, came into view, the EM/SPEC began to generate interesting pictures. Larry and Richard were among the lucky ones who were on duty at the time. A small group gathered around the lighted console, while the navigator tapped coordinates and computer commands on the key board. Ernst who was there at the time, began to give them the low down on what was happening. In his Swiss German accent he began to speak,

"Vass, we have here, is a close-up of Yupiter. Much closer than any one has yet seen, or any camera has recorded, with the exception of de Hubble probe some years ago."

The screen filled with a breathtaking view of Jupiter and its larger moons - four in all, but with two of them hidden. Set against the blackness of space the planet looked like a luminous ball of coral and white. Ernst spoke again,

"You see the planet is streaked with four weiss bands off clod,"

He went on to explain that the clouds are stacked in decks of different chemical composition and are interlayer with Hydrogen and Helium Gas to the depth of a hundred Kilometres in thickness. The layers make up three weather zones, the first being water and ice crystals and the two gasses, Hydrogen and Helium. Next comes Ammonium Hydrosulphide crystals, and the last outermost band consists again of Hydrogen and Helium gas. Finally for good measure there is an icing or sprinkling of Ammonia Crystals."

As they watched they observed that near the equator - a row of white horse tail clouds had broken open, to allow masses of Jovian heat to escape from below. The most spectacular of these was a great red spot, which resembles an eye. Larry thought about the foam at Tramahon beach and could it be related to this Jovian world!

The heat and redness are supposed to be due to phosphorus organic molecules being transported from below. Ernst told them that Jupiter in Roman mythology was know as King of the Heavens, and it does live up to the name. Just then Hiroshi pushed his way into the group. Larry watched his expression of awe as he gazed at the screen.

Ernst continued, "Now look," he said,

"See, here are the first two out of twenty moons of Yupeter, these ones are larger and called Galilean moons, Io and Callisto - our name sake."

The moon, Callisto, was now clearly in view sitting quite dark and crystal like, but distinguishable by its light beige patches – impact marks made by huge meteorites. These hits, explained Ernst, caused concentric ridges to spread like ripples in a pond. Its dark slurry crust is reckoned to have formed four and a half billion years ago. The largest meteorite to have hit the moon, blasted a crater over two hundred kilometres in width, and unimaginably deep, but this is hidden by the immediate infill of the moon's ice crust - that poured into the cavity and froze.

The room glowed from Jupiter's light. Then Ernst drew their attention to Io, saying,

"Before we look at Io there is a phenomenon that is not visible to the naked eye and must be electro-magnetically enhanced. It shows the interchange of energy between Io and Yupiter."

With that he asked for permission and the punched in several coordinates on the keyboard. Within a split second, the whole picture turned a brilliant blue, splashing its light through out the chamber. Some of those on the higher levels were distracted and turned to look. At this point Larry noticed a familiar white clad female approach the scene. His heart gave a Jovian jump, for it was that pretty Lieutenant Everina Spazola, who had issued him his billet. Looking quite athletic and fit she bounded towards the group. As she peered down at the screen, her face became bathed in the magnetic blue light. To Larry she looked like a disco queen. In that instant, Larry imagined she and he were sipping tequila in Cancun, to the sound of blaring trumpets and guitars. She turned momentarily and looked at Larry and gave a knowing smile.

The screen now displayed a magnetosphere image of the planet only this time it had altered. It was now completely alive with moving lines that quivered in wide distorted arcs radiating, left and right of Jupiter. Ernst reminded them, that this activity was the actual magnetic field of the Planet, and that it was invisible to the naked eye and could only be seen through their 'Maggie 500 Sx' to which he added again - was a Swiss invention!

Just then Hiroshi moved over to Larry and said quietly,

"Larry, do you remember what Dan said about Eldron's paper? He talked about the great torus that surrounded Jupiter? That it forms a doughnut shaped circle around the planet, and that there was also a great flux of electro-magnetic positively charged particles - transferred from Jupiter to

Io, and returning as negatively charged. Here it was happening right before their very eyes. The sight was mind-boggling. The whole process conveyed by a massive arch that carried the particles one way charged, and the other way uncharged."

Hiroshi was now quite excited,

"Larry, look all this is a simile of George Kuhn's Mandala. He had used this very system as an example of how the whole universe is sustained from a greater dimension and suspended in time. It bears similarity with a great arc combined with a rotating flux!"

He pulled out Kuhn's picture once again and pointed to the key features.

The ship was now in its second space month of travel. Every portion of the horizon was being photographed and computerised and analysed. In the evening as they called it most people watched 3D/dvds from the library, or played chess, or read. Larry had little opportunity to meet Everina as she seemed to circulate in a different world. The electromagnetic Atomic-turbo charged motors had been turned off and only used when needed to make adjustments to their direction.

The Callisto was being merrily whisked along by gravitation from the deepest of space. They were now close to the Oort cloud and the consolation of Sirius could be seen straight ahead. Hamish and Raphael, the two dark horses, along with their group of physicists, were working hard doing their calculation while also peering regularly straight ahead. The Navigator also permitted them to observe through the EM/SPEC but noted that they did not show much appreciation!

Chapter 7

A polite voice called for the Skipper's attention,

"Captain Sir, we have a difficulty which I have checked and rechecked and reported to Ernst and the Flight officer. They said to get this information to you immediately."

Dave narrowed his eyes and waited,

Lionel spoke firmly,

"The ship has suddenly been drawn 27.5 degrees off course by some object or draw that lies up ahead. As we speak the ratio of degrees is increasing. The source appears as an indistinctive blurred area just beyond the Oort cloud."

Dave responded,

"Gravitational anomalies must see what Mr Coughlin has to say!"

He then asked to see the log and to know had all calculations been verified. Lionel rechecked the EM/SPEC and confirmed adding,

"Sir in addition to this a few of the crew have drawn our attention to strange phenomena. As the velocity had increased oddly some products on the ship had began to shrink. An example of this was natural fibber wool sweaters, and some food products have become noticeably smaller."

Lionel passed a large photo of the blurred area, for Dave's inspection. Dave looked puzzled as was to be expected,

"Lionel, are you implying that certain items are shrinking, or are we increasing in size and also being drawn towards an uncharted zone?"

"Sir, I am only sure we have a problem but don't know the answer!"

Dave then called an emergency meeting that included Dr Casper Mantz, Ivan, Ernst, Richard, Lionel and all who were versed in flight navigation. It was Richards first time in the Boardroom and to his amazement there was a birdcage standing in one corner of the room. Inside was what looked like a canary? It was yellow and as Laura entered the room it let out a cheep. Despite the emergency, she immediately went to the cage and dropped some food in through an opening saying at the same time,

"There my little Kiki, eat up!"

Then she turned to the group and said,

"Kiki, I am glad to say, has not shrunk one centimetre, she is one of us. She will also let us know if our atmosphere becomes any way infected, you know I still do not trust computers!"

Then she winked and sat down. Dave looked like he was about to explode. He wanted to get on with the serious business on hand. Dave's first question was whether Laura had contacted EUSARUS yet? She said she had but they had not replied yet! So Dave asked her and Lionel to send a detailed report about the problem as soon as the meeting is concluded. Naturally they agreed.

Then a debate erupted about the nature of the blurred area, and what made it draw them in the first place! Why was material shrinking or is ship and its fixed contents growing in magnitude? Samples were brought to the room for examination and remarkably some were now quite small. Mantz said he believed that the ship is expanding at an inverse square of the Hubbell constant. If that were the case, then as they increase they will be within the equivalent speed of light to their size – this may lift their speed barrier of 299,792, 458 m/per/sec (1) and permit them to travel even faster then that! This also means we will contravene Einstein's theory Relativity! Then he added,

"As a solution to this contradiction, we may overcome it by causing his law to stretch!"

No one uttered a sound, but their expressions said it all. Then he cautioned that at a certain critical velocity the ship could become trapped in time, like a rubber ball at the base of a waterfall? He stopped for a moment, but again no one intervened. Then in a low voice he said, that at those hypothetical speeds the Callisto could be catapulted into another dimension!

Laura was uncomfortable and spoke up,

"Well Casper, at least the latter is only hypothetical."

Mantz scowled at her. Then Ernst was asked if the engines could be boosted to alter their course by at least 45 degrees in an effort to turn away from the stricken zone. He agreed and the meeting ended as quickly as it started. Laura and Lionel went to prepare their SOS for EUSARUS and Ernst scurried off to fulfil his promise. However as he went he kept repeating,

"I see trouble ahead, I see trouble, trouble!"

Down in his spotless shiny control room, five of his technicians were on stand by. Ernst looked at them and said,

"Menche, prepare to ignite all emergency pods on port side. Olivia set one. Karl set four zero seven."

"Ya vol Ernst."

Then he wiped his forehead and said in a shaky voice,

"Commence building."

With that there was a hum that slowly increased in strength. Soon it became a whine. At this point Ernst began to move between the turbines feeling them and observing idiosyncrasies. The when he appeared satisfied he called out,

"Novak fire all."

There was a roar and a shudder, which meant that all motors were working overtime and all pods on the port side. Ernst immediately left the area and went to the EM/SPEC. Dave, Laura and Lionel was watching events on the screen. Lionel had learned to take an interested in Earnst's moods, as the navigation of the ship relied so much on him and his crew. Ernst stood in silence staring at the spectre. The ship slowly began to turn to the East. Then as if caught by an even greater force it was quickly drawn back to north nor-east, the direction of the blurred area. Everyone let out a gasp. The Callisto was not achieving the latitude they were seeking. In other words they were 'Kaput'. Ernst looked at Lionel and then turned and said directly to Dave,

"The engines were not strong enough to deflect the ship from the source. The only alternative will be a reverse thrust."

Dave who did not like to retreat - needed time to think. He instructed that yet another SOS be sent immediately with the hope that it might eventually get through. Mantz was once again the bearer of bad news saying,

"You know it is likely that gravitation from the draw is distorting our messages – they may never be received!"

Quite upset Dave drew aside and gazed at what lay around. Jupiter was far behind and already buried in the 'Milky Way', which in turn had reduced to a disc set in an even greater scheme of filaments of galaxies and stars. Great webs of matter were stretched all around like cotton candy. The Galaxy in which earth is positioned was now beginning to take on the shape of a giant fried egg. He thought who ever saw a fried egg with ice crystals floating all about its extremity? These ice crystals are enormous and packed close together forming areas as large as our moon. As he watched, one such chunk of ice appeared to become dislodged. It immediately began an inward journey towards the Galactic centre. As it did so it began to form a plume of ice vapour - the birth of a comet!

Dave was alerted by the sight. He did not want the Callisto to fall like a comet into the blurred area. He may have to do what Ernst suggested, reverse thrust and head for home, but he did not want to do it without one final check. He turned and requested another but more detailed spectrographic survey of the problem area. Larry immediately went to work and in ten minutes produced his report. The area was somewhere beyond 'Abell 370' a recently discovered cluster. It was an astounding 15 million light years from the Callisto point of departure. That meant that they were being drawn to the threshold of light and universal expansion. This was indeed a daunting prospect and with such intense gravitation the area may be laden with dark matter.

Amazingly Larry observed that the area had both a red shift (2) and a blue shift (3) simultaneously. This means that it is either a rotating quasar with an incredibly strong gravitational field or that it is an object with an inflow and an out flow. Mantz on seeing the report found the latter terrifying!

Larry had not been in the Boardroom before but when he saw the birdcage tried not to look at Richard for fear of laughing. Clearing his throat and then taking a sip of water; Mantz addressed the team now sitting around the large conference table,

"Dave, Vice Captain, these pictures are of great interest to us. In the medical field they use technique such as obstetrics and diagnostic imaging to achieve what you have just done on a larger scale. I propose that we link up so as to help one another. Now if our guess is correct, we are now in confirmed danger? "

"Please elaborate?" said Dave.

"Gentlemen, Ladies, in simple terms we are about to be siphoned out of this dimension in one gulp!"

Ivan scowled, and Dave looked shocked once again by the frankness of his comment and responded,

"Look Casper, listen for a moment."

Mantz scowled as usual but Dave insisted,

"Lets not jump to conclusions. First, I accept that we are in some sort of danger but we need more time to ascertain its extent."

"Hell!" shouted Mantz. Oh, excuse me, but if we flounder it will be too late, if not already!"

"Ernst butted in on the side of Mantz and asked to test a reverse thrust if only to ensure that they could execute a departure at will. He guaranteed that he would only require about twenty minutes to confirm or otherwise! Reluctantly Dave agreed looking at Mantz who now seemed relieved. Laura then made an official announcement informing the crew of Ernst's manoeuvre.

While waiting for the reverse thrust maneuver, Hiroshi sat in beside Richard as Larry was in the Boardroom. He asked Richard to give his undivided attention and explained. He had another letter from George Kuhn that had been lying unopened. It contained comments about the importance of the forces of nature as a key to the final frontier. It also cautioned about the effects of extreme gravitation. It cautioned how they might be sucked into a draw or sinker in space, and also how anti-matter could harm them, as they increased in size, due to the equation - mass by velocity by distance over c [3].

Then he said that Thales a Greek Philosopher from Asia Minor said in the fifth century B.C that the earth floats on water that stretched downwards limitlessly. The Egyptian world at the time also held the same belief. Now while we will laugh at the idea in a sense we will discover that they were correct - no philosopher is ever wrong. Kindest regards. George Kuhn.

"Well I'll be dog' gone, here we are 'up the creek', and old 'Kuhn face' can just sit on his butt and lecture us with theories out of the inferno!" said Hiroshi to which Richard added,

"Hiroshi, where did you learn your slang?"

Hiroshi giggled, "TV, where else!"

---

(1) C = the universal symbol for the speed of light 300,000 km per second. The numerical 3 would increase it three fold. P

(2)Red Shift; Measurement of light frequency in recession

(3) Blue Shift; Measurement of light frequency advancing

Chapter 8

Meanwhile down on earth, Dan, Larry's Father turned in his bed, awoke and looked at his watch. It was four a.m. and Maria was sound asleep. Something was disturbing him! He had not had word about Larry for several months and therefore he was perplexed. Since they had gone out of range of the S-mail, both he and Maria had become quite depressed. They had eventually received a group message to relatives that assured them that all was well. From then on, there was no more word and when asked, asked both the agency and EUSARUS knew nothing. On Dan's last communication, he had been told the Callisto was then out of range of communications. However, there was a possibility that the long range Hubble Probe launched at the end of the century would be able to relay back some messages but it would be on a wait and see basis.

He got out of bed and walked out on to the balcony. The cold from the night air stung, just like paddling out through a winter wave. Also memories of his earlier life in the Rocky Mountains of Alberta flooded into his mind. He recalled the sting of freezing snow hitting his face and of the blazing sun glistened on the ski slopes. He imagined the Husky Tower in Calgary and the buzz of the city he loved. It was a long time since he had worn his Stetson or lined danced during stampede. His mind returned to the present.

He looked up at the sky, and was awe-struck by the beauty. A million tiny specks of light studded the heavenly vault. Dan thought, how can any human manage to travel up there, it is fantastic. Yes this is why he was wide-awake - it was what he had been reading before going to bed. The article in the science magazine reported that back on June 4th 2000, a team of scientists claimed that they had broken the ultimate speed barrier; the speed of light! (1)

"The work was carried out by Dr Lijun Wang of the NEC research institute in Princeton, who transmitted a pulse of light towards a chamber filled with specially treated Caesium Gas.[2] Before the pulse had fully entered the chamber it had gone right through in and travelled a further 60 ft across the Laboratory In effect, it existed in two places at once, a phenomenon that Wang explains by saying it travelled 300 times faster than light."

Dan well knew that light travels at 300,000 km per sec, receding from you no matter how fast you travel!

Meanwhile in Italy, the National Research Council reported on an experiment performed by physicists had managed to propagate light at a speed 25% faster than the known speed of light (2). The implications of this could upturn Einstein's Theory of Relativity, the second law of thermodynamics, and Causality, it could probably simplify Quantum Physics and explain the famous paradox called Shrodinger's cat (3).

As if to justify his thoughts Dan recalled his own theory (4) and that he had read that physicists have already created a hollow atom. What they have done is move the inside electrons out to the outside thus creating a void where they had been. It is very difficult to dislodge these insiders, and therefore scientists have tried to literally re build the atom! First, they get a bare nucleus and as it possesses a natural requirement to have electrons, it is directed towards a metal sheet. Electrons are automatically whipped on board the nucleus but they remain in the outer regions just as the doctor ordered. Atomic manipulation is something real these days. Efforts are being made in CERN Switzerland to produce an actual anti Hydrogen atom with the intention of producing an efficient fuel for space travel. Therefore a reorganised atom could be necessary if such a transformation out of the universe were ever to occur! He pondered will the Callisto experience any of this!

The following day at about two thirty the phone rang as Dan was about to go out. The call was from his old friend Fr Paddy Carroll in Elkton, who bellowed down the phone,

"Dan how yah'bin? How's Larry doing up there? I've read a lot about the flight also got your letter and newspaper cutting about the space trip."

Dan replied,

"What do you think about it all?" Paddy replied,

"Incredible, I'll bet you're a proud parent, I've given you lots of brownie points."

Dan then responded,

"Say, on another matter. Do you know the Padre on board the Callisto, he is Don Travis, from St Lawrence's in Tallahassee?"

Fr Pat replied,

"Sure I do, he is actually from the Dominican Republic, but he's a hum dinger at Basket Ball. Also he's the right sort of fellow for the trip he's very deep into metaphysics and eschatological studies, though you would not know from looking at him. Well Dan I must go, just want to say I have quite a few prayers being said for your family and I'll be over in the summer as usual and we can split a few beers, Give Maria, Jill and Amy my good wishes and also your mom and Mrs de Laundre."

---

(1) (Sunday Times, 04/06/00; Jonathan Leake, Science Editor) (1)

(2) Dictionary of science & technology 1996 chambers Ltd Cambridge University Press 1988) "Caesium gas is alloyed with antimony, gallium, indium and thorium and is generally photosensitive. There is also a caesium cell, a caesium unit, caesium-oxygen cell and such thing as a caesium clock, using caesium-ion resonance of 9192631770 Hz."

(3) Shrodinger's cat, Relates to an experiment where gas may or may not enter a chamber in which there is a living cat, and which in turn may or may not perish!

(4) However Dan's own theory called Trinitivity gave credence to Fermions who have a spin of $[(n+ half) h$ where $n = 0,1,2$ and h is the Dirac constant] now trusting this it meant that fermions travel in and out of existence their movement yet undetected. The reason for this is that their light is back before it goes, thus the observer is unable to detect any evidence of gaps in the sequence. If one is to say what happens if this process shifts or slips out of synchronization, the answer is inhalation or in human terms - death. Dan could quite easily toss this physics around in his head because he had done it so many times, yet the price was it kept him awake.

Chapter 9

Larry told Everina that they could observe the ship's turn about better from the stern. Once there they sat on soft seats by the observation area and viewed the star studded vault. They obediently took the precaution of fastening their safety belts. Larry thought that this was almost like a real date and he was going to break with regulations and make the most of it!

Before any others arrived he asked her about the reasons for becoming a space cadet. She said she had been fascinated since childhood. He then asked more personal questions about her family and learned that her father was from Guam and her Mother came from Mexico. She had a brother who was a lawyer, and a younger sister in college. Her parents had raised her in New Mexico, but her father he had been killed in military service when she was fourteen.

Though Everina displayed a tough exterior, deep down she was tender at hearted. As if to emphasise that point, she shed a tear making Larry feel bad for raising the family question. Right now, her career was the most important thing in her life. Larry wondered would she ever have time for family! He thought that she was the most courageous girl he had ever met, and since she was so pretty it was likely her offspring would also look superb. Though that would also depend on her partner! For a moment he wondered, would he be that Guy? Then he remembered that before any of that could happen they would have overcome the nasty predicament that lay ahead. To Larry's delight Everina had also quizzed him about his family but she had gone a step further and questioned him about girlfriends. This played into Larry theatre and so he invented a few so as to keep her interested. However he refrained from asking about her boy friends, as he knew she would tease him back, but he did ask had she one at the moment. To this question she replied, "That's for me to know and you to wonder!"

By then several of the crew had arrived and sat in. Larry felt quite juvenile, but it was the price he would have to pay for having a cosmic crush on the right person at the wrong time.

All of a sudden there was a tremendous roar and a lot of vibration. Ernst had just fired the pods on the port side. The ship began to turn till giving a panoramic view of the great star studded domain that lay around them. It stopped when the stern was directly facing the critical blurred area, still webbed in mist, and still the cause of their plight. Then the main engines roared into life causing intense vibrations and a high pitched roar. Now the nose was pointing towards home and the way was open for their departure! Larry waited with baited breath, but felt no sensation of movement! They were looking right at the blurred area which by now should be shrinking as they went. However it was not and worse still, it appeared even larger than before! As if to confirm their failure the engines shut down, gradually the ship rolled back to its original direction. All this meant the Callisto was hurdling out of control into the unknown. Just then Hiroshi came running in, eyes wide open and a look of grave concern. Larry unbuckled and said,

"What's up Hiroshi? You look shocked."

"The Blur has just cleared for a moment and we saw inside!"

Chapter 10

An official warning light indicated a, "Code Orange – done RP Gear."

Hiroshi was too excited to explain, all that he could do was to beckon, for Everina and Larry to follow. He went towards the main concourse and control area and front of the ship. A group had now gathered as usual at the EM/SPEC. There was an eerie silence, only broken by the low click, clack, from the spectral visor and the control team calling out soundings for the Captain. Ernst was also there but had now had given up efforts to reverse direction. The Callisto was therefore moving at extra high velocity, to a rendezvous with possible disaster!

Then without warning the blurred area cleared again to disclose two enormous tunnels. They seemed to be set in reflective wall that might be the extremity of the universe in the act of merrily expanding ever outwards. The tunnels were portals to the unknown! Everyone gasped. The odyssey that lay before them was identifiable because it was punctuated in the space fabric with webs of stars and streaks of silver mist. These stars stretched around the circumference of both cylinders in a mystical curve of dancing lights. Perhaps they were being welcomed into the realms of a newly discovered spatial dimension! The navigator spoke hesitantly, as he found it difficult to reconcile the whole situation. He described the vista as being tunnels, one of which was attracting inwards, the other outwards. Dave could see the inflow was spilling clouds of very bright matter and energy back into the universe. It seemed that they were witnessing a cosmic enrichment of enormous proportions. The universe was being fed with cosmic scale nutrients, carried by incoming material of high luminosity. Every now and then there were flashes like lightning, and rainbows ranged from blue through green, ending in shining gold. But there was still something else!

Hiroshi asked Larry.

"Is all that activity occurring because of the influence of unprecedented levels of background radiation?" Larry shrugged and said,

"I guess so, but there is a deeper question to be investigated. Casper, Dave, Ivan, I see on the EM/SPEC that 'Dark Energy' is also billowing into the universe at an enormously high speed from that inflow tunnel. If this is so, then we have found its source, and now know what fuels universal expansion! What do you think?"

They gathered around the screen and gasped in amazement each one nodding in agreement. Dave marvelled and added,

"I think this whole ensemble is one massive presenta or umbilical system!"

This was greeted with horror and silence from the onlookers.

The wall of the outflow tunnel was shaped in an enormous curve; this was the tunnel into which they were being drawn. The stars were grouped in curved ribbons and filaments that were now engulfing the Callisto. It was like entering a tubular universe, tapering off into the distance! The EM/SPEC was now registering particles that were tracking alongside the ship. One such particle identified was a called a Tachyon. It was most amazing as this is a virtual particle, supposed only to exist at velocities in excess of the speed of light. Does that mean they had broken the light barrier? Background radiation was registered as some 40% cooler then the average. The EM/SPEC also registered info from the alternative tunnel where streams of leptons and quarks were arriving with a density of a rain storm. The spectrum called both areas an exotic void!

As if to give some reassurance, an aroma of freshly brewed coffee seeped through the ship. A radio in the background began to play a dreary melody – I'm on the road to nowhere. Some of the crew made their way to the galley. Mantz on the other hand had no time for niceties. He was looking very concerned and was keeping close to the Captain. He had predicted the Callisto and crew would be emulsified by now. Yet amazing that was not yet to be their fate!

One of the flight officers made a curt announcement,

"This is our second alert it is mandatory that all personnel put on RP gear and strap in, I repeat RP gear and strap in."

There was a click. Larry moved over towards Everina, reached out and took her hand, squeezing it gently, before they departed to kit out. As she went her way, she turned, and smiled as if to say - everything is going to be all right. Then she turned away. Hiroshi sprang into action; he gave Larry a push, saying at the same time,

"Larry come on, wake up, she's gone, and get going boy."

With that, Larry regained his motivation and strode off at high speed. The task, to be performed was the putting on of a single piece safety gear. They must now wear the asbestos based, anti-radiation reflective suit retrieved from under their hybos. As Everina had said, these are designed for in-ship activity but not for prolonged space exposure. These lighter suits were dubbed R.I.P. gear, but the joke ran thin as the situation deteriorated.

Once fitted, Larry and the Hiroshi went and clicked into their seats. The computer banks buzzed and lights flickered. Lionel's voice could be heard reading out information,

"Magnitude is steadily increasing - now reaching 998 times that of earth scale"

People gasped and Larry hissed to Hiroshi,

"This is a violation in laws of scaling $Y= a M^2$. They are saying the Callisto has increased more than 75% thus entering a scale of 27 orders of magnitude and that's incredible!"

"Yeh," nodded Hiroshi.

"On the plus side we may have a slower metabolism and may gain longevity. We will experience less heat loss from the surface of our bodies unless of course there is any alteration of our structure! This might be good news, but it poses the deadly question - can the process ever be reversed?"

Some of the group looked around curiously; Larry wondered why they had not already figured it out for themselves! Then as if to answer what was on everyone's mind a Chinese fellow, called Quan Chew, was brought to the EM/SPEC to address the group. He cleared his thought and said,

"Scale is like a one-way street; there is no going back. It is like Mohammed Ali, deciding he was going to join a junior boxing league and start again! He could not! This also brings us to the question of time! If I may suggest, with respect, that you pack away your watches, because we have already leaped into the future and from here on our time calculations are irrelevant!"

Chew continued,

"The trick is never to travel too rapidly or you outpace the natural increase of your surroundings. It seems we have done exactly that! Our greater magnitude is altering our overall velocity to the degree that we are over advanced."

Mantz could not be contained and insisted on having a word before they hit what he called the proverbial fan,

"Consider on the good side, that becoming caught in this tunnel may contribute to stabilizing our expansion! Also there is another startling aspect, a near miss! You see because of our increased size and that we were becoming alien to our surroundings, our silicone tracker has detected streams of anti-matter moving towards us. This was just before we reached the entrance tunnel. Luckily they were deflected because of the intensity of the electro-magnetic field at the entrance. This was the blue effect that you all witnessed. All this estimation was made possible with the assistance of Larry Coughlin's Epona particle detector."

Mantz looked at Larry and then went on,

"A clash between anti-matter and the Callisto could have reduced us to a stream of intense Gamma Rays. Thankfully this did not yet occur and it looks like we may escape. Now there is one other peculiarity that is worrying us!"

There was a murmur from the group listening. At the back of the concourse some cooks, still dressed in white, and a female mechanic dressed in green had joined the audience, and were listening with intent. They had not yet put on their RP gear; perhaps they were in a state of despair! There was now silence in the spacious enclosure. Captain Dave Mc Cluskey looked at the Doctor in anticipation. Mantz coughed, and then continued,

"In view of all that had happened, so far to be precise we expect next that our atoms, will reverse and turn inside out!" Ivan nodded his head in agreement.

There was roar of indignation from the listeners. Mantz held up his hand,

"Now don't panic, hold on a moment, I believe it will happen without causing us any injury what so ever! What I mean by this is that the nucleus will move out and the electron field will move in. The reason I am predicting this is because of a thesis by, D Coughlan, and G Kuhn physicists, which state that a reversal is quite likely when leaving the confines of our three dimensional continuum. An inverted atom or molecule is seen as a possible solution to human confinement. You see, also an inverted atom is speculated to have a greater heat loss, than a conventional one! The hot nucleus will not be shrouded by the electron cloud, and will loose its heat more rapidly. This will facilitate greater mental activity than possible at present. It can be compared to a computer where the very operation, causes heating that in turn can cause damage. If a computer was designed that could function without heat building up, it could function hypothetically forever. In our situation, hopeful that will also be the case! Therefore this inversion could be our making! You know it has often been said, that our world is both upside down, inside out, and backwards! It has to be experienced that way to be understood!"

Then he attempted to hand out a paper on hollow atom experiments (1). There was uproar once again. People began shouting up objections as they felt Mantz's scenario was not acceptable.

Hiroshi whispered to Larry,

"There goes my metabolism theory!"

Larry smiled.

Just then Hamish Cauldron, stood up at the back of the group and in a loud voice shouted out,

"We propose that we draw lots so people are allowed leave in the repair crafts that lie dormant in the hold. They have enough power to get within the rescue perimeter of EUSARUS. This way at least some will be saved."

Three or four voices shouted up in support,

"He's right and we want to go home."

Dave immediately sensed trouble and articulated clearly over the intercom, that there was no evidence of their lives being endangered. To protect the crew was his job, and therefore the idea is appreciated, but not acceptable. From now on the ship is going on Red Alert and near silence will be expected.

---

(1) Hollow atoms; (Ref new scientist June 1995 Ian Hughes and Ian Williams Queens University, Belfast.

"Scientists take nature's building blocks back to the drawing board; the atom is being rebuilt. In laboratories in the US and the Netherlands, physicists are ripping away the electrons that clad atomic nucleus, and rearranging them into a series of hollow shells."

Chapter 11

Now as a result of their being enlarged and within this cylindrical world while travelling at enormous velocity; optically the stars seemed also on the move. They looked like thousand of glow-worms travelling in the opposite direction. Suddenly the Callisto must have come under new influence, because all at once, the lights throughout the ship began to blaze. Every electric gadget became activated. Music blared, and the emergency siren squealed, of its own accord. The computer banks illuminated, and even the Hybos lit up. The crew of the ship began to turn the equipment off, but could not! The computer operators instantly began to run emergency copies, for fear of a shutdown.

The Navigators and both Captain's clustered around the flight console. It was strange, because the EM/SPEC was the only piece of equipment that seemed compatible with the world they were entering. Larry noticed Hiroshi was drawing a sketch of the activity in the ship. He looked up at Larry and smiled, said quietly,

"Did you know that cameras do not work up here? The shutter speeds do not synchronise correctly with the scaled up situation, I don't know why! Oh by the way, we never showed the Mandala to Mantz."

At that, the Navigator called out, "Peculiar sighting ahead!"

It was in the form of a transparent barrier that resembled a great membrane blocking their path. It looked like a segment of the same universal perimeter they had already observed. On the other side of the membrane there was a vague sign of flowing liquid, moving from left to right. What did that mean?

Lionel then made a judgment call,

"My readings show that that movement is liquid under the influence of gravitational and electromagnetic gravitation!"

Just then the ship's dire emergency siren sounded. This was a serious red alert plus one. People instantly pulled up protective hoods, and drew oxygen masks from their seats. The ship hurled towards the transparent barrier. On close inspection it had a surface like a bubble, and by now it appeared so enormous that it blocked their path filling the entire expanse of the cylinder.

"Good heavens," Larry exclaimed,

"This must be singularity, let's go for it!"

The transparent barrier was also reflective, as for a fleeting moment the Callisto was seen like a golden flash on the bubble surface. Just then every clock in the ship began to spin backward or forwards and that included a set of digital atomic clocks in the control area. Then they all stopped completely. That was at that moment the Callisto hit the membrane and the Captain yelled,

"Impact!"

The occupants felt great shudder and suddenly could see silver streaks like dancing rain rising around them, penetrating everyone and everything. Then from the front of the ship a wave of light moved from fore to aft. As it went, it warped everything in its path. The silver streaks became thinned out and then disappeared, and were replaced with a strange tingling sensation and a sound like a cascading water fall. Larry thought he heard Hiroshi cry out, but could not investigate as he was overcome with dizziness! He felt like he was intoxicated and about to faint. He opened his mouth to scream, but could not utter a single sound. Then he opened his eyes but could not see. It was as if he was underwater without diving goggles, yet he was wearing an oxygen mask! Like what had happened to Richard, when he said he cleared his mask in Crystal River and could only see blurry blue.

"Oh good God," Larry thought. He had just remembered Everina.

He tried to look around for her but couldn't. He began to feel sick and throughout his body felt a ghastly vibration. Then he passed out!

Chapter 12

Everyone on board the Callisto, must have shared the same experience. This was evident because they were slumped in their seats, some groaning in discomfort. Lionel and the Skipper were sitting strapped in beside the EMSPEC both of them also looking quite limp. At first Larry pulled off his mask and then noticed the silver rain had disappeared. He looked down to see if he himself was intact! To his utter amazement, not only was he in one piece, but also his vision was clearer than it had ever been. He could see right across the room, pick out the tiniest detail on the control panels and also hear with incredible sharpness. Even stranger, he had inherited a capability of knowing what was going on behind him, though looking the other way! He thought to himself,

"Oh! How strange and wonderful, I feel so light and disembodied!"

To Larry's dismay he could see partly through his own hands, he had turned semi-transparent but also one hand was pale blue and the other pink! He looked over at Hiroshi who appeared unconscious but with his mask removed. He had an agonised expression on his pasty face and his oriental colouring had altered, and replaced it with the same blue tinge to his left and pink to his right. Larry examined himself and was relieved to notice that he was not completely see-through, as he had feared. At least his bones and veins would not be on display to the general public!

Then Hiroshi made a sound and twitched his nose. He turned slowly and looked at Larry. Surprise registered on his two tone face. Larry thought he looked quite ill! Then perhaps a little over confident, Larry tried to move, but in vain. He tried to speak but could not even form a word. It was like being an infant, and having to start the learning process all over again! A feeling of hopelessness took hold. He began to command his fingers to move, and persisted, until they began to respond. He heaved a sigh of relief and began immediately to attempt at forming words. At first he could only manage to utter a grunt, but within several minutes his voice returned.

He looked across the room at Richard, who was also in the process of self-reconstruction - grunting and trying to form words. Larry felt the scene was almost comical, and began to laugh while exclaiming out loud,

"Great Buddha," Then a pause, and then with great effort he managed to say, "What have you done with us for we are all blue and pink?"

He unlinked his safety harness, which was also quite transparent, and stood up. The deck below him was soft like 'Lime Jello' and the walls were the same. The computers blinked, and though they were now see-through, they were working once again. Larry stood up and extended one hand to Hiroshi, who even looked a little afraid to touch him.

"Come on Hiroshi, how do ye' feel? Are you okay?" Hiroshi responded slowly, stretching out his hand and saying,

"Yeh! Larry, how are you?"

The handshake was quite normal, but there was no doubt that if one squeezed too hard the hands would have meshed together! Up here there will be new rules of contact to be learned. Larry now intrigued with their state, tried poking his finger through his own hand. To his amazement it sank inwards without causing pain or damage! Then he pushed on his chest but stopped because it began also to give away. He decided to leave well enough alone. He proceeded over to Richard who was still sitting,

"Are you Ok? Rich?"

Richard replied slowly rubbing his eyes,

"Larry, what the heck has happened to us? Everything is so bright and clear, but are we dead? You know we are inside out according to Laura and Chan. It's a crock of you know what, and none of us are going to make it. Also I'm not going to see Clearwater and Pat, and the children ever again, we've had it!"

The words struck terror in Larry's heart. Richard looked terrible underneath the haze, and Larry was worried. He replied,

"Maybe you're right, but it couldn't be like this to be dead! Everything is way too normal, apart from the transparency!"

At that Richard gave a wail, because he had only just discovered his see through hands. Larry immediately tried to pacified him but to no avail. Then, as if to help matters, the intercom crackled and Laura's voice came through. Larry was not sure whether she was speaking, or just conveying a flow of messages and ideas that everyone naturally received. The message sounded like this,

"Congratulation, we have survived this encounter and I'm glad to say our damage report, is zero, we are intact and are moving ahead. If anyone has any difficulty, press your emergency buzzer and a medic will be immediate assistance. Please remain on full alert, because in five minutes we will be hit by a series of Gravitational waves that are believed to exist at the edge of the sphere of influence of universal extremity, and that is just where we are right now. If I may add that they will hit mainly to the port side."

Richard now seemed more reassured, and some colour began to return to his opaque cheeks. Larry could not remain still for long his breaky heart was thumping and he had to find out about Everina! He knew she was with other cadets, somewhere up back. He shuffled that direction, and ran right into her, as she was coming to see how he had survived. Larry was elated to think she would have considered him. She was smiling as she walked, and resembled an intoxicated clown. Larry laughed at the sight. He noticed that like the others her garments had taken on a clouded plastic appearance. It meant that the outline of her figure could be seen through the fabric, like she was a super model. Having gone through so much drama, Larry could not resist the releasing of his emotions. Though it might be a violation, he just threw his arms around and kissed her. He made sure not to press too hard as they might weld together! She did not have a chance to object, nor did she try. The kiss felt perfect, just as good as on earth, but one had to be gentle. Then while she was still in his embrace Larry whispered,

"That's 'cause I love you, and I also did it for science."

He let her go, and she responded by giving him a very quick return kiss. Then she looked at him sideways with a teasing smile and exclaimed,

"A small kiss for Larry, a giant step for mankind!"

With that they both giggled. Then from the adjoining area someone shouted,

"Shhh, quiet you should be seated." Everina whispered,

"We better return be good, see you soon, marsh mallow man."

Just then the cook's radio played Madonna's I am a material girl.

Larry rolled his eyes up to heaven and they both shuffled off in different directions.

Larry could not help thinking of a 'Richie's mints' commercial the he saw on TV when he was a kid. In the commercial, everything was soft and white and springy, just like now on board the good ship Callisto.

It was just at that moment that they hit the first standing wave. Suddenly the Ship lurched to starboard. Larry was hurled along the isle, but managed to climb into his seat. Hiroshi turned and shouted,

"Larry where have you been, you must be a bit soft in the head. You could have busted your neck. Do you realise we are hitting the first of those standing waves."

Larry grunted and strapped himself into the seat,

"You forget Hiroshi, these are not ocean waves, and we will probably plough right through them!"

However, Larry was half wrong and so was Laura. As it turned out the waves were coming straight at them. With that the ship's nose was wrenched upwards as they began an endless climb. Then it turned and like a roller coaster tore down the other side of the enormous precipices. As it hit the trough there was a sickening jolt and all loose objects in the ship went flying in many directions. There was a crashing sound from the boardroom. Things had gone from bad to worse!

The navigators knew his job, he did not leave the helm and he stayed on course, never letting up for a moment. It was like nautical history being repeated. Then the waves began to settle but were now beginning to come from the left. From where they were sitting, Richard got a bird's eye view through the front portal of what lay ahead. He saw a bright blue patch there was hope at the end of the tunnel. Immediately the cylinder widened, like the beginning of an entrance to another world. Above and around them the stars disappeared and the sky opened, and an electric blue ocean formed below them. In an instant, they had vacated the tunnel and glided out onto an impressive expanse of open sea. They were not flying any more but gliding on a flat plane.

Just then there was a loud exclamation from the Boardroom. The hypnotic moment was shattered. It was Laura,

"Dave, Kiki has disappeared. Oh my God, has anyone seen my bird?"

Chapter 13

There was misty sky above the Callisto while the abyss seemed to shimmer and radiate blue ultra violet type of light. The Navigator attempted to ascertain their position in the new environment. He worked feverishly on the EM/SPEC and eventually with a grunt of satisfaction, got a result. To his amazement the machine had now adopted a mathematical portrayal of the landscape and it looked remarkably like Hiroshi's Mandala.He turned around and stared at the anxious faces. He told them that they were positioned at the lower central region of an immense triangle. Now Mantz stood beside him slowly nodding his head but saying,

"What's this about Hiroshi's Mandala?"

Hiroshi blushed and pulled out a copy.

"Sorry sir we never got an opportunity to show it to you!"

Mantz looked closely at the picture and compared it with the EM/SPEC. Then a reluctant smile crossed his face and he thrust it back to Hiroshi saying,

"Well done. I see Lionel has a copy? Lionel nodded and began to philosophy where about where they had landed. It was then for the first time that Don Travis came to the fore. He was fascinated by the Mandala and the EMSPEC by comparison. He asked could he study them both, did so for a few minutes and then cleared his throat,

"Look we are in a world of forms and ideas similar to Platos's Eidos."

"Explain," said Larry.

"Well all this will govern our earthly geometry, this is the ideal triangle the first and last of its kind. This is non-corporeal eternal and real. Somewhere up ahead we will encounter more forms and that I can now say with certainty."

Then he continued,

"In the 'Timaes', Plato said that geometrically solids are bounded by planes, and the most elementary plane figure is a triangle. From two types of triangles he envisaged all solid bodies. To Plato they were Earth, Fire,

Water and Air. Putting it in very simple terms, this triangle is certainly the generator of all air and water but what generates fire? I think we will find out when we get further north!"

Hiroshi cut in,

"Thanks for that Don, I have something to add,"

Don raised his eyebrows, and listened intently.

"From what we have seen it looks like we have discovered a truly divine form! We are privileged to gaze upon a perfect inelastic collision (1). There is no doubt that as you said this is the form of all forms and would remain as such even if the universe were to disappear. Now Don what do think of that?"

Don Travis looked at him in amazement!

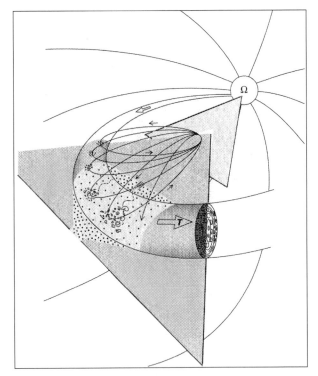

What the EM/SPEC recorded.

The humming sound from the EM/SPEC indicated business as usual. It now showed that the triangle was generating immense negative electrical current! Amazingly the magnetic compass was working and indicating that north was directly ahead towards the apex of the triangle. Lionel again compared the Mandala with the assimilated version and said,

"This is a piece of sensible material, it will be a great help in our navigation." Hiroshi repeated,

"Keep it safe it's precious."

Lionel taped it at the side of the console. Then said,

"Our estimates concur and show the universe lies to the south in a cut out section in the centre of the largest triangle, the one we are now in. That puts us situated in the middle of the of the EM/SPEC picture."

Mantz and Ivan were making frantic calculations and when ready explained their findings, it was Ivan who spoke,

"As you know we are now beyond the threshold of light. This begs the question, how can we see? Well this zone produces its own glow – quite amazing! The EM/SPEC generated info for us to say that this triangle was one hundred and fifty times larger than the universe! Depending on the size of the triangle we could be anything from twenty to a hundred times larger that when we set out on the mission. Therefore we have grown beyond the bounds of human imagination!"

Mantz nodded in agreement. Dave, Larry and at least a dozen others let out a sigh of acceptance. Richard asked,

"Is it certain that we are also atomically inverted?"

"Yes Rich, that's for sure but our medics are going to confirm that shortly."

Then the atmosphere was abruptly shattered by Hamish Cauldron who pushed up from the seated area and said out loudly,

"Now where is this God that you all talk about? I don't see any evidence."

There was a dramatic chill in the air and several stopped work to listen.

It was Travis who fielded the question,

"Hamish you are looking at an intimate part of God, the force field of the AMGOD. This is part of the Trinity in the act of being midwife and keeping our world alive and allowing it to develop. Take this triangle away and we would have no light or life of any sort because there would be no electrons, no neutrinos and thus no atoms. In other words we would be snuffed. Be patient we will get to the source of power in easy steps, and right now we are in her lap!"

Raphael now arrived and joined to support Hamish. Now having an alley he responded negatively,

"Tell us another one Padre!"

They shrugged and walked away.

One of the crew who was listening said loudly as they went,

"Hamish some of us are atheists and non believers, but we are scientists first of all and we do not subscribe to rude challenges like you have just performed. Be clear, you don't represent us in any way so please have some respect!"

Dave appreciated the loyalty and things settled down again with people just gazing out across the expanse and relishing the benefits from their improved senses. However the question about the inverted atoms was still foremost in everyone's mind. The scene was enchanting with the water altering in colour to take on every tone of blue and turquoise imaginable. Then to add to the exciting beauty there were the flashes of lightning every now and then being emitted from the sea.

One of the Medics named Burnette, approached the Captain,

"In the light of what has happened, it is our intention to do medical checkups on all the crew. We have already checked and analysed tissue from donor's hair and nails and can confirm the inversion is in evidence – it really did happened! However we could not delve as deep as the atomic structure, but at molecular level it defiantly has occurred. We do have powerful microscopes on board, but have been only able to see DNA at 1/10,000,000 of an inch in diameter, universal scale related. We have found them to be completely opposite structures to what we know. They are inside out, and less compact than before. Molecules are therefore more spaced out, but they are in the same string configuration. We are concerned to know if all the chemical actions 20,000 per cell are taking place, and we would like to have many other questions answered."

Dave nodded in agreement. Burnette continued,

"We intend setting up clinic immediately that is with the Captains permission, and proceed with health checks for everyone. When word got out this brought about a general sigh of relief, as at least it was 90% certain that they had inverted.

Then the EM/SPEC made its usual clacking sound a report was printed out its first report on the composition of the new territory they had entered,

"Gravitation- zero, replaced by negative electro magnetic gravity. There is an abundance of Dark Energy in motion. Landscape Topography – triangular force field. Contents; photons and one only primordial electron Identified. There is an abundance of Neutrinos and a consistency of newly un-identified particles and unknown Dark Energy."

Lionel was the first to read it and immediately alerted Dave and Larry.

"Sir did you see that 'Dark Energy' comment?" Larry reacted,

"This means that 'Dark Energy' is a bi partisan of Electromagnetism, wow!"

A dozen of the physicists quickly gathered around to speculate on its meaning.

Someone said,

"You know the void is denoted by the Greek letter Lambda Constant. This is the symbol for Gravitational repulsion. The equation reads like this; $G = Aq = 8$ omega T."

Richard looked around to see it was Raphael who had made the comment. He could not complain as after all this was Raphael's specialised area. Everyone was quite patient so Raphael now joined by Hamish, continued,

"This is the equation that Albert Einstein introduced but later regretted. However, it turned out after his death that he was not wrong. What he had done was not in vain because study of the speed of light (2) showed that it could alter with time. This is something that we all discovered on our journey here, so they must be correct in this assumption."

Then Jean Moreau, added something more directly related to energy,

"The equation was later used by science when calculating how dark matter though up to now still only theoretical, would hold galaxies from moving apart. Therefore physicists had assumed that it was Lambda that was holding the universe from over expanding and dissipating to emptiness. On the opposite end of the scale 'Dark Energy' fills 74% of space and is said to fuel expansion. This is what we are looking at on the EM/SPEC at this moment, it's wonderful!"

Despite this burst of enlightenment nothing seemed to change. People still had their feet on the deck. An alternative force had now taken the place of earth gravitation. Richard said it must be electromagnetic generated gravitation and then turned his attentions skywards,

"Look Larry we are free for the first time from that Torus of gravitation that seems to be flowing from somewhere way above us. Being curved it must bend everything in its path, space included. Therefore space now bent, in turn must bend motion and perhaps light? Hoop-la it would look to science that gravity is no more than a track in space fabric, where as it is actually the other way around. Just look, for yourself, it is plain for all to see!"

A physicist who was listening butted in muttered some disagreement,

"Richard, you can't defy Einstein's statement that mass bends space fabric and that creates gravity."

Richard looked at him and nodded but said,

"With respect, I'm postulating on the premises of what we see around us. As a reassurance, Einstein's saddle shaped universe will not be effected, as any section of the torus taken in isolation is already saddle shaped!"

The physicist nodded, this time in agreement.

Richard then got close to Larry and said,

"Hey Lar, I've noticed you and Everina are sort of an item! Does she like you a lot?"

Larry quickly brought Richard up to date like he was a brother, and then said,

"Rich, you're an experienced guy with family, what do you think of her, or am I mad?"

"Yep Lar, your crazy alright, but she is worth every hallucination. Go for it, but of course not on company time!" Then he laughed.

The team now turned their attention to the outside void that spread above. Due to the thinning mist they began to notice that the sky was quite black, but also alive with activity. Something was not right; there was a hostile feeling in the ether. Then like a bolt out of the grey, a swirl of inky substance moved across the sky behind them and descended towards the universe. It was the rear observer who alerted them. This was like smoke from a burning oil well polluting everything it came in contact with. It was a case of black substance moving on a black background. Then they began to hear sound for the first time. It was sudden and penetrating like an artillery shell rushing through the sky. Then it was seen penetrating the outer layers of their cosmos. Moments later there was an implosion deep down in its fibre! Something awful was happening!

At that very moment Everina thought that she saw the source of the venom - a dark object floating low in the void, only visible because of the light from the implosion. She let out a shriek!

"Did you see that?" she said.

"I saw an object directing an attack on our poor universe!"

Just then Don Travis intervened in a sympathetic tone of voice,

"Everina, from here it looked to us like a nuclear attack, but it was not. It is no secret that there are dark powers always trying to derail humanity. Some people deny that, but here you see it for yourself. We on the other hand are praying for salvation from exactly that sort of peril. Don't let what you saw bother you as it has been happening for eons. Just take note and continue doing your best that is protection in itself."

The others also tried to observe the object - but to no avail. Everina nodded in appreciation and moved from the window, unprepared to discuss any further just what she had seen! Larry and Lydia who was one of the cadets, followed her trying to provide comfort. Then as they watched the scene altered. There was no further encroachment and the universe began to take on the shape of an unborn child and then it faded out of sight. The group marvelled.

----

(1) Inelastic Collision; a Platonic description of Ideal form or the laws of nature.
(2) It was further discovered by John Webb of New South Wales that the spectrum of electrons in a number of Quasars showed that though they had been apart in the early universe, never the less they had been within the same light threshold. All this proved that light therefore must have moved at a greater velocity than the present estimates!

Chapter 14

Though the engines were turned off yet amazingly the ship did not loose speed but was merrily drawn along in a northerly direction. Dave discovered that the natural wool cloths in his office had by now shrunk beyond recognition, and what did all that mean, and would they grow even more? Just then one of the crew spotted what looked like a flock of magnificent white doves swirling above the sea. A moment later they disappeared, perhaps they were not supposed to be seen. Then from somewhere towards the apex of the triangle the sky began to glow red and orange just like an earthly sunset. Silver arcs of light could now be clearly seen shooting up and over their heads and descending towards the universe far behind. Then in an instant these same streaks returned to their source at enormous speed. It was as if the world was a holograph; a three-dimensional film being projected on to the curved interior of the torus! These were the same streaks that had been like rain and then thinned and disappeared as they broke through the membrane. Hiroshi looked disturbed by this feature as he said,

"What will happen if that machine is turned off? Will people become pillars of salt?"

This did not please Richard, because it gave him pangs of fear reminding him of his state before he had become strengthened. However, on the plus side, Larry said,

"Hey we cannot see it as a machine, remember it is a living entity, giving us precious life. Also those streaks look as if they are quite impervious to the fiendish blackness."

Richard looked relieved. Larry then added,

"When I was a kid we went to 'Jack and the Bean Stalk' a Christmas pantomime. Young Jack, climbed up to the land of the giant. The Callisto has just performed a similar fete. Why have we not yet met a giant? Or are we now giants ourselves!" Richard again looked disturbed.

The Callisto remained on the smooth central trail that led towards the apex. The only problem was that things were going too well. The electric equipment was generating more power then ever before and the luminosity in the ship was carnival like. The crew's misty soft textures, shone more vividly than before and there was much jibing and joking about their state. Their personal vision had increased enormously, they could see for hundreds of earth miles in this newfound 'kodachrome' world. It was as if a mystical energy was sweeping the Callisto ever onwards.

It was then that they began to hear the sound of chimes in the wind, and the chant reminiscent of the South Sea Islands. It was what one would expect in Tahiti or the Hawaiian Islands; but it was also quite weird and wonderful.

"Enihi ka hele mai ho'opa. Mai pulale I ka'ike a ka maka.
Ho'okahi no makamaka 'o ke aloha. Oka hea mai'okalani a'e kipa." (1)

Then the sound abated and silence descended. Richard turned to Don Travis and said,

"Don, what's next?

Don answered giving the impression that he had prepared for the question,

"Now Rich, you have been through thick and thin, and have directed your mind to eschatological questions. On the other hand, I have become saturated with physics. However things are moving so fast that I'm a bit confused! Travis gave a laugh and then got serious,

"Look Richard, I am startled by all this. It leaves me spellbound. However if I muster all that I learned I can attempt to put the following spin on it. This is an intermediate arena where the divine principle is transformed into qualities that can in turn support life in our three dimensional continuum. To correct my self, the universe may not be a continuum as generally perceived, but contiguous and sub-dividable. The 'Apeiron' (2) that makes up this blue world seems superior; all one and not sub dividable. I believe we are now in the working body of the Spirit - the mid wife of creation! Others will call it their Nirvana and some will see it as Chi-energy connecting everything everywhere like a computer."

As if to confirm the Padre's words, the mist retracted, to a point in front of the ship. Then with out warning the ship stopped of its own accord and a whispering voice was heard. It was female and resounded in everyone's understanding simultaneously. It began much like the sound of wind. It was ghostly and everyone was startled as she said,

"Shalom, Shalom!"

With that some of the group went to their seats and clicked into their safety harnesses. Some pulled the zippers up high in their RP suits; others just stood their ground. The voice spoke in many languages, because later everyone agreed that they heard it in their own native tongue. At this point the white birds re-appeared flying in circles around the ship. To an onlooker, if such could exist, it must have been a pretty sight. The golden coloured Callisto set against a sea of many shades of blue, under a black sky that had streaks of phosphorous clouds webbed about the horizon. The light provided for this event as they had discovered, did not come down from a sun or a moon but was generated from below; by the triangle itself. This entire splendour coupled with the flock of snow-white doves and enhanced with the sound of wind and musical chimes, added up to a speckle of magnificent proportions. Then the background sound abated and the voice spoke again,

"Let me introduce myself as the one known as the Paraclete (3). Little ones, you are the seeds in which we place our trust. You are welcome to my world. Please be advised, you got here only by a stroke of good fortune. Do you know you have accidentally violated many laws of nature by coming? This would not have happened but only because nature itself has waved its laws and permitted your arrival. Nature is your friend but never defy it! God always forgives but it does not and can be a cruel opponent. Despite that Nature has its genesis in me and springs from the world of ideal forms; myself! Perhaps you arrival is a sign that the time is right for further human mutation and elevation!"

There was a long pause, which prompted the Vice Captain to speak. She asked with respect, would the violation cause punishment? Then there was a further silence. People did not know if a reply was possible in these circumstances. Hiroshi dreaded the answer. After several minutes, just as if all sound was delayed via satellite communications, there was a reply.

"My people, you have suffered enough anxiety, we are not beings who are bent on punishment. We are beings that that take pride in forgiveness and are supportive and eternally curious with all we behold. As you have come this far it would be sad if you did not have an opportunity to experience our fullness of time. Therefore do you want to continue with this journey? Alternatively you will be returned unharmed to your original status, thus all these events never happened? The choice is yours, trust me and deliberate amongst yourselves. You may not realise it but you are in a state of prayer by the nature of this very discussion and as a result you will make the right decision. Now take time, relax, discuss, drink and arrive at a unanimous choice, and then call out to me - I will answer your call."

Then there was another prolonged silence. Larry prayed that Laura would not ask about Kiki! Then the voice said,

"Did you realise it is safe for you to open the doors of your craft, and to bath in the ocean? You will come to no harm and will enjoy the experience. Your guardians have much power up here they are your mentors, and now I bid you Fi man- illa" (4)

---

(1)E NIHI KA HELE-ref The Gabby Pahinui Hawaiian Band. Vo; 1
"Be cautious on your journey, don't be over anxious
Don't be overwhelmed by what you see
There is one companion of love
When the sovereign bids to visit."
(2) Apeiron; Both principle and element that steers all things, according to philosopher Anaximenes
(3) Paraclete, Christ's Spirit that also generates the feeling of peace, forgiveness and tranquillity. (John 14;16)
(4) Islamic goodbye in Iraqi.

Chapter 15

The sweet fragrance in the ylem bore testimony to the presence of a heavenly being. The Captain went to the EM/SPEC and asked for a rewind of the last events. The replay was interesting because it showed the triangle lifting at its apex. Then like a peaking wave it peeled upwards and rolled towards the Callisto, increasing in height as it approached. At the top of the rising mass a magnificent female face appeared. Then from the left and right sides, two arms with slender hands protruded. They were covered in blue waves just like the rest of the body. Then the figure bent forward towards the ship. Her face came so close she could have breathed on it. At this point she appeared to speak, and that would have been the conversation they had already heard. While this was happening the waves and the flocks of snow white doves moved across the great body as if in total defiance of her gravity. Then she slowly rolled back and the triangle returned to its original form.

There was silence and the ship still remained at rest. People wondered what next!

"Oh bye the way," said Laura, "Do you realize that none of us have eaten or drank since coming through the tunnel?" Dave noticed that she looked still quite upset by the disappearance of Kiki. So he forced myself to be congenial and said,

"Laura I am really sorry about Kiki, but let's hope she turns up, I know she will, this is a strange world full of surprises. So look you go first I'll take a break later." She responded,

"Thanks Dave for that, the only need I have apart from seeing Kiki again is to have a drink, but I could not face eating!"

The crew therefore got busy with the task of refreshment which consisted solely of fresh water from the oasis systems. Some went to the canteen and got their water a la carte with ice cubes, while some preferred juice. The cooks were heard to jest, that if word about the trend got back to base, they would be made redundant. One of them began to suggest that water should be charged for, but was booed out of it.

There was concern that their supply would soon diminish, but on inspection the level in the tanks never seemed to drop! The physicists said that they wondered had a new constant been discovered. They said in jest they might name it h_2/o where h equals Heaven!

The Captain remembering the Ladies suggestion, requested for two volunteers from the crew to test the sea before people got wet. They immediately stripped down to their shorts, as they did not have swim trunks as part of their kit, in fact no one did! On a command from Ben, one of the computer people tapped on a keyboard. There was an immediate hiss, and the door began to roll back. Instantly there was a strong aroma of perfume, accompanied by a musical sound that amazingly came directly from the sea. The interior of the Callisto became bathed in shimmering lights of blue and gold. Everina thought it was like a beautiful discothèque in a tropical resort. Everyone gasped in delight. Then the two designated crew members cupped their hands and withdrew some water. They stood up and said, still holding the water.

"Major Sir, this here water, does not even wet our hand, it is like blue mercury."

Dave instructed that a sample of the water is taken for later analysis. It was then that they discovered that the ship was sitting on a golden pallet of light, perhaps that is what had delivered them this far. It appeared harmless and tended to retreat when people investigated so it was not interfered with any further.

Quite a few of the group began to swim in their fatigues. Some shouted out,

"It's solid it's real and just like back home!"

Richard and Hiroshi were quick to join in the fun. Larry ploughed in with a big splash. Being a surfer, he could not believe that he was back in the ocean again. He then made a duck dive to see what lay beneath and just what he might find! To his relief it was not unlike the Caribbean and far below he could see the golden expanse of shimmering sand that glowed quite brightly. The effect of rising light was amazing. Shafts of gold burst from the seabed along with streams of blue bubbles. All this rose and invigorated any thing or anyone in its path. The texture of the water was slippery and grain like, one moment it was flat and placid, while the next moment brought waves. Richard was convinced that they were experiencing first hand Quantum theory in action. Hiroshi decided to take a sip of the water. He did so reluctantly but then swallowed it. Immediately his eyes opened wide and he called to Richard,

"Hey Rich, try drinking some it's great."

With that he hiccupped and several golden bubbles popped out of his mouth. Those who were watching roared with laughter. Richard sampled the water and competed by sending a shower of bubbles in all directions.

"Gee!" He said, "It tastes sweet."

Just then, Everina splashed into the water and swam up beside Larry, smiled and pointed downwards. He instinctively made another dive, and she followed. They both met face to face allowing ample time for a gentle kiss and a moment of embrace. For a brief second they were suspended in a world of blue wonder. It was like midnight in the Caribbean - as bright plankton like objects appeared and illuminated the liquid. Time stood still and they slowly drifted to the surface at the speed of the rising bubbles.

They were in a trance, and when they broke the surface Larry fond himself whispering to Everina,

"Praise to the pneuma, theion, theon, theou pneuma" (1)

"Praise to ruah" (2)

As he did not speak Greek or Hebrew, he wondered how he conjured up the words. Everina looked at him in puzzlement.

"Larry,"- she said jokingly,

"You speak in tongues, did I cause that?"

As people climbed back on board, to their astonishment they found their cloths were bone dry. Everything about this extra universal discovery was palatable, accommodating and everyone loved the experience.

---

(1) Spirit and divine reality in Greek
(2) Ruah – Spirit in Hebrew.

Chapter 16

It was Larry who again noticed that several people had not joined in the fun. They looked quite miserable and kept away from activities that were not directly related to duties. The more exuberant the crew became the more dejected these people looked. Hamish, Dalia and Raphael were apparent leaders. By enlarge these were normal people who for some reason or other did not fit with the new experience. Some of them were crew and one or two were cadets. As a result, they seemed to find consolation in each other and therefore began bunching together. Larry discussed the observation with his colleagues and between them some worrying thought immerged. What happens if there is a crisis and they don't do what is required of them? No one could answer that question. Everina suggested that the grotesque object that had attacked the universe might have something to do with it! But then Larry said, they had been like that from the beginning. Just then they were interrupted. An announcement called for general assembly, a town hall meeting. Dave the skipper addressed the entire group,

"My dear fellow explorers, as you know, we have come a long way together. I thank my God, that no one has been killed or injured and there is no need to assume that this will change. Now what do you people want to do? We used to say in situations like this, that we are on a mission and absolutely must carry on. Now the goal posts have changed. The rules of the game have altered and we are extended far beyond the call of duty; and it's up to you as individuals to say what comes next! It is obvious this is our last chance for to return and rewind the situation. If we chose to go on, there will be no turning back and we will have to continue to the end, what ever that may be! There are various options open to us, we can have a show of hands, or a secret ballot or I can say let's try it and see does anyone disagree!"

A most unexpected person stood up and walked forward. It was Cadet Everina Spazola. She moved forward in a gliding motion, slowly turned to face the group and then looked at the Captain. She spoke in slow deliberate words saying boldly,

"You have seen by now the terror that lurks in the void. It is driven by a mysterious dark personality, an agent from the abyss that we do not admire. From that ebony inferno comes the devil in the machine the ones that plague the earth. This is what has warped our natures and continuously distorts everything one does. There is but one force that thwarts that fiendishness and that is the power of this triangle. Already we have been enlightened from the moment we entered the tunnel. As a woman, I for one feel elevated by what we have experienced. I trust and identify with the blue lady and her kind voice. I feel whole and entire and in better health than ever before. I feel forgiven, washed clean and my spirits are high and I perceive a very bright future no matter in what form it comes. If we do not proceed, we will erase all that has happened and can never relate it to our universal kin. We will have failed those who we love, and above all we will fail those who love us. I vote we continue."

These rallying words coming from a girl, and a cadet, seemed to tip the scales. There was another thunderous applause and people spoke out loud saying,

"She is right, let's carry on!"

With that there was a jolt and the Callisto began to move forward once again.

It was now a much more united crew that peered north. A column of mist had been leading them up the centre of the triangle. Richard thought it was quite biblical. He recalled some text from memory,

"During the day the Lord went in front of them in a pillar of cloud to show them the way, and during the night he went in front of them in a pillar of fire to give them light, so that they could travel night and day." (Exodus 13.21)

Up ahead, there was still a red glow which by now was deeper and broader. A visit to another triangle was imminent. As they travelled, the water became swept by the wind that increased and blew towards the apex. The source of this seemed to be a ribbon of bulbous mountains running up both sides of the upper one third of the triangle. As the triangle narrowed to a point, the mountains seemed to close in on both sides. There was also the faint line under the water that may have been a spinal section with some intersections, which ran off in the direction of both mountain ranges.

It was so strange that Lionel produced Hiroshi's Mandala to find a meaning but there was none in evidence. Hiroshi said he thought it looked like part of a mammoth breathing system. However both the EM/SPEC and the Mandala agreed showing that up ahead there was another triangle- the king pin of the matrix. Then as quick as it had appeared, the column of mist began to vaporise, it had completed its task.

Now they reached the narrow point of the blue triangle and glided between high peaks and onto the broad lower end of another surreal land. In contrast, the new environment consisted of a molten mass of red and maroon eruptions. Every few moments its substance belched coloured spheres that were linked together with strings that vibrated. At each eruption hot matter unleashed a strange cocktail of anti-colours - turquoise, mauve, green, grey and mustard. They rose as bubbles and then dissipated into its atmosphere.

The navigator was now resting in a reclining seat. He looked like the events had quite worn him out. However he drummed up fresh energy and introduced a scientist who wanted to bring the group up to date. This new personality was most informative and gave his commentary while examining the screen.

"Most of you know me - I'm Calan Spencer, from Tweed Head in New South Wales, Larry I think you have surfed there!" Larry smiled and nodded and Calan continued,

"I'm a physicist suffering from a serious dose of information overload like most of you. Now look here at the screen, it states that we are receiving images from this new fangled triangle. This territory appears to consist of a mass of quarks, gluons and also free what's called, quark activity. There is evidence of a super strong force with supped up protons, inverted of course and baryons of three different spins. Then there is an anti-world with supped up inverted anti- protons and anti-quarks."

As he spoke there was an amazing sequence in which the triangle alternated through the colours of the rainbow blazing finishing at pure white, turquoise, mauve and green.

Calan commented,

"White is the eventual outcome of all colours being mixed. Now remember on the scale of things, we are quite enormous compared with our original state. Therefore hold your breath because these quarks must then be larger than anything imaginable. This will cause an overwhelming proportion of strong nuclear and colour force but all in a reverse configuration. Just like us they are most likely inverted. Also there is no sign of any atoms just their fundamental components. To sum up, we are in a giant atom free, inverted world of the metaphysical kind!"

He took a deep breath,

"Now here comes the crunch - temperature! The readings are in excess of (100 million, degrees Kelvin) x3. Why then are we not burned to a crisp? Well there are three possibilities, one that we are protected because of inversion, that our EM/SPEC is faulty, or divine intervention!"

No one asked any questions, and many found the irony of their situation more than amusing!

Chapter 17

It was about then, that Hiroshi announced that he had calculated it must be his birthday. Larry and Richard were in no mood for festivities, but were obliged to play along. Hiroshi said that they should come to his billet and enjoy some vacuum packed Mochi-Gashi cake that his mother had sent him before departure. It was not Japanese tradition to have cake, but he was doing it for his friends. Therefore they gathered for the celebration, as did Everina and a female neurosurgeon called Navine Bakr who had become her friend. Their main concern was their appetites. Everyone wondered if they could manage to eat cake after their watery experiences. However Hiroshi was so excited by his birthday that he quite forgot their state. With one swift movement he opened the cake pack and sliced it carefully. He passed the cake around on paper plates and everyone took a slice. Then at the given word they sang Happy Birthday, and began cautiously to eat. To their astonishment they had no difficulty. The cake was delicious and they all had seconds.

Then Larry asked,

"Hiroshi do you realise we are eating once again?"

Hiroshi responded with a whoop and said,

"You see my cake has cured you!"

He then showed pictures of his family, but when he was asked had he a girl friend he took out a picture of Jill and said,

"That's her, isn't she lovely? Larry you know her well – your sis."

Everyone agreed that he was a lucky guy. Larry on the other hand was taken aback yet pleasantly surprised.

Then the party became quite solemn as Navine, who was an Islamic became eager to talk all about their experiences. She naturally got on to the subject of neurology, but in relation to the new reality. Sitting on Hiroshi's Hybo with one slender leg on a swivel chair, she began to talk freely. The others squatted wherever they could find space as she spoke,

"You know we have witnessed an infant shaped universe. Well there is a school of thought promoted by Francis Heylighen from the University of Brussels. He says that we are developing a global brain. He sees the Internet and E-mail as its beginning. Since then we have S-mail which is a photon boosted and magnetic transformed telepathy communications system. Next we could well develop a world soul and above all a world thinking process will enable it to evolve. Should we welcome this global brain or fear it? That's the question?"

She moved to one side and sat on an unused stool,

"Now from what we have seen his theory must be correct as our universe shows every sign of being a living entity. To succeed, there will need to be a super organism that can foster vast amounts of information so as to facilitate a central brain. There is a process that is called 'transivity' where the internet begins to look at what it has in the way of information and at where there are information gaps or shortfalls. Then it begins to question users to make good the missing knowledge. It is thought that humans will be a secondary part of this brain I hope not a disposable part. Now this is where we come into the picture."

She paused and sipped some water,

"You see, I am convinced from what I have seen that the human is like the sum total of all its parts and therefore its soul. We will be the manipulative force that will always monitor and control, rather than leaving it to Internet. On another level we as Muslims are perpetually ready to submit and surrender to Allah. We therefore are open to what ever he shows us, no matter how difficult it may be to understand. We are quite sure that he will keep it simple and reward us in the end!"

Another swig of water,

"As we know, the brain of the human has a left and a right side. Each side controls the opposite side of the body. Information travels through the nervous system at up to the speed of 6.66 km per second. Now this looks to us as being much slower relative to the speed of light 300,000 km per second. Consider that the universe is reckoned to have a volume in cubic miles of 4.2×10^{69} Imagine 10 with 69 zeros, quite a mass! Now the human is only the size of a grain of sand by comparison which means that our nervous fluid travels as quick if not faster relative to the size of our bodies, QED!"

She took a breath,

"I know I don't have exact figures but it is a valid point. Do you agree?"

"Okay, we can't argue with that." Said Hiroshi and so Nadine went on,

"This means that each of us is a dynamic universe of our own and combined we will have a synergy value of extra ordinary proportions. Mentally and through the media our combined knowledge is able to see and understand things that we as individuals could not comprehend. So the net should just be a tool at our disposal, and we must keep it that way.

Again on a different subject; in the Qur'an we are told that the Lord created man from a clot. Now that we are in such an extra-spatial condition, one wonders will we receive enlightenment about his statement? The only comparison that I can find so far is the preoccupation that Christians have with blood and passion. However we differ because I like my compatriots do not believe in democracy, as you know it. We believe in obedience to a hierarchical order above, which comes ultimately from God. The Persian poet Rumi wrote,

"Oh God do not leave our affairs to us, for if you do, woe to us!"

With that there was the sound of voices from the main concourse. Navine concluded,

"I have said too much, let's see what's happening and Happy Birthday again Hiroshi."

Chapter 18

There was a distant sound of thumping that grew louder as they glided into the interior of the new triangle. The thud was so persistent that it reminded Larry of stories about running Zulus warriors on the warpath. Then as the rhythm grew even louder, the gentle scent of rose perfume penetrated the ship. Larry looked at his compatriots who ever since the tunnel, took on a distinct blue hue to the left side of their being, and a pale pinkness to the right. He noticed that some of the females had begun to play with make up perhaps for example, some pink on the blue side and blue on the pink. He chuckled to himself thinking just how fast people had grown accustomed to the new phenomenon. Everina came into view as she went about her duties. Larry snatched a look towards her and gasped at her extra radiant beauty. She looked fine as an earth girl, but now he thought she was breathtaking.

The ships bells jangled. The Captain stood wide legged at the EM/ SPEC and the computer banks became very active. Larry looked at the screen and noticed vapour following them from the blue territory. The vapour was there perhaps because of a temperature difference between both masses. It was certainly being absorbed directly into the maroon triangles structure. Perhaps all this was purifying the texture, the elixir of life of this strange world!

A range of mountains loomed up ahead. It's mass seemed to vibrate ever so slightly and in time with every thump. As they listened, one of the medical people made some calculations. He determined that it made a thud once every .857 of a second - timed on their earth watches. They were struck at the resemblance it bore to the human heartbeat.

The mountain range appeared smooth and rounded like the back of a turtle shell. It just rose before their eyes, perhaps because they were travelling faster than realised! Lionel exclaimed,

"What do you know – this is like the famous Ayers Rock in the Australian's northern territories, what do you think Calan?"

The volcano section now became more noticeable. It could be seen protruded through the centre of the surrounding hills. This super pandemic vortex was undoubtedly the source of spiritual and even cosmic energy. It was the epicentre for the silver streaks that they had watched for so long. As they became more accustomed to the evolving oddity, Larry noticed that the incoming streaks were purple and that the outgoing were a vibrant mixture of blue and gold. As if to confirm the importance of the experience, some of the crew said out loud,

"Good God, is this the powerhouse of existence? Another responded,

"Why yes, it must be, and where the heck else would you see a sight like it? Ernst exclaimed " Es ist einnen hertz!" Mantz muttered,

"Le Coeur du Universe, et Le Sacre-Coeur!"exclaimed Jean Moreau.

The navigator again compared the Mandala with the image of what lay ahead. He was again reassured by the near similarity. Then his curiosity was rewarded. Just as if to answer his question; a city was sighted, nestled on and around the base of the mighty rock,

"City ahoy," yelled one of the Ship's crew.

"It looks like Rio, you know Rio de Janeiro!"

It seemed to be spread across the planes and up the hills leading to the higher peaks. There were reflections of moving objects which gave the impression of traffic of sorts. Maybe this activity was caused by their arrival, but who knew!

As they got closed its dwellings appeared sometimes white or beige in colour and many had arched windows and orange tiled roofs. Many possessed balconies so that it was all quite Spanish looking. The dwellings were varied, some were of low design like homes but others were taller and like apartments or commercial blocks. There was also aerial activity - specs of light could be seen rising and descending like fireflies. There was the twinkle of water - a lake to the south west. Some of these fireflies were circulating above the lake and disappearing, perhaps into the rear of the Ayres Rock Style Mountains. Just then the EM/SPEC gave a reading,

"$T = 300,000x3\ T\ Avum = .00005\ T\ Eternitas\ as\ absolute\ Zero$ -.00005. Contents reverse Hadrons Deuterium and Super Strong Gravitational Force."

Richard read with interest and then stabbed a finger in the direction of Deuterium saying,

"That is the first time we have had confirmation about this element. No one ever knew from where it came from or if it existed. Now look this is where it must have originated!"

"Your right," said one of the physicists,

"But look it records the temperature is much too high for Hadrons to be, this strengthens the case that they are inverted as otherwise they would not be here? Then there is super strong gravitational force, what is that?" Larry took a guess,

"It must be the total of all local gravities otherwise we would be floating around by now."

The navigator managed to magnify the imaging of the city. A new feature became apparent. All around the outskirts there were plains of golden colour that resemble those of Manitoba, the steps of Russia or the fields of Athenry!

"Could that be wheat for bread?" asked Everina.

"Could be!" said Larry

"I wonder what else?"

Luckily, the immediate area around the city was free from eruptions, as that is where the Callisto came to a stop. As they were now very close the thumping diminished perhaps muffled by the mountains and the buildings.

Chapter 19

The Callisto had finished its multi billion light year odyssey right in front of a mysterious city in a world that could only be justified as imaginary! Everina had been correct; it was wheat that was growing around this almost real metropolis. After being deposited on firm ground the golden pallet of light withdrew and retreated south becoming just a shimmering line on the horizon before disappearing. Then from out of the town several vehicles made an approach. Above them were several flying bird people that made a musical sound as they came. It appeared that all transport was quite transparent, to the extent that their interiors could be clearly seen. They were like two tiered limousines their surfaces smooth and therefore reflecting an array of colour from the surroundings. They arched in a wide turn some of them cruising over the wheat without causing any damage! Then they came to a standstill beside the ship. Without a sound the four flyers landed gracefully and flick switches to turn off the power. They were wearing head visors like halo's - which they pushed back to reveal young friendly faces. They wore white jet packs with even whiter wings partially outstretched. The effect was clearly angelic.

The transporters were like Delorian sports cars, because they had gull type doors to allow access. Most of the drivers appeared to be in their mid twenties and were obviously of both genders. They were also subtly coloured like the Callisto people, with the now familiar pale blue on one side, and pink on the other! Some were dark or black skinned but nevertheless the colour tinge was obvious. Despite all of this peculiarity, the overall effect was one of beauty.

Larry noticed that a few had mature faces and in their case the hair was golden – perhaps denoting age! Most were dressed in contradictory gear, which indicated an element of freedom of choice. There was a girl in a long white dress whose styling was medieval. There was a fellow dressed in a bush shirt and shorts. Another was in combats and a tee shirt and one was in a one-piece flyers jump suit. One of the drivers was quite Arabic looking with a dark beard and moustache. The girls wore various hairstyles, ranging from ponytails to long flowing. One had a punk style orange haircut and large hoop earrings, while another was dressed in a black linen suite that looked oriental! They were a very individualistic bunch and not quite what one would expect so close to the pearly gates.

They briskly alighted from their vehicles and walked towards the ship. By now the visitors had gathered outside and were looking quite puzzled and a little shy.

The leader of the host part was a fellow who resembled a gardener with a straw hat and denim dungarees. He stepped forward and extended his hand to one of the group and smiled,

"I am Garcia and this was about to be an historic moment."

Lisa the Cadet was the first human to shake hands with this divine being. She gasped with fear, and then almost cried in the aftermath. Next to shake was Ben with his flashing white teeth and big hands. All this caused people to applaud. Larry drew a breath, his heart was pounding and he almost felt faint. Everina gripped Larry's hand so tight that as usual her fingers sank in, and it hurt. All at once there was the sound of trumpets from the city, as the significance of the moment had not gone unappreciated. Then Garcia said in a booming voice,

"Welcome to our city!"

Then they and the visitors began to mingle and shake more hands in warm-hearted friendship. There was no language barrier, and the conversation flowed. The flying people were introduced as Jet Packers, from the Angle tribe. They wore grey green suits and arm patches with the word 'Cherubim 71st. These new celebrities were also all quite tall, one was a girl and the rest were male. They explained that the power comes as light waves ricocheting from one wing to the other while ejecting inverted photons to the rear. Someone asked were there saints in their group and were told, perhaps, but to remember no one is allowed to know that! One person asked the name of the city and he was told Purgosia. People turned and said to one another,

"Purgosia, did you hear that, Purgosia; or do you mean Purgatory?"

Garcia smiled and said,

"You can call it that if you like!" Then someone asked,

"What's the name of the mountains and do they really move or is that an illusion?"

The leader answered,

"They are the Sangrias, and yes they move, all is alive. They propel time and energy throughout existence."

"Sir, said one of the girls, why are we two tones?"

Garcia said with sympathy,

"Because of the incoming and out going flow of the volcano, heart of reality, but be assured you all look beautiful that way!"

People laughed. Then when asked what the triangle was made of he said,

"Skrauq,"

No one questioned further but the Captain wrote it down as spelt. Then he wrote it in reverse, and it made more sense. When asked if they had ever gone to the edge of the triangle, they were told that Purgosians had often gone over the edge and back on the other side. This task was performed frequently by Jet Packer, work parties on seismic missions and for better observation of the deeper void and the occult!

Garcia, asked if everyone was now out of the ship. The skipper said no, that there were a few who felt shy and unworthy. He asked the Captain's permission to enter. This was agreed and several of them entered and extended gestures of friendship to those within. Hamish, Hiroshi's non-friend was so shaken by the experience that he clenched a fist and thumped the table. However, after encouragement from Garcia they reluctantly emerged and joined the others blinking in the brightness of the day.

Then the visitors were ushered into the vehicles, which were suitable for up to twenty passengers. People climbed on board but found everything so transparent that it was difficult to see the seats. However there were small dots that seemed to float in the ether. These were attached like markers for safety to the upper corners of the seats. Larry and Everina sat up front beside the girl driver who wore a long dress.

She glided onto her perch, which was turned sideways so she could look around at ease. On the dash board the word 'Drof/trillinium' and this was evidently its brand name. There was a screen on which she could control direction with device like a fast moving computer mouse that she called a felluca (1). She pressed the felucca and the panel lit up to show a map. She then clicked once more and they moved forward. As they did so a red arrow on the screen depicted their position. She then turned to the group and spoke. Larry and Everina reckoned that the language was Latin but they both fully understood. She said in a musical voice,

"I am Pepitra Palcevska, when I was a little girl it is recorded that I was sent here by a terrible earth quake. Of course I do not remember anything.

Most people say that is how it is! However there are some like Russell who is driving the vehicle behind us, and he wished he had never been where you come from. He suffered what you call pain before he was released and he never wants to go back. Of course he never will be asked. Some have been asked and I believe a few did return! The incredible truth was beginning to dawn on the visitors; these people had once lived on earth or near it!

Then Pepitra turned and looked at Everina and said with a smile,

"You are so beautiful, is he the lucky fellow?" She turned her brown eyes towards Larry and nodded slowly. Larry spoke up promptly,

"Yes I am for sure, very lucky and hopefully for ever!

The people in the bus hooted their approval and even Larry blushed.

"You both appear not to have had any real hardship in your lives. I hope that continues and that you will come here as soon as possible."

Then she winked and turned to the group and pointed ahead. The city now came fully into view. Someone asked Pepitre if there were many accidents. She replied,

"No accidents, because vehicles sweep around each other like your physicist envisage the motion of colliding monopoles."

As she spoke she entered onto the main street where by coincidence two vehicles slid around each other like they were made of a gelatinous substance.

Larry asked about the 'Drof/mellinium' to which she replied,

"This car is very cheap and reliable. It comes in any colour you desire, as long as it's transparent."

Everyone knew she was kidding.

They drove up an incline a sort of entrance to the city. Then they continued on an upwards sloping avenue lined with trees and lots of onlookers. The city was paved and firm, no erupting ground like in the surrounding territory. There were strange sidewalks on which people were being carried along on both directions. There were moving at quite a speed, had ribbons of moving lights at ground level and evidently pedestrians could hop on or off at will. Every now and then a new person would join the moving throng. It looked like a safe efficient way to get about town and also quite some fun. Larry noticed signposts with prominent names. There was Avenue Rue de Pythagoras, Place Desmond Tutu, Avenue Descartes, St Benedict's Pavilion, the Plato Memorial, The Bono/Geldorf Auditorium and the Pagoda of the Dalai Lama to name but a few.

The City population looked young and carefree much like the transport drivers and through the throng, jet packs were to be seen as they strolled about. Then Hiroshi spied children, amazingly they all looked to be about five years of age. Pepitre then explained that people were divided into distinct age categories. Those who came, as infants or embryos or very young children were all rounded up to five years of age but in compensation are given the fully developed adult intellect. Those who were older were advanced to eighteen, earth years equivalent, she added. Everyone else became about twenty-five and the very old become golden-haired. How'zat?"

She said, and everyone nodded in agreement.

---

(1) Felucca; a traditional fast moving fishing boat on the Nile

Chapter 20

The vehicles turned into a palatial building ornate with Greek pillars that resembled the Parthenon in Athens and Pepitra commented,

"You are now arriving at the Euclidia. It is a meeting place and a resting place for travellers. Enjoy your time here your visit is a landmark in history, many are anxious to meet you. Oh! By the way, I should have told you, things here are very comfortable most of the time but at night the temperature drops and everyone gets cold for a few hours. Then by dawn the temperature rises but eventually becomes pretty uncomfortable for a while. Now the angel tribes and saints are not affected, but all others feel the discomfort. However, we must bear it in retribution for being here. You will just have to resign to it, as there is no escape. Adding or shedding clothes will make no difference. However, it is bearable and the rest of the time here is quite blissful. Oh but the way, Islamic people will call this Barzakh." [1]

She drove through an opening that was like a carport. Inside was paved in what looked like very large terra cotta flag stones. The walls of the building were deep amber in colour, and decorated with murals and mosaics depicting great events in eschatological time. There were also etchings of flowers, creepers and palms. Larry was impressed by the fact that despite the lack of variety of natural growth, its people obviously had an appreciation of horticultural beauty. Pepitra told them that there was another mural in the lobby that might be of interest. They alighted from the Drof/Trilliniums and were ushered into a reception area - from which they could look out through broad openings and see the Callisto parked on plains beyond. Pepitra pointed to a roped enclosure at one side of the lobby and said,

"That is where you stand when going to your rooms."

No one quite understood what she meant Larry and Hiroshi looked around and there behind the Front Desk was a great mural. [2] They gazed at it in amazement as this one showed a stratum beyond where they now stood. It was of a world beyond in which there was two enormous people one sitting and another standing. Then two others were kneeling while looking down on the triangles in the act of creation. In the lower corner it said,

"Divine Euclidean Geometry beckoning us on our weary way, By G Kuhn and O Kwang."

Richard grabbed Larry by the arm and pointed to the inscription.

"Would you believe, Old George Kuhn painted this?" Larry responded,

"By golly, he must be up here somewhere!"

Then they turned their attention to the Front Desk where two monitors gave continuous financial information. The currency quoted was not familiar and was quoted in 'PQ's'. An analyst referred to today's 'Praque' value on the 'Praydaque'. Larry was intrigued, but before he could ask about it Hiroshi interrupted,

"Larry, it's your turn next"

Larry stepped forward to sign for his accommodation. Within moments, he was issued with a card to say his accommodation is room 1004. There was an instruction that said,

"Please enter the roped enclosure and state your room number."

He noted that a key did not seem necessary and with card in hand he entered the roped enclosure along with some others and stated his number. Immediately and without even moving he was delivered to a smaller roped area on the tenth floor. Everyone was fascinated by the fete of engineering.

Larry just like a child, went up and down several times trying to discover the split second he and his floor was whisked upwards, but there was just no way of finding an answer. It was like trying to open the household refrigerator so fast that the light was not yet turned on! However the basis of an explanation was later forthcoming. Larry was told that each floor transformed into another, as it is 'super quark' based - and quarks transform regularly. One of the Uclidia floor people in a Mauve Uniform gladly elaborated,

"As we are not caught in any rotating flux, time here, does not flow. It occurs across a broad front. The either at this level is so expanded that many events can occur simultaneously, and not evaporate as on earth. We can be retained any event in such a way, that one can walk around and examine them from afar, or rewind. For example if we willed it, you could be returned to the moment you arrived at Pergosia and view the event over and over again. Your very presence can alter outcome, but not in any detrimental way."

He smiled and continued,

"Therefore it is quite normal for the floors to do gymnastic at your beck and call! However no one can go beyond these super quarks as they are the last frontier and have a momentum that no one can fathom as they are particles that come directly from the Father. They obey to a point but only at hyper velocity. You won't get behind them! Larry thanked him for his time and induction and went to his room horridly for fear it would disappear!

Naturally, everyone had a room to themselves, but there was a booking mistake made. The two Captains Dave and Laura were delivered to the same room. Red faced they explained that Captain was not their name and so they needed separate rooms. Richard said later that they were being tested; had this been Bangkok they might have said nothing. Everyone doubled up with laughter at the thought.

Larry found his room to be quite basic that is, it had a bed and a view. There was nothing else except four objects - a computer type screen that almost filled one side of the room, a fresh water dispenser, a table and a normal type bed - rather like a thick mattress with no legs as it rested directly on the floor. There was no bathroom because neither he nor anyone else had a needed ever since inversion. On the table there was an envelope and a box beside it a curious transparent container. Inside the container there was continuous changing aspect of nature. For a while there was a waterfall, then it changed into an ocean then a forest and then curiously it depicted a strange world that Larry did not understand. Larry then opened the envelope and read the note; it was from the Euclidia management!

"Dear Mr Coughlin, You are invited to a reception at 18.00 hrs. Please meet in the Lobby - optional attire. Zahura Ronge Ji (General Manager Euclida Inns)."

He opened the box and in was clothing in lieu of his RP gear. Shoes, Navy pants and a white shirt and they looked about the correct size and obviously on loan. He immediately went to the computer and extended his finger to press a button. However, before he could do so the screen sprang to life. A voice spoke from it and asked,

"May I help you?" Larry responded,

"Yes I would like to speak to a guest - Everina Spazola."

With that there was a musical sound and a few moments later Everina appeared on the screen.

"Oh Larry, you've cut in on me, I was surfing Purgosia, for shops and boutiques. Pepita's sister Agnes is here with me showing how it works."

Standing behind Everina was a very pretty girl. She had plum coloured hair and a tanned face. Here eyes were like green pools that reflected lots of light. She smiled and said in a Latvian accent,

"Hello Larry." Larry responded,

"Nice meeting you Agnieszka" Agnes laughed and said,

"I see you speak Polish!"

Larry knew he was being silly and ignored the comment as he was now a little flustered and said,

"Everina, I hope you have money for your spree!"

Then he gave a laugh, just like he had caught her out.

"Yes Larry, no money, no travellers' cheques, but what do you think I have? I have a hotel welcome pack, with a complimentary charge card. I'm going to be a real earth girl - and shop, shop – none stop!"

Larry was more surprised than anything so far, and raised his voice,

"No Ev you can't do that it's not right."

Then stifling his apparent outburst of jealousy, he said in a softer voice,

"How can you waste time in shops on an occasion like this?"

Everina replied amidst kinks of laughter,

"We can do, and will do, and never mind, we're not going to miss - your occasion like this either!"

Then as an after thought added,

"Larry, did you get your invite to the reception?"

"Yep."

"Well then my marshmallow man, will you escort me from my room at 17.75 pm as I don't want to go there alone. You know that the same as 17.45 to us as they use decimal time here!"

Larry agreed and then smiled in disbelief and the screen went blank. He felt cheated and immediately checked with the front desk about the charge cards but was told cards were only for females! This rendered him helpless, completely deflated and so he had no further questions!

---

(1) Barzakh – The Muslim people believe that all souls go to a patrician or state where they dwell till judgment. In this state even the just will receive some torment because of small offences in the past.

(2) This mural can be seen on the back cover of the novel.

Chapter 21

As planned, Larry collected Everina from her room. She was wearing an eloquent midnight blue gown. It was just one of her many purchases but really suited this occasion. Also to make matters more interesting, it had been delivered to the Hotel by the boutiques at no extra charge. She now looked so radiant that Larry found himself admitting,

"Gee you look wonderful, it was worth it after all" She looked at him winked and took his hand saying,

"I knew it would, and you look sharp did they give you a card also?"

"Yep, they did," said Larry, his first fib in paradise!

She then said,

"Good, c'mon lets go down."

Some of the group had already gathered and it was apparent that all the women had been on the town, the style was incredible while the males were dressed like Larry. At the appointed time, several vehicles turned into the Euclidia entrance and a large group of people alighted. As the entered the Lobby, Everina let out a gasp and squealed,

"I cannot believe what I see, Mamma, Papa, Dana, Lauretez, Carlos!"

She ran straight into the arms of the approaching figures. She hugged and kissed them, and asked over and over how they got there. They were just a surprised as they had not been informed of the full significance of the event. They gasped and in trembling voices said,

"My God Everina we thought you were gone for ever!"

Though she was equally taken aback, never the less, she tugged Larry over, and introduced him. Then she ushered them to one side of the lobby for an intimate discussion. From afar they looked overjoyed yet bewildered. Larry realised that this is what being in the future really meant. It means meeting people who have already passed away. Why then do the crew of the Callisto not meet themselves? Larry pondered! He watched the goings on with fascination and then suddenly his eyes focused on familiar faces. Why they were the faces of his, own family!

"Is that you Larry? By God! it i'zzz!"

There in front of him was Maria, Dan, Jill, and Amy accompanied by a fellow holding Amy's hand. Everyone embraced and tears rolled down their cheeks.

"Larry dear" His Mother said,

"We never heard from you again I cannot believe you're here!"

Larry was spellbound. He could not move. He felt faint then falling over and being caught in strong arms. He had no control over his being trapped in a coma - something from which he could not escape. His mind re-lived the past, being in West Cork with his family, college, flight school, university and then the Callisto blessed with Everina's smiling face. He awoke with a jolt and found he was sitting in a chair.

Larry was now looking in the blue eyes of his mother. Her very young face beamed down at him with unconditional love and affection, like he had not experienced since he left home. Beside her with tears in his eyes was Dan. They introduced Zachary who was Amy's husband back in the 'auld sod'. He was a very friendly fellow and over the years had become just like one of the family. They drew aside from the crowd so as to talk and reminisce.

By now the Lobby was awash with other heart rendering meetings, as more and more of the group assembled. Larry noticed the arrival of a beautiful Italian looking girl. She was in the company of three young people who must have been her children. Richard sprang to his feet and rushed across the room and gathered them in his arms. This was Pat, his wife, and children without a doubt, and Larry hoped that Richard could bear the shock. He had been very emotional on the Callisto, and now he must be in bits!

Larry took up the conversations where he had left off,

"Now Mom and Dad, I told you how we got here, but that we will have to leave before we can ever return. This is because as you know we are still corporal beings. All this happened in error and an exception has been made on this occasion. It will last only for short duration - just like Cinderella at the ball. All the intrigue became possible because of the inversion of our atoms otherwise we would have been too dense to survive!"

To this, Dan responded,

"Larry, is everyone in the group in the same condition? I heard that one was killed."

The statement startled Larry, his mind raced, who could that have happened to? Then like a bolt in the dark, he thought about Hiroshi and his cry of pain at the moment of inversion. He remembered Hiroshi's strange facial colour that seemed now to be so permanent. He felt his heart missed a beat but he managed to say,

"Dad that might be correct, I'll have to do some checking. Now come on you guys tell me about yourselves, and how you got here?"

There was an awkward silence them Maria spoke,

"Well, it was your Dad. Soon after the Callisto was lost he began to go down hill. It was not immediate and it was also a little comical. To cheer him, we went back at Trahmahon, you know our summer haunt. Now he had been very melancholy and sad about your disappearance - now about seventy-five and still able to ride the odd wave. Amy's kids were staying with us on that vacation. As per usual we went down to the beach. After they had swum for a while, I tried to suggest something for them to do. I said to Dan, why doesn't he and the gang act like marines in the Pacific and attack those sand duns! You know, they did just that! It was a nice sunny day, and I was laid out picking up some rays. I heard laughter and when I looked up they had donned old combat jackets and Dan's old USMC camouflaged helmet and went zigzagging up the beach. Dan was carrying a piece of driftwood as a gun, shouting orders to his little buddies who always seemed to do the wrong thing, and run in the wrong direction. It was quite a funny sight and I suppose it only happened because the beach was quite empty - no spectators. It's all right to laugh now but at the time it did not seem that way.

He made it to the dunes and began to fight his way to the top, all the time gesturing for others to follow. Then at the top he reeled backwards and let himself tumble as if shot. He lay there and did not move though the kids prodded him with their driftwood guns. Quite alarmed, one of the children called for me to come. I got to him and realised he was suffering a massive heart attack. He died a day later."Then Dan spoke with deep respect,

"Now this is the part I don't like to think about. You see after being a physicist and a surfer all my life I had become a sort of a brash hombre - who never had a set back. Now this heart attack caught me right off guard. After I woke up in hospital I was in awful pain and was so attached to machinery that I had a feeling of closterfobia! That was bad but things were to get worse, and in my last throws while I knew everyone was around me I could not breathe. I dreamed I was under a wave and could not get to the surface. They gave me oxygen and but it made me more alert to my predicament."

Larry looked at Dan he was holding Maria's hand very tightly and his brow looked wet. He then bent over and spoke very quietly,

"Now I always was a religious person, but I was distracted so much that I just could not pray, but then in the distance I heard Maria do it for me and say - Padre Pio look after my Dan, Padre Pio send your angel to bring him to safety, please help him and bring him to heaven. At this point a great calm came over me and I slid peacefully into this world."

As I departed I could see them gathered around my bed. It was sad but there was no way back, and so it became the beginning of a fantastic voyage. I was conscious of my guardian guiding me here. The angel whispered that it would guide me over the River Styx delivering out of the great flux and into the Chasms of Yahweh that lies quite near here! I never saw my angel face to face, but since then I think I know who it was. On arrival a beautiful person wearing a maroon cape and called the son took me in his arms and helped me on to my feet, where I walked into the company of my parents and friends. They had been waiting for me following my every move up to that. What a reunion!"

Jill and Amy leaned over and hugged Dan.

"Yeah!" he said,

"I'm really sorry to have given everyone such a start, and it was foolish and it was my vanity that made me capture that beach for your Mom. Now let the others tell you how they faired."

Maria then spoke up,

"Well, I was lonely with your Dad departed. Jill was my companion, and she looked after me till the end. I slipped off in my sleep. It was a strange feeling. I dreamed about Dan and flying to the south of France. The plane jolted and I rolled out the door. Actually I loved the falling feeling and I did not want to go back, and there you are I didn't! Jill went many years later in much the same way. She was very old and staying with Amy at the time, but she didn't have a dream - just woke up right here! Amy lived to a ripe old age, and her children and grand children; who by the way are now visiting the mountains and lakes along with my mother and father. Now Amy tells us that she cannot remember much about the ending, isn't that true dear?"

Amy just shrugged and gave a smile. Zachary then spoke,

"I'm ashamed to say it but I earned lots of loot and liked betting on the horses and drinking too much. I guess I was having too good a time. Then at forty-two I was wiped out in a car accident, dying was an unhappy release, as I left my family to fend for themselves. But Amy and the kids have now forgiven me and so now I'm perfect, thank God."

He slapped his chest,

"This, however, is just my plasma body, but we are assured that at the time of amorization and deliverance we will get our earth bodies back, they will be as good as new."

Larry then said,

"Look folks, this is the most fantastic meeting in history. I hope this moment is never lost or forgotten. In fact I know we can replay it in the future. All I can say is that I am delighted to find you safe and well and I know we will enjoy tonight - come hell or triangles" More laughs.

Everina brought her family over to meet the Coughlin's and it was evident that both she and Larry were very united.

"Gee, it's a pity we did not meet sooner,"

Jested Manuelle Spazola, Everina's Dad. To which Dan replied,

"Just as well we didn't meet we wouldn't have understood each other like we do here!"

Just then, Hiroshi arrived. He did not bring over his parents because he had seen Larry's sister and his dream girl – Jill. He was thunderstruck and overcome with the discovery. He just stood unconscious of Larry and the others and quite speechless as he admired her radiance. There she was, just as he remembered - bright blue eyes and silky blond hair looking at him with a slender smiling face. Hiroshi could not find words to describe how he felt. Larry jumped to his feet saying,

"Mom Dad, you remember Hiroshi, Hiroshi meet our family again, and also look here are the Spazolas."

This was wasted on Hiroshi and all Hiroshi could do was glance around and smile and then he turned back and exclaimed,

"Jill, is that really you? I cannot take it in."

Jill jumped from her seat and embraced him with tears in her eyes, while clinging to him like he was her childhood teddy. Hiroshi then ushered Jill away, saying,

"Please excuse us, Jill please this way just for a moment."

The others smiled at the unrelenting love that had just been displayed and watched their departure. As they reached the side of the room Hiroshi whispered,

"Jill, I know now that I love you and I never want to let you go, will your husband be angry?" Jill blurted,

"I have none. I came here alone!"

Hiroshi's eyes opened wide, and at that moment he did not look very Japanese. He decided that he had waited long enough, perhaps five billion-earth years and he was not going to wait any longer and therefore said,

"Jill, will you marry me here and now - as soon as possible?"

Jill looked stunned. She began to smile as if fascinated by the curious offer.

Then she said,

"But how Hiroshi, we are now of two different worlds and all those married were married before they arrived".

Hiroshi, undaunted, said,

"Look if I can arrange it, will you agree?"

Jill smiled again; equally fascinated by the originality of his wish, and then she began to nod her head at first slowly and then very fast, blurting out,

"Okay Hiroshi, you asked for it, okay, okay!"

Hiroshi overjoyed with her response took a ring from his own finger and slipped it on to Jill's quivering hand. It fitted perfectly.

"How did you know it would fit?"

He just winked, kissed her hand and immediately brought her along with her family to meet his parents.

The Meguros were a serene group of people. Their lives as a fishing family had made them physically strong and open, and friendly by nature. There was Hiroshi's sister Shohko and his little brother Jinkichi and his Father and Nasko his mother.

When they were introduced and began discussing each other's lives, Dan became intrigued with Hiroshi's Father. He was a tallish man and no doubt that was where Hiroshi got his physique. His name was Soju. He said he was born in 1926 and had been fighting for the Japanese in Saipan. Dan reacted with surprise. Here was a true warrior from the past, someone with whom he could identify and have common interests! They both began to chatter excitedly about history and aspects of warfare. Soju told him how he had been ordered to direct a group of the local inhabitants to shelter in some caves at Nafutan Point. In the process he fortunately ran out of ammunition, was knocked out by an explosion and taken prisoner. He was mesmerised by the humanity of his captors and considered him self lucky.

Dan listened with intent all the time, knowing that as a boy he had played war games with his friends. In those days war was more popular and Star Wars had not been invented. Using thin planks of wood, the boys built a fleet of attack transports for the purposes of an invasion. This included Higgins boats with drop fronts to carry hundreds of toy marines to invade the flower beds. These were imaginary Pacific Islands - the Gilberts, Marshalls, Carolines and Marians the latter which included Saipan – all defended by troops of the Imperial Emperor! However he declined to discuss these battles so he put the memory to rest and continued with a different conversation!

---

(1) Amorization, Pierre Thillard de Chardin's belief in a state when love transforms the universe for transformation in to the realm of Paradise.

Chapter 22

The Group was invited to a reception room by several of the Euclidian personnel. Doors were rolled back to reveal what looked like a bar adjoining a banquet hall. To begin with they were given refreshments presented by polite young people dressed in light weight uniforms that alternated colour from black to grey-blue; depending on the light. They looked ever so crisp and stood out in the crowd.

There were delicious looking juices, perhaps mango or papaya, along with a variety of wine, ranging from white, amber, pink, blue and reds. To Larry they tasted like the non-alcoholic Alpine wine known as Traubensaft. However, it was not long before the ship's cook and Ernst had bets to see how many colours they could manage to consume. Larry noticed that none of Raphael and Dalia's group had attended, perhaps as he expected!

As an appetiser there were platters of very light toasted white unleavened bread spread with a variety of vegetable purees. This delicacy was designed primarily for the Callisto group. The servers told them it was manna bread - to sustain them on their travels.

Then there was an announcement by Mr Zhu, a Chinese director of the Euclidia. He introduced a guest of honour, the City mayor and several other dignitaries. The mayor was an attractive African woman who said she was honoured to be at such an historic occasion, and praised God for his goodness.

They strolled into the dinning room where Larry realised that unlike the experiences of the blue triangle he now had an appetite. A small orchestra played soft music that was enhanced with the voluptuous sound of harps being strummed by ladies in flowing white dresses. There was a head table that had places for the mayor, dignitaries, the two captains and some of the Callisto management team.

Dave gave a reading before the meals - reading from the Book of Wisdom 7;

7-11: *"I prayed, and understanding was given me; I called on God, and the spirit of wisdom came to me. I preferred her to sceptres and thrones, and I accounted wealth as nothing in comparison with her. This is the word of the Lord."*

Then a man dressed in white and wearing a white baseball hat came into the room and introduced himself,

"I am Pedro Blouet, your chef for the evening; I am at your service. There is no secret that the food has been imported, as this land does not produce most of the products you are about to receive. Our food is for gratification only and not a necessity. It literally refreshes and dissolved in one's mouth so pray enjoy our menu and bon apatite!"

To begin, there was a starter of exotic palm hearts with sour grape and fig sauce. This was followed by soup like Gazpacho in a dish chilled with smoking dry ice and an accompaniment called quark cake wafers. These were hot to contrast with the soup and resembled garlic toast but tasted like anchovies. This, along with vapour rising around the bowl created an exciting start.

As a main course, there was a darn of pink fish like salmon. It had been poached, then brushed with honey and seared golden brown. The slice of salmon was sitting on a bed of blue spinach and topped with a slice of chilled caviar and lime-flavoured butter. As an accompaniment there were gently fried pasta spheres, tasting like the Swiss spaetzle and a salad of rose petals in frangipani vinaigrette.

For those who wanted an alternative, there was a hot vegetable substitute - a potato and corn based dish that had a sort of hickory perfume like pine smoke. It was flat like a pizza and served in slices accompanied with tangy apple piquant sauce.

Accompanying all this there was an amazing chilled white wine called "Au bord de Sangrias 80." It was chilled and said to be fermented grapes with a hint of powdered pomes stone. Though this was true and its aroma was of the hills, nevertheless Larry thought it tasted like a good Chardonnay.

Then there was a pause and with that the conversation became boisterous. As they were towards the end of the meal Maria sat back in her chair and said,

"That was excellent the food literally melts in your mouth. Dan and I have always wanted to dine here, but never had the opportunity!"

Dan studied the triangular plate which to his amazement was already shiny clean and quite dry despite being used. Then the dining continued.

A sorbet of peppermint water ice was delivered. Following that there was Cheese made from sap of the heavens with buck wheat wafers while all this was capped by a dessert consisting of multicoloured berries on a bed of sponge soaked in la crema cristi flavoured caulis. On the side there was a mini jug of pouring cream. There was a hot brew that looked like coffee but was called Dankus and was made from a sort of dried broad bean and corn roasted. Lastly there were petit fours baked on rice paper and flavoured with almond, angelica, cinnamon and many unfamiliar flavours. That as it turned out was 'Le Fin'.

Maria asked the group at their table,

"How do you visitors find eating our disappearing food?" Larry responded, "Mom it is delicious but the fish was not as good as yours used to be!" Maria laughed and leaned over and tossed the front of his spiky hair and added,

"Mine was the salmon of knowledge, the salmon of wisdom, you know the Celtic folklore that tells how Fionn Mac Cumhail (Finn mc cool) burned his finger while cooking the special salmon, and put his thumb in his mouth and thus received wisdom, the gift of a second sight and the vocation of a poet. Well my family has been fed on just such food. That's how you got here Larry; you have the luck of Fionn!"

When the dinner was over Vice Captain Laura thanked the Management, Chef, Cooks and General staff for the excellent evening, and added her appreciation that the City had made them so welcome. Then it was announced for everyone to meet in the morning - there would be an outing to the mountains.

The group then retired to an adjoining room where there was a quartet who played music and seemed to know every ethnic song ever composed. Dan appropriately, sang the Auld Triangle while some of the guests joined the chorus. He was delighted to have the opportunity to establish his identity in an otherwise very cosmopolitan world. Soon people retired to rest.

When Everina retired, Larry went to his room and immediately waved his hand across the front of the screen saying to the computer,

"Compo, Compo on the wall, find me the finest girl of all!"

The computer buzzed into life and right as requested Everina appeared on screen grabbing a bed cover around her and squeaking,

"Larry don't do that without a warning!"

They chatted about the evening, but soon began to feel cold. However, as there was no known protection, they had to accept it as the price to be paid for their condition. It was dark outside but there was a red glow coming in the windows and filling their rooms making for a deceivingly snug atmosphere. It was a nice setting and despite the chill they drifted into their slumbers leaving the screens still on.

There were of course some wild cards in the society, who needed more activity than the average. They would meet in clubs where they could, chat and sing, listen to music till they tired. However, there was absolutely no liquor or vice nor people who were even capable of such at this stage of their being. It was in one of these dens that the withdrawn group Hamish and comrades from the Callisto descended. To them this was the closest they could get to home and they felt they could talk or scheme more easily in such an environment!

---

(1) Noosphere, A state proposed by Pierre Thillard de Chardin where intelligence can be harboured, but where animals may also reside

Chapter 23

The next day found Hiroshi feverishly trying to arrange his wedding. He went to see the Captains who agreed to co-operate in every way possible - bearing in mind that they also were mere guests. He was given an interview with the Lord Mayor who remembered him from the night before. She said it was very unusual, but she would see what could be done. Even if the marriage occurred, the pair might end up separated as Hiroshi would have to return and Jill could not. However, the pair quite undaunted said they would worry about that when it happened and continued with their plans. Hiroshi looked for a Buddhist to perform the event. Jill said she would also like Fr Paddy, her Dad's friend to share the celebration.

While all these manoeuvres were taking place Larry and the group went on the sight seeing tour of the Sangria Mountains. It was called Le Tour de Grace. Though the trip was for visitors, as usual some of the group chose to stay behind. The tour guides, were called Luca and Faustina. Luca looked like a man of deep integrity and experience and greeted them as if he knew them all his life. Faustina spoke with a Polish accent and was quite frail.

Agnes, Pepitra and the fellow who resembled a gardener were the drivers. The trip proceeded south westerly along what was called Spazinski Avenue, one of the main thoroughfares. The traffic was varied and consisted of vehicles similar to their own, or larger. There was also many Angel Brigade transporters, smaller individually manned vehicles, and bikes of every description. As their vehicle slowed at an intersection, the group saw a man dressed in a red kilt like a Royal Stewart. He was playing a magnificent haunting version of Scotland the Brave on bagpipes that he held with pride. Another man who must have been a Romanian rendered sombre notes of 'Ciprian Porumbescu's Aria Dochitei-Hora'.

Larry looked at Everina and asked,

"Did you see many people shopping last evening? What did they use for money?"

"Yes Larry," Agnes said from the driver's seat,

"They were using Praque and it's our form of currency. In some cases people use cards that are funded by the success of trade in the stratum. You will learn about it later."

Then suddenly Everina pointed to an elegant looking boutique and exclaimed, "Look Larry, that's where I got my gear, pointing at her clothing"

Larry looked in dismay. He had not realised that she was not in uniform! She glared at him and said,

"Ha Larry I caught you, you didn't notice."

She leaned forward showing a label on her black blouse that said in tiny writing - 'Klaus' Larry forced an embarrassed smile and said,

"Sorry, I had not realised. Gee it's beautiful." She looked relieved.

"Did you buy anything else?"

Everina responded rapidly raising her leg to show black jeans and a slim black shoe.

"Yes, all this and the shoes can alter colour like the chameleon depending what I'm wearing. Perhaps that is why they are now black."

After admiring her gear, Larry leaned back and became absorbed in the City. It had all the trappings of an earth City; an Opera House, several Museums and a Concert Hall. They drove past a Basilica with a Spanish tile roof, surrounded with tall waving cypress trees. Richard leaned forward and said to Larry,

"Did I hear that your Mom had a devotion to Padre Pio? Well it turns out that my wife Pat's Grandmother was from Pietrelcina, and she knew him! She did not make it to the reception but we may meet her later!" Larry was amazed,

"Let's hope we do."

Soon the boulevard petered out and the vehicles entered the countryside. It was at this point that that the road suddenly widened like an airport runaway and vehicles began to become airborne! There was consternation amongst the visitors as they watched vehicles rise with them and glide off in various directions. They noticed that all heavier vehicles remained on the roar which now narrowed to two lanes. Agnes commented casually,

"Cars are not permitted to fly near the city. Heavies must always stay on the ground."

As they went, the sound of thumping gradually returned. The mountains could now be seen heaving with every beat - quite strange and frightening. Its surface colour was still maroon but also higher up it was blue with crevasses and valleys of pink and gold. From this vantage point they could see the plains spread out below. One interesting feature was that the draught from the blue triangle was still blowing into this territory. It caused swirling surface patches that erupted with every colour in the rainbow. It became apparent that other than doves, there was absolutely no animal life. This was first noticed when Laura's Kiki mysteriously disappeared.

When they reached the very high ground they were met by peaks capped in pink snow that glowed against an ebony sky. Now for the first time the extremity of the void and the new hemisphere came more clearly into view. They could see the heavens above and witnessed a peculiarity they had not seen earlier. It took the form of an x shape of monolithic proportions, called rose lines - spreading to the three corners of the vault. It was identical to the mural in the Euclidian. It divided everything visible into three segments plus an external one, the one that they were presently within. The whole geometrical matrix converged at another blurred area just as in their previous experience! From this area the same great Torus (2) emerged curving around all of Creation like a corridor in the sky!

They arrived at the panicle of the volcano and alighted from the vehicles and were directed to gather at a safety fence that encircled the massive outflow from the volcano. Larry thought it was like Niagara Falls in reverse! There was also a similar opening for its return from completing its fantastic round trip. There was an attendant who Luca introduced as one named Theophilus who did a most excellent job keeping people safe at the site. Luca then told them with a loud voice that they had now arrived at the fountain of life, L'Arc de Triomphe. Then he cleared his throat and took a prominent stance on higher ground to attract more attention,

"One granule of this substance takes three times less than a 'Plank moment' to journey to the universe and back. It is the geyser of reality - the bee all and the end all of everything. It's the quantum vortex that is responsible for action at a distance because it binds all things (3) whether far or near as they rotate."

He said that this phenomenon enabled information about its own composition to be broadcast universally; thus a homogenous world evolved. It is a fabric of quark strings shot through vibrating Leptons. All this impacting on a super gravity saddle shaped screen - the torus! It is the time flux that enables this happening. The continuous motion moves all objects out of the way making space for new – a so-called continuum. The movement dictates time and - time flies!

Mantz looked at Lionel who had a puzzled expression, and then to one of his astrophysics team - who was nodding his head in agreement. Luca then said,

"If one wanted to return to the universe, theoretically all they would have to do is jump into this spray, and it would carry you into the matrix of existence. On the way down, your plasma being would become potential matter - and in an instant one's logo would become implanted in someone's embryo. Reality is balanced on the knife-edge - just a little to one side!"

Then on a theological note he continued,

"There is the question about how our creator entered creation? There are two trains of thought. One says it happened when he embarked into the flux in pure obedience. Look there is a mark on the ground where, it is said that he stood in burning passion just before his departure. There burned into a stone slab was the word Cristu."

Luka then continued,

"Remember he descended here which is inside himself to perform this feat. That is hard for you to imagine but this mountain and triangle are his greater body."

Then with a stern expression he said,

"Remember only he has a right to tamper with the Arc. If any mortal disengages from it by their own actions, the outcome of this is undisclosed even up here quite unknown! It is only the Father and the Son who are the custodians of that knowledge!"

No one tried to question that statement as Luca was correct and it was truly hard to imagine.

Luca continued,

"On that occasion the blue triangle moved right overhead causing the whole arc to turn the colours of turquoise and gold. Nine earth months later com.saint@himmel.pa who are based above, took over administration."

He pointed upwards to the blurred area and continued,

"The lasers of the Citadel directly assisted in his human delivery. People on earth called it a star. But call it what you like - it did the job. The Messiah was then delivered in good health by his mother Miriam." He drew a breath,

"Now get this – according the scenario, the Son stepped to the flux, whole and entire and in both his plasma and a human body. Remember as I told you the flux was his very own property – himself! Then according to his own laws of metaphysics he diminished on the way down, and became both an embryo and a logo implanted in his mother. He was therefore a stand-alone product, yet totally humanly evolved. And to quote Scriptures;

John 1."Before the world was created, the Word (Christ) already existed; he was with God, and was the same as God. From the very beginning the Word was with God. Through him God made all things; not one thing in all creation was made without him. The Word was the source of life, and this life brought light to humanity. The light shines in the darkness, and the darkness has never put it out."

People nodded their heads, and Larry then interrupted,

"Just a minute Luca, according to your story, the son was an implanted embryo which would make his mother a surrogate. None of that was ever taught to us and if it was; it would be a schism."

"Okay look, Miriam was his mother and she bore him whole and entire and what's more the conception was unique, and was performed by the one you all met in the blue triangle along with laser assistance from above. This will fit either scenario" said Luca.

Faustina agreed but said there was an alternative. Then she added in something that was on her mind. As far back as 1931 she had a vision and encountered a flux of energy flowing from the son's heart, and she could not see a difficulty for him to have a divine yet earthly body as well as possessing a logo from the most high. After all humans are fundamentally made from star dust and we don't worry if it came from Jupiter or Mars!

Luca nodded and went on,

"Now I'm only telling you what was said up here. The second belief is more like what happens to all humans – that it was only his Logo that travelled down. The outcome of this is; divine logo in a human body derived completely from his earth mother. In this case he would have inherited all the genes and traits that come from the family line into which he was born. Now does that sound better or not? It is a trade-off situation, so take your pick. Either way, it gives you guys more hope that your human bodies have some value and hope of resurrected. Isn't that right?"

Larry nodded, and even those non Christians found it agreeable. Luca then said in a hushed voice,

"When we heard what eventually happened, we were very upset. His death was watched in detail in our 'Kinograph' which is like a Cineplex. We saw the excruciating whipping and his descent into hypovolemic shock (1). Then we saw his slow and painful death on the cross from suffocation. Finally we observed him being entombed. So we went into mourning and gathered within this mountain, to welcome him on his return. However, when he arrived to our surprise it was with both spirit and corporality intact. All this happened on your Easter Sunday and was a glorious occasion. To our amazement he also did not delay but got busy and descended, into the lower regions of the void, but that is another subject.

Then Everina spoke up,

"Luca, will we get to meet the son? We have seen the lady Spirit already though she was a bit too large for us to handle!" Luca laughed,

"Yes, you will see him in the Chasms where we are going shortly and much later you will meet the lady spirit." Then he went back to his earlier line of conversation,

"Things here before the redemption, were very dull. The world population say around the ice age was only about 10,000 beings. But since then things have really livened up. The population has quadrupled. When you left to come here the population was about six billion. That has increased by 78 million plus, every year since then. As we speak it is at almost twelve billion and climbing. That is like adding every three days, a population the size of San Francisco. You wouldn't think it but our Purgosia has massive potential to expand. They say a twin city will be built on the corresponding side of the triangle, with direct under angle access. The Sangrias also rise on the underside." He paused.

"Mind you the people coming up here these days are becoming a lot more interesting. In fact some of them come here with more information than some of the locals ever had. There is something good going on in your worlds, just hope it stays that way. You realise of course, some never make it to the triangles at all. I've been told that they are ones who never wanted to come in the first place. No one who ever wanted to come here got disappointed, just the ones who reject us. They become detuned from the silver arc and slip out of its frequency, and so they just flit away into the void. Where they go after that is a mystery that only Thormentus from Tartarus really knows!"

He frowned.

"Oh by the way, Thormentus is our traditional enemy, who along with his allies has become very active in the past week. We are concerned and hope it is not because of your visit. He has already sent his agents hovering dangerously close on at least two occasions."

These words caused a chill in the ether. Those who were at the back of the group pushed forward asking what had he said? However, no one was prepared to repeat it and Luca carried on,

"One other point of interest; do you know I have seen this arc turned off! Yeah, one moment it's there and the next moment it had disappeared causing time down below to stand still! It happens on occasions when there is serious universal repair work needed to be carried out. Then great beams of light streak down. That is from the blurred area above. They cauterise, heal, melt objects or deliver coded messages and so on. They do it very quickly and then the arc or flux is turned back on, just like nothing has ever happened. It is like removing a disk from your computer. You see when it is turned back on humans can never detect that it had ever been off. That's the system used in many miracle cases, after all how else would a miracle get performed? Oh don't repeat what I told you."

Some people looked at each other, and smiled and made helpless shrugs. ThenRichard asked Luka,

"How are you so knowledgeable yet still remaining here?"

"I hope I don't give the impression that I have superior knowledge because all that I am telling you is just general knowledge up here. Actually I do live above the blurred area but come here to work. This is a job that I and John who you will meet more or less began on earth. It's a devotion to the son and that is why I still promote him as best I can. Now while we are on the subject of above; only Saints, the venerable or Jet packers and Cherubs (child versions) are authorised to leave this confinement. All others will remain till the universe is unified with both here and the above. People are anxiously waiting for that time when there will be a great convergence. It will enable everyone to share in the same domain – the halls of Montezuma, or the garden where the praties grow; you know seventh heaven and all that!"

Everyone laughed, it all seemed so logical, they must be dreaming. He then added,

"Oh, by the way, did you notice there are no animals here! Well, that's because when they die they stay in a state or phylum known as a noosphere. They too will be liberated at convergence."

Several people clapped their hands, said, "Great."

Luca and Faustina gave broad smiles and Luca chirped,

"Lets all move closer to the flux."

He turned the group followed to the viewing fence around the edge of the volcano opening. It was quite daunting to move so close. This inward flow was basically blue tinted with purple in colour while the outflow some distance away was bright red. One was now only a few metres from a great projector showing the movie of life.

"If one were to fall in," Luca said,

"They would be whisked into the unknown and maybe born again, God knows where! Would that differ from death?"

No one attempted to answer. Then Luca looked like he had cunning plan to deliver,

"One last thing, if there is any lovers amongst you; it is your turn to have fun!" A few of the crowd looked at Dave and Laura, because of the blunder the day before. They said nothing and just looked straight ahead. Then Richard gave Larry and Everina a shove. They stumbled into view. Once Luca saw that happen there was no escape; he knew they were perfect subjects.

"Both of you two beautiful people should cup your hands together and hold them into the flow, you will get a pleasant surprise, along with a wish as a bonus."

Obediently the loving pair held their hands together and carefully reached into the deluge. It was like touching a moving plastic sheet. There was no impact or splashing yet their hands penetrated the substance. Then the surprise some of the stream hitting their palms from a particular angle produced a television like picture. The crowd pushed in for a better view. The picture generated was of a star studded universe. Then Luca tilted their elbows and suddenly the new angle appeared. It was of a street in perhaps Beijing. People could be seen walking with cars moving beside the throng. Then they moved their hands and the new angle generated a picture of deep space with an exploding nova in the midst of its birth. Another twist and they were right on the surface of some unknown planet, covered in gas. Then finally they moved their hands once more. Millions of pink and gold dots appeared.

Larry turned and yelped out to Luca as they withdrew their hands.

"Hey, what are these spots - I hope they are not radioactive!" Luka quickly replied,

"Please put back your hands you will loose your wish. Those are only the logo that I talked about. Is that okay?"

"Nope." said Larry like a kid,

"It's not okay,"

Everina scowled at him and thrust his hand into the flow both making a silent wish. They withdrew their hands quickly and examined them for spots but there were none. They embraced for a moment the group hooted and applaud and Everina blushed.

Faustina who had been very quiet, now took her turn to speak,

"You all may have forgotten that this theatre will never harm anyone. It is bent on the continual recognition of the son's unfathomable mercy. He has promised nothing or no one will be lost and you must trust in his continued forgiveness. Are there any questions before we take you to the Chasms of Yahweh, the highlight of our tour?"

---

(1) Hypovolvic Shock; Derived from terrible pain and the loss of large amounts of blood.
(2) See back cover of book.
(3) Possibly the string theory at source.

Chapter 24

Their vehicles were whisked down a steep road leading to the western side of the mountain. As they descended they saw the lake spread out beyond, and low flying aircraft sweeping in and out of the mountain just like they had guessed. Larry wondered what all the activity is about! Now the sound of thumping grew to an overbearing level. They parked at an opening and the drivers promptly produced devices like what the Jet Packers wear.

"These are called sound halos," Pepitra said with a smile.

"These contraptions rest on your shoulders at the same time sitting upright behind their head. There are control buttons on a collar so as to adjust audibility. Now you will all look the part!" She giggled.

The drivers said that the busses would meet them at a different exit on the east side. Luca led the way, walking the group briskly in through a large imposing entrance. The darkness seemed intense for several moments, but as they shuffled forward; they felt warm ether and a pink glow appeared ahead. It then opened up to reveal a great chamber; like a gigantic Cathedral with walls that shone. There was a noticeable aroma of incense that indicated adoration to God of the most high.

Luca said,

"This is the Chasms of Yahweh also called Grand Central Nation."

It looked the part with hundreds of people milling around, while several stopped to look at the newcomers but then continued on their way. The enclosure looked as large as half of Lower Manhattan, and the ceiling as high as the tops of skyscrapers. Now they were down where the arc was manufactured. The incoming one was now closest to them was the now familiar blue tinted with purple edges denoting spent energy in need for renewal. It crashed with a mighty roar into the nearest of the two sub terrarium lakes.

"Wow!" said Richard,

"What a display after all we said, this is like Plato's Phaedo revisited?"

Further away the arc rose in an upward moving column from an adjoining lake which lay to the north. This time it had taken on a bright red colour with flecks of gold denoting refreshed life. The incoming lake was churned from impact and but the edge was crystal clear with sand beneath. There was a sign that said,

"Dedicated to Patrick and the Lakes of Derg – please exercise caution."

Periodically young people ran in and out of the water evidently enjoying the experience. Luca said that it was quite dangerous and just as St Patrick had warned - there were tunnels connecting the two lakes. Some time ago in the north lake a child was swept away and became born in the universe quite by accident. He had to live a life all over again,

"What a drag! Now the triangle generates but a few products, wheat and wine, exports all forms of quark like particles, and most importantly it passes on logos derived from the Spinal Optic Canal which connects us with the above. This I will show you very soon."

Richard popped a question,

"Does the triangle get anything in return for the exports?" Luka looked at him with wide eyes. He slowly stroked his chin and then smiled,

"Yes, Richard, it's called - People!"

There were three tunnels; the one to the left was transparent and opened to the west side of the mountain. Aircraft could be seen entering and leaving. It appeared the tunnel had a circumference large enough to take several Callisto's. The tunnel on the right opened into the enclosure and was busy with people coming and going in small transporters. Then there was the centre tunnel, also quite enormous but it was delivering a cascade of liquid that was both speckled and sparkling into the northern lake.

"Look," he said,

"This is the sap of the dynasties a mixture of substances from the three super powers up above. The gold and the pink logos hit the rotating arc and are lifted up whereas the blue continues on to become part of universal matter."

Then he related with reverence;

"Then the dust returns to the earth just as it happened to be and the spirit itself returns to the true God who gave it. (Ecclesiastes 3; 18-22) The word spirit is translated from the Hebrew word ru'ach, meaning the life force that animates all living creatures, human and animal." (Ecclesiastes 12; 7)

"You may have noticed the gale blowing from the blue triangle when you arrived. It blows across the plains and under the hills even beneath where we are now standing. This hurricane of metaphysical energy shoots through the matrix of spinning élan, or liquid and re energizes everything. There are no bubbles because it is inverted or reverted opposite to your natural earth state. The re-entry is at a velocity of $2.69440024 \times 10^{25}$ m^3 sec^3, relative to the universe. This comprises of is the universal speed of light 22,792,458 meters per sec is multiplied by itself three times which is the scapular constant of creation!"

"Oh stop it Luca, you'll confuse them" said one of the drivers, showing furrows on her brow!

They walked to a large paved area from where they could see over the city from large openings. The area was filled with parked vehicles of all sizes and many people were milling about. They were shown the massive cinema like complex which they had been told about and is called the 'Kinograph'. Inside was like a football stadium. In the centre were four giant screens on which world history was played. One of the screens was dedicated to past and another was current affairs. People keyed in requests for topics or to find family and were given almost instant results. This meant that you could follow the exact movements of anyone at any given time. There was also a probability factor, which could be played. This showed what might happen with future events. If several people than requested a particular event, it would override a less popular one and they would lose priority. However, when it got busy the screens could sub-divide to service more requests. The most popular requests were from relatives watching for loved ones, so that they could be there to greet them on arrival. Everina asked, what was meant by arrival. Luca smiled and led them back to the lake.

Out of nowhere, a couple of children, who had been swimming illegally, ran up to Everina. They took her by the hand, and said, "Hola." They both appeared to be five years of age with brown eyes and black hair one was a boy and the other a girl. Everina asked their names!

"I'm Janette and he is Rico. We from Cusco in Peru. Where you from? You so pretty like our madre!"

Everina looked taken aback but asked the children all sorts of questions about their experiences. It turned out that their parents were most likely still on earth, and that is why they felt so lost. Lionel gave chewing gum and told them to wait around their mother might come soon! The gum had improved with inversion as it was expanded in every direction. It was filled with large holes, was very spongy but the flavour was still good. The children began to chew and blow and stretch it giggling at the new experience. However they ignored Lionel's suggestion about waiting, as instead they tagged behind the Everina and the cadets.

Chapter 25

Luca said they must witness the arrival of mortals. On closer inspection of the incoming area, they noticed a gantry extending out into the water. It was awash with thunderous deluge that covered its extremity. They could just make out a large circular area like a giant lens immersed in foam. There were figures of people emerging out of the deluge but it was not yet clear what was happening. At the side of the lake there were tiered seats and large screens with names moving across them. People were letting out shouts of approval every now and then. It seems they had been anticipating the arrival of their close friends or relatives.

The visitors gazed in awe, as a blare of music alerted them to an increase in what may prove to be human traffic or perhaps a major event. It sounded like a score had occurred in the super bowl. People pointed to the lake. To their amazement, they saw a very large group emerging from its lens. At first they seemed to appear as shadows. Then they materialised like part of a holograph and then became real walking people. They appeared to bring with them whatever calamity occurred as they departed their world. Just then a dozen people emerged with evidence of severe shock on their faces. They were accompanied by one of the angel brigade guiding them along. Almost immediately out of nowhere an immensely tall man in a maroon cloak appeared. There was silence throughout and even the mountain seemed to miss a beat. The audience bowed their heads in reverence and the then continued with their music. The man went forward and embraced each and every one of the arrivals. The background seemed to shimmer in his presence just like a tar road on a sunny day. At this point Luca said to his group,

"There is the Son, the Christ, the one I said you would see!"

The Son then turned allowing his face to be seen by all. He was young and swarthy but above all his features shone with a brilliance that only the ultimate spiritual being could produce. He then turned back to the task of comforting the arrivals. In doing this he converted horror into the joy of salvation a moment that would never be forgotten by the audience. Just then an equally astonishing person in a blue dress arrived as his aide. It was a woman who also possessed charismatic charm. She joined in helping those who were most disorientated to meet their friends and relatives waiting on the side line. They continued relentlessly, never letting up at their wondrous task of comforting. Luca reminded them that the lord comes in many forms and can perform many tasks in different states simultaneously."

The concept was so great that people just accepted it and watched in silence.

By now there was a constant flow of people arriving on to the gantry. They were clad in the cloths they had when their number was up. Their clothes looked shrunk and must have also been inverted, thought Richard! Some were in robes, some in torn military gear, and others in pyjamas. Some wore shrouds and others seemed blackened or even deformed or with the loss of a limb. To console the victims in this situation, new limbs were provided instantly. Some times there was a deadly clinical silence as a person arrived – their last memory being an operating theatre.

Then there was the arrival of tiny babies. This devastating sight mellowed into a happy state as they grew to become the healthy equivalent of five year olds. There were even containers with embryos that arrived carried by their mentors, guardians, fathers or mothers. Within moments even the tiniest foetus materialised and grew to become a child thus causing a frenzy of joy and relief to their nearest and dearest. It was miraculous and exciting and tears streamed down the faces of all who watched.

In the first moments of people's arrival their eyes were often closed. Then they put a foot forward and found 'terra firma'. They opened their eyes as if in shock. They looked down and examined their bodies, stretched their hands out in front of their faces, and then some made the sign of the cross, others went on their knees as if praying to Allah or adoring Mohammad. Then they stood and gaped at the scene around them. Without exception, a colossal smile spread across every face, and some began to cry with joy. Every few moments a Pergosian would shout out the name of a friend or a loved one, and there would be a reunion like no one could ever imagine. Some of them were heard to say,

"Is this a surprise party?"

The crowd was jovial and the message projected to the new arrivals was to say,

"Look it's all over, don't take things too seriously; forget the past you are here to be loved."

Then a young fellow emerged with a gaunt look and with tears streaming down his face. He was wearing a back pack with a breathing apparatus. The mentor the Son was holding him very tight and told him something. Immediately one could see the boy take a deep breath followed by several more gasps. His lungs were now free from the grips of his cystic fibrosis. Then an extraordinary smile crossed his face. He uttered "Sixty five roses," and began to laugh like he had discovered some new freedom. His mentor then ushered him towards family who began to wave and shout welcomes. The mentor now satisfied that the boy was in good company, turned and quickly melted away in the crowd.

Luca ushered the group towards the north lake called upper Lough Derg. Many looked back finding it difficult to leave the scene behind. Now they began to meet scores of Jet Packers and others who Luca said in secret - were saints. Luca then pointed to the centre of the lake. This was the outgoing area where the liquid rose upwards, red and replenished with élan from the blue triangle and the effervescence of the mountain. Here there was a smaller gantry with tiny lens through which one could be inserted into the system. Now they witnessed several jet packers slowly swaggered outwards. They were laughing and kidding each other, because some of their esperanto language drifted back. Words like,

"During my next break I'll do that for you," and another said,

"I hope my next assignment is a good looking!" Then with a laugh - one after the other stepped into the flux and was swept upwards.

Ernst asked Luka what affect the arch had on time in the universe. Luka replied,

"I did give you some dope on this, when we were top side. The question of time is complex. Remember time energy and light are inter related and interchangeable."

Then he continued,

"We move at thousands of times slower than universal time yet we are ahead – we cover more ground. Think of music. You are like semi quavers and we are semi-brave. It's all a matter of proportion. Existence beyond the Omega is subdivided and experiences complex time and tangent time. Complex is local omega time but is influenced by what is happening within the void, and that includes the triangles. Tangent time is Eternal and influences the acreage that is beyond our imagination but within the imagination of the Three Dynasties. They command scores of template ships that trail blaze the great outreach. You will learn more of them later. Now when you as a group flew from earth you went back in time, but then you grew and this brought you forward in time. There is little more that I can say for now!"

Ernst piped up one more time,

"I have one last question. Do the saints and angels also alter in size when they travel between Dynasties and the Cosmos?" Luke replied,

"This will have to be the last question. But yes, everything will increase or decrease enormously with inter-scalable travel. There are five magnitudes; Micro, Universal, Triangular, Deity and Eternal Deity. You have experience of three of these magnitudes but the last two will be harder to comprehend."

Chapter 26

Luka turned back towards the centre of the car park. Through the great opening on the east side they could see the roofs of Purgosia. He pointed to a very large Georgian style house perched in the middle and said,

"Here is where the tough side of life is played out. Now read my lips!"

He widened his eyes and said,

"That is a reception centre where incomers receive counselling. There is also a recovery area where complicated cases can rest after being treated. One prime example is when a mother arrives in childbirth. In that instance the process continues here till the birth takes place. All the toil becomes worth it in the end. However, sometimes it is just the mothers that arrives or even a single father. Sometimes there are parents who have left a young family and who require very gentle treatment and a lot of assurance. They also are given a special faculty that allows them monitor their family's progress through life. People respond to this with great gratification. The building is where the records of the city's citizens are retained. Some people are here as a result of repenting their violations at the last minute, yet atonement is still necessary. In many cases a meeting is arranged between a victim and a violator (who has repented) and always has incredible results. At first it is a dreadful encounter, but with time, patience and spiritual healing, that can only happen here - all can turn out well in the end whether dead or alive!"

He paused and then said,

"It's pretty hard to face a mother after an incident on earth where your car ran over her child. We call the process metaciliation."

Luca then described it,

"This is a metaphysical equivalent of your earthly confession or conciliation. It has its origin in ancient times when Celtic people had an 'anam cara', a name friend, and it took the form of one, to whom you confessed. The process was psychologically rewarding not to mention the many blessings that go with it. The effects of being confronted publicly are painful, and many souls remain for days trying to face the causes and effects of all they did wrong. Eventually they recover by accepting and apologising for the grief they caused others. The councillor and the victims are called soul friends when introduced to a new arrival who almost always wants to express remorse for deeds. Most people here have gone through this process and benefit from it. They describe it as a cleansing fire."

People of all denominations understood what Luka was saying they all had their own equivalent. Larry did not have time to request George Kuhn's address, because they were now about to leave. Luka finally said that the management of the operation was run by a specially appointed committee and chaired by a fellow named Michael, who was the Arc's senior citizen. Some of its management comprise of astute financial earth trained business people who are now Purgosians.

As it was now becoming twilight – l'heure bleu. They climbed on board the transporters that had been brought around to the south east side. The then joined the steady flow of traffic descending to the city - now a blaze of lights. It was evident that almost every vehicle had picked up a new arrival. There were also people on foot, merrily cruising along on moving sidewalks. When they were half way down the hill, Agnes slowed the vehicle, and pointed back from whence they had come. There on top of the mountain was the gigantic Corcovado like statue with its arms outstretched delivering protection to dwellers below. It was illuminated and despite its stony edifice there was a smile and an appearance of slight movement!

Chapter 27

Now quite tired and mentally exhausted the group returned to the Euclidia. Hiroshi and Jill were in the Lobby and bursting with excitement. They announced that tomorrow would be their wedding day. The City Fathers had agreed and so they will be married in an 'Ecoversal' celebration in St Gabriel's 'Churtorium'. They were not sure what it meant, but word had already got around town and it would be a big event. Hiroshi then arranged for his parents and close friends to gather in his bedroom for their official announcement. He had arranged that there would be drinks and mouth watering hors d'oeuvres. When everyone had arrived, Hiroshi took Jill by the hand and began to speak,

"Thank you all for coming. You are all invited to our wedding."

Everyone applauded and the pair got embraced by their families - who also looked a little bewildered. Hiroshi lifted his glass smiled at Jill and said,

"Now this will be a unique event in more ways than one. It will take place no later than tomorrow because we only have limited time. Then you will ask when the fun is over how can I remain here or must I go and leave Jill? Well it is with great sadness that I can answer that question because I am already one of these people. The City hospital confirmed today that I was killed at the moment of impact as we entered the blue triangle. When we inverted and hit gravitational waves in the tunnel I was killed on impact. As we all were inverted at the same time, my state was not noticed. You see all at once the Callisto had moved into this life where I would have gone anyway. Amazingly not unlike the Gods, I entered here directly, bypassing the flux and the Chasms of Yahweh. My death has enable this marriage to become possible"

There was an outburst around the room, Everina groaned and immediately put her arms around Jill. Larry drew a deep breath, his worst fears had been realised.

Everina exclaimed,

"No, oh no, Hiroshi, that cannot be true!" and began to sob.

Jill moved over to console her. Then two by two the relatives departed but Larry and Richard stayed back to talk to Hiroshi in private.

Larry asked,

"What you going to do boy? Are you coming back or staying?

Hiroshi didn't know, so Larry laid it on thick,

"Hiroshi, look though you are RIP now, when we go back that will change."

Hiroshi looked puzzled.

"We will have the skipper ask that the Callisto be returned to the exact time it came here. We have a right to have this granted as otherwise we will be lost souls! If granted we will be back to just before the accident occurred and so Hiroshi you will not have died. You can therefore return with us and read my lips – marry Jill back on earth!"

"No", Hiroshi exclaimed,

"I must stay I do not want to take that chance. When you go back down, it's simple I will just not be there."

Larry then said,

"Then we will have to report you as a missing person and earth Jill will be told. That will make her life a misery."

Hiroshi looked from side to side and then asked hesitantly,

"Without sounding facetious, could that be the reason why she never married?

"Yes it was," shouted Jill who had just come back into the room with Everina. She threw herself into his arms sobbing.

"It is quite simple Hiroshi never asked me to marry, he must in his mind's eye have known there was trouble ahead! However now we must live the moment and that is to marry here and now.

"Yes." confirmed Hiroshi,

"We intend to live the moment and put aside the issue of whether I return with the Callisto or not!

As logic was not popular on this occasion, both Larry and Richard retreated from their original positions and agreed the best course of action was to just go ahead with the wedding, and let things sort themselves later. Then Jill lamented,

"Oh where will I get a dress at such a late stage?" To which Everina responded,

"Don't you worry Jill, I still have the Uclidia charge card and we will use it!"

There was a cheer from the group - this was like pouring oil on troubled waters. There were smiles once again with everyone anticipating a great and memorable festive occasion.

Chapter 28

Seldom, in the history of creation had there been so much excitement in Purgosia. Communications were second to none, because people were blessed with the great power of telepathy. They knew the time and location of the wedding and all about the groom and bride to be. It was to happen at 'Le Place d'Elevation' at the intersection of Centre Street and Fifty First Avenue, at 16.00 hours following the hot spell. Fifty First Avenue was like all the others; running horizontally across the city and parallel to the mountains. On the other hand the streets ran vertically connecting the Chasms of Yahweh with the lower city. The population knew from tradition that they should converge in accordance to their family names. The A's were allotted to Fifty-First Avenue, the B's to Fifty-Second and so on, all along the route.

The people who were invited to the wedding were the relations from as far back as four generations. The visitors from the Callisto were included in the guest list and some volunteered to assist. The two Captains were asked to participate at the readings and the cadets were used to usher people to their seats. No one would miss seeing the wedding couple, as their vehicle was routed to pass through most of the town. Following the wedding and after a small reception they were scheduled to go to a honeymoon destination high up in the Sangria's.

The city had by now taken on a festival atmosphere, and was decorated with streamers and lots of imported flowers. This was to be called the marriage made in heaven. Small floating airships glided in from nowhere, each one bringing families or groups to see the event. They circled and then descend at one end of a parking area adjacent to the wheat fields. Then the tempo increased as hundreds of Jet Packers arrived. Word had it that they comprised of two squadrons the 62nd Cherubim and the 201st Seraphim. The 201st was legendry because of their active service in <u>word </u>war one (1) and their constant appeared at important occasions. The 62nd were children whose piece de resistance was their divine voices.

At the appropriate time the cavalcade began to ascend the hill to where the ceremony would take place. Hiroshi and family were in one vehicle, and Jill was in another along with her Dad. The destination was different than expected as instead of a traditional church, there was an enclosure known as a 'Churtorium'. It was of open air design, surrounded by Cypress trees and Greek style pillars, while at one end there was an altar and an elevated area for a choir. It was quite reasonable for the enclosure not to have a roof because; the view of the heavens was always of prime importance and bad weather non-existent.

At four pm. on the dot the cavalcades arrived as planned to be greeted by throngs of well-wishers. There was a white carpet laid out to their arrival point. The entrance was decorated with green garlands, and there was a great arch made of elephant's tusks. Hiroshi said that the display was a Buddhist Tooth Relic from the Haloed White Elephant who in legend became Buddha in a dream. He was fascinated to know how they had procured such artefacts. As the party alighted from the vehicles two members of the crowd leaned forward and grasped Dan's arm. To his surprise it was George Kuhn and Father Paddy!

Paddy was tall and portly and had a broad smile. Kuhn was quite the opposite, as he was thin with a bushy moustache and bore a great mop of golden hair that in his earth time would have been snow white. Kuhn had a hooked nose and he wore wire glasses through which squinting grey eyes peered. He wore his Yiddish scull cap which must have been made from synthetic fibre otherwise it would have shrunk coming there. Dan broke from the party and welcomed them. There was back slapping, jesting and hand shakes. Dan then said in haste,

"From this moment you are both to come as our honoured guests. Do you guys live down here or up above."

Fr Pat laughed and said,

"Now that would be telling you!"

Then Dan swung around,

"Hey, Larry, Maria, look who is here!"

Hiroshi went to the front of the 'Churtorium' while Jill and Dan prepared for her grand entrance. As they waited there was a tremendous peel of bells which were evidently housed somewhere in the hills - as there was no bell tower in sight. While waiting for Jill, Hiroshi noted to his pleasure that one side of the enclosure had lots of Buddhist memorabilia that he had only now noticed. There was a picture of the Lotus Sutra from the 10th

Century. This was believed to contain the final sermon of the Buddha who preached at Bodhisattvas. There was a picture of Avalokitesvara - the forty-armed Goddess of mercy. This one was very appropriate on the occasion, as she reminded Hiroshi of the woman of the blue triangle. The people on that side of the 'Churtorium' were mainly of Japanese origin. On the other side the guests were relatives who were from Australasia, North America, and various parts of Europe which included Ireland.

Some of the guests wore national costumes. For example, Pepitra and Agnes were decked in Latvian attire. Their hair was tied in pigtails, red ribbons and wearing embroidered pillbox university style hats - white blouses, black waste coats and long striped multicoloured dresses.

To everyone's delight, Amy and Everina had been chosen as her senior bridesmaids along with Hiroshi's brother and sister, Jinkichi and Shohke. The trainbearers were none other than Janette and Rico whom they had met in the Chasms. The females were dressed in graceful cream dresses, with tiaras made of fresh flowers. Their shoes were golden and they had light satin trains flowing from the back of their arms. In effect they looked quite angelic as they walked. The locals had that familiar blue and pink tinge which in effect was a little punk, yet attractive. On the other hand, Everina had a pinkish to copper tone complexion, much like she had returned from a ski vacation. It was incredible to think that these beauties were from worlds apart!

---

(1) Word as in Genesis 'In the beginning was the word'. Therefore Word War not World war.

Chapter 29

Then with great pomp and ceremony the Cherubim choir began to sing a south sea island style chant that sounded like, 'here comes the bride'. Then Dan and Jill began to walk up the isle. She held a bouquet of pink and white flowers and was wearing a long flowing dress of electric blue that shone like a million suns as she came. The material was like nothing ever seen, because it had a three dimensional texture with light sparkling from within its depths. The material also caused a swishing sound like the wind as she glided along. She was topped off with a pale blue veil, stitched with luminous thread creating points of light that shimmered in its texture. The trainbearers came behind her diligently holding the veil from touching the ground.

Hiroshi was now sure that he had done the right thing, love would triumph and he would live with Jill for eternity. Tears welled up in his eyes and he managed to wipe them away hoping people would not notice. He stared up the isle in fascination. Jill and Dan were silhouetted against the garlands and framed with the great tusks of the Buddha. The white carpet leading to the altar was strewn with the most beautiful flowers they had ever seen. They were called 'Trinitivias' and were like very tiny roses. Each flower was multi coloured. Their buds were of pale pink, turquoise and avocado with a pale lemon outer leaves and a lime green stem. Then as decorative points near the altar, there were exotic upside down plants. These plants had extended roots that fanned upwards while their greenery was firmly spread out on the ground below, acting as a base. Evidently they received their energy, from the atmosphere, like fresh air plants on earth. They were called 'Brain Plants' because it was said they resembled humans or Gods as their brains were uppermost just like these plants! Also both normal plants trees and Gods are similar in a strange way. Their roots either in the ground or as in the case of the Gods, up in space intermingle creating unity.

On the altar stood Father Travis, dressed in white clothes with a black tie and a golden tie clasp with a cross in the centre - his badge of office. Much to his delight, Father Pat, arrived and was given his place on the altar quite prepared to join in the ceremony. There were two women ministers and also a Buddhist Priest who was standing centre stage along with several of his monks. Normally Buddhists do not have a marriage ceremony but Hiroshi was having a Christian gathering with Buddhist blessings. The gospel reading of the Mass section was from Hebrews 10:11 and was read by one of the two women,

"To have faith is to be sure of the things we hope for to be certain of things we cannot see. It was by faith that people of ancient times won God's approval.

It is by faith that we understand that the universe was created by God's word, so that what can be seen was made out of what cannot be seen---------

-- It was faith that made the walls of Jericho fall down."

She then spoke about events when faith was in evidence, and reminded the listeners that faith had brought Hiroshi and Jill together and it was this faith very same faith in love that brought about the creation, which in turn enabled us all to gather here today. Then there was organ music from Handel's Messiah, with the amazing accompaniment of tambourines played by the monks. Then Father Travis was delivered pink coloured earth and liquid from the lakes of the Chasms of Yahweh. He elevated them on a platter and a chalice and said,

"God the Father you are most holy and we want to show you that we are grateful. We bring you Earth and fruit of the vine and ask you to send your holy spirit to make these gifts the body and blood of your Son. – When on earth he took bread from the table – gave you thanks and praise. The he broke the bread and gave it to his followers and said- Take this all of you and eat it – this is my body which will be given up for you."

Then he lowered his voice and said,

"Hoc ist enim corpus meum (1)"

Then he again spoke,

"When supper was ended he took the cup and filled it with wine and said – Take this all of you and drink from it this is the cup of my blood the new and everlasting covenant it will be shed for you and for all. So that sins may be forgiven – do this in memory of me."

He concluded with,
"Hic est enim sanguinis mei" (2)
A gong was sounded and a sanctimonious hymn known as 'How Great Thou Art' was sang by the Cheribums. Their Angel voices rose like swallows in the wind ascending ever upwards in glorification of the Almighty. ,

"O Lord my God, when I in awesome wonder,
Consider all the works thy hand has made.
I see the stars; I hear the mighty thunder,
Thy power throughout the universe displayed
Then sings my soul, my Saviour God to thee
How great thou art, how great thou art.
Then sings my soul, my Saviour God to thee,
How great thou art, h o w- g r e a t - t h o u - a r t."

The specimen of earth and liquid of life were both left for all to see, but not to be consumed. Larry turned to Dan who was sitting beside him and asked why did they not use bread and wine that the souls could receive? Dan who was now triangle wise, tried to explain in a whisper,

"The souls here are already in the Son - we have been consumed and do not need to consume further. The bread of life as you know is only a necessity for living humans as you have not yet been consumed and should therefore consume as often as possible so as to bring him within. This is a necessity for Christians but not for other creeds. They can achieve the high status through good works and living to their own dogma.

However the principal is a sort of trade off; if we consume him, the son, the heart and nucleus of nature - he will in turn consume us by assuming us into his body, which is here!

"You see, to be consumed is to be saved!"

Larry nodded and then asked in a whisper,

"The dead sea scrolls tell you that a Jewish sect named the Essenes celebrated what was known as a messianic banquet akin to the Lord's Supper in which a priestly Messiah placed his hands upon bread and wine, which was blessed and distributed. All this is believed to have happened in the first century B.C."

He finished abruptly, as Maria kicked him in the shin.
"Shush, Larry you're distracting."

---

(1) Hoc ist enim corpus meum, This is my body.
(2) Hic est enim Sanguinis mei, This is my blood.
(The words of Christ as quoted in scripture of the words of Jesus Christ at the last supper.)

Chapter 30

Don Travis and the Buddhist Priest beckoned for Hiroshi, Jill and their parents to come forward. Both priests in turn said,

"Hiroshi, do you take Jill to be your wedded wife?"

Hiroshi looked like he had been asked the $64,000 question on a quiz. He rolled his eyes and then in a quivering voice answered,

"Yes, Yes I do."

Jill also agreed in a less dramatic way, and they became man and wife.

The Buddhist priest, who was dressed in an orange robe, then spoke. He raised his both arms and opened his hands above his head and said,

"Aloha, may the spirit go with you both where ever you go."

Then he talked about the four noble truths of Buddha,

"First all existence is suffering, the 'O Bhikkus', is the name of this noble truth. Next this suffering, or 'O Bhikkus', arises from desire or craving. It arises from earthly desires here and now, in gratification of the passions, or craving for life, or the craving for success. Then there is the cessation of desire, which brings the end of suffering. It is the getting rid of, and the freedom from craving desire. Lastly all this is achieved by following the eight fold path, controlling one's conduct, thinking and belief. This is what Buddhists call the middle way. This is a way that enables people to enter Nirvana, though they may not be too religious or may even be atheistic. Thus enlightenment comes, not from God, but from personal effort in developing right thinking and the performance of good deeds."

Then he turned to the married couple,

"Hiroshi, look after Jill in this heavenly domain."

At that moment, the surface of the triangle began increased eruptions that caused a million rainbows of to emerge. The mountain above seemed to glow and vibrate even more that usual. Simultaneously there was a roar of approval from the congregation. From the city streets music was heard, as people began to celebrate. Amidst a hail of white streamers, confetti and 'Trinitivia' buds, the two made their way to the vehicle. Jill then turned and threw her bouquet back over her head and into the crowd. It landed fair and square beside young Janette who grabbed it and danced around with Rico. Jill appreciated the children's mirth and Joy. Then she waved as the cavalcade departed slowly down Centre Street.

The reception took place in City Hall and its purpose was strictly to allow all the relatives meet. The only food was a wedding cake made from very light rainbow sponge and covered in icing that sparkled silver. On top it had a miniature bride and groom standing beside a model of the Callisto. This was shared with the guests along with the usual varieties of beverages. The speeches were short and when all was over Dan and Maria extended an invitation to the Captains and their relations to visit their home. The wedding couple then said good-bye and departed for a two-day sojourn in a secluded dwelling in the Lake District to the west of the Sangrias.

Chapter 31

"Now you must see how we really live up here," said Dan. A courtesy vehicle brought Dan and Maria with family, to their home at 'Tramanna'. It was located in the lower south western regions of the Sangrias. The house was triangular in plan with lots of transparent walls and a flat roof with stairs leading up. To everyone's amazement it slowly rotated to accommodate a changing view of the lakes and mountains beyond. Other places they passed were more compatible with earth designs; some looked quite Greek or Roman with pillars and some were like Californian Ranches. Everina in her generosity took young Janette and Rico along to share the experience!

The interior of their home was quite minimalist. There were bedrooms around the parameter. They had open arches instead of doors. Catering was almost none existent, and plumbing was not required. The tables and chairs were what they call on earth art deco and there were musical instruments everywhere - a Celtic harp, a set of bagpipes, a flute, and a recorder. There were many oil paintings one depicting their beloved Tramahon Bay in West Cork. Maria had painted it from memory. Larry noticed that though it was very good, amazingly everything was backwards! Things had mellowed and changed in time! She also had several pictures painted by Monet one showing a child with a hoop standing in front of his home. Also there were renderings from Renoir, Turner and others. Maria said she got them from kind people in Purgosia for a good price.

Larry asked Maria how she and Dan had become reunited. She said she was greeted at the chasms as the authorities had advised Dan about her imminent arrival. Up to now, there has not been marriage in Purgosia - people have been quite happy to live alone or just share with others, and some with their original earth spouse, some with a relative or just a friend, and singles live in apartments closer to town; it all depended. As there is no reproduction or appetite to do so, and no threats to people's security - marriage is therefore not needed. Then she added a note of triumphant observation,

"However, since Jill and Hiroshi's wedding, attitudes may change and who knows who might have a shine on someone – even up here!"

She laughed. Dan welcomed the guests by offering wine, or piping hot dankus and a tune on his flute. As night had now descended he pressed a switch and stopped the house turning with the front facing the lake. Then Maria asked everyone to come to the rear patio window. She smiled and examined a list of garden types; Kew, Suzhou's, Buchart, Brookside, Monet and many others. She selected Monet, flicked a switch and voila; the back yard transformed into a holograph of his garden at Giverney 1872. People looked and clapped happily. She led them through a huge Nympheas Studio filled with potted plants and an old straw hat hanging on a peg. Then out into blazing sunshine like earth on a bright summer's day. They were walking into an exciting simulation. Janette and Rico let out whoops, and began to run in all directions, they had forgotten what earth had to offer.

There were archways of climbing plants entwined around brilliantly coloured shrubs. To make matters more authentic, there was a water garden that had a magnificent Japanese style bridge that led to an island covered in a mass of wisterias and azaleas. There was lilac, pale and delicate, flaming yellow cannas and aromatic white calophyllums. Everina dipped her hand in the water and found it quite real as it was wet and chilling.

Maria told them that the system was called 'Gardex' and may be procured from Bellingham's on Fifth Avenue. She told them that once she had cut some of the flowers and shrubs, but when the holograph was turned off they just disappeared! She pointed out that as one walks along the paths, you reach its end in just a few steps. In effect one could traverse the whole garden in seven steps, where on earth it would take thirty five!

Then she pressed a sound control and the garden filled with the din of birds singing and the scent of freshly mowed grass. Finally she made the sun go in. It seemed to hover above the garden then disappear in clouds causing summer to depart. Then a gentle breeze bent the lime green trees to and fro, and some leaves began to fall. With that Maria turned off the 'Gardex', leaving nothing behind but a neatly cut lawn. Larry asked would all this disturb the neighbours and was told it was only short wave and neighbour friendly, but that anyway they have great neighbours!

There was a balcony where one could sit and gaze on the lake that was now glowing with effervescence. Out beyond and to the North there were shimmering lights moving in the sky. Dan announced,

"That is 'Lake Mudnauq' and the bay nearest to us is 'Tramanna Bay'. It was called 'Tramanna' because of the whiteness of the sand on its beaches.

The white is a simile of manna from heaven. The moving lights are our equivalent of your Aurora borealis." (1)

Dan then said,

"Can anyone guess what 'Mutnauq' means? Well my dears, it means Quantum,"

Richard picked up the buzzword and began to listen intently.

"At certain times the lake becomes rough. When this happens it is a most eerie experience."

Just then, as if by co-incidence, the tranquillity was disturbed - the bright blue liquid suddenly began to produce sets of tiny waves. Dan called for everybody to look. The waves were now getting larger because they were generated from the surrounding land by increasing vibrations from direction of the Chasms of Yahweh. Dan explained,

"These are advanced waves (2) something unknown on earth. They move inwards and not outwards. They travel in concentric walls towards the centre of the lake, where they dissipate like magic!"

Then, just as predicted, the waves did just that! However it was ever more exciting because wind from the Sangrias caused distortions – one side feathered from the off shore effect, the other just rolled. Larry was fascinated but couldn't turn away from the enchanting panorama. He fancied that if towed in on a board, he could ride a full circle! Dan interrupted his thoughts pointing a finger towards a cluster of lights from a vacation village quite near the lake and saying,

"Don't forget our honeymooners Hiroshi and Jill - are right over there!"

Everyone held up their cups in that direction and toasted the pair.

As darkness descended, the hills turned red and the land stopped generating its spectacular rainbows. The lake continued to roar and the howl and the wind whistled from the caves. The water was as bright as a lighted swimming pool, and the sky above was stitched with streaks from the silver arc crossing overhead. The golden torus could also be seen swinging in a curve across the sky just as the Milky Way does to a viewer on earth. Maria switched off her simulated garden and everyone turned in.

---

(1) Aurora borealis or Northern lights caused by charged particles waves hitting the earth's atmosphere which are carried by the solar wind to collide with the earth's magnetic field.

(2) Advanced waves are only known on earth through James Clerk Maxwell's equations on the quantum behaviour of wave time asymmetry. These waves are very different from earth waves

Chapter 32

While the family and friends burned the midnight oil, both Jill and Hiroshi had sat gazing at the romantic antics of 'Lake Mutnauq'. They had been so close to its fury that they had been almost hypnotised. Then they kissed and caressed and sipped a syllabub and then slept in blissful content. The next morning they awoke in each other's arms. The land was also awakening; as it began to shimmer with the great expectations of another day. They arose and wandered out on the terrace smothered with vines. They picked grapes and enjoyed the sweetness of the juice. By now the lake had turned quite flat and placid- from whence it got its name. However there was a very gentle breeze like a Chinook (1) just enough to cause a herringbone effect on its surface.

By the waters edge there was a marina. It was somewhat different from earth. It was designed to be quantum proof. It simply had a glass roof and consisted of two harbour walls that that widened as they went creating a large entrance. This was because all waves travel towards the lakes centre, and so a narrow entrance was not necessary. As a precaution there was a series of mirrors set at intervals close to the shore to break up any waves generated inside the harbour. There was a sign stating,

"Sailing allowed during calm periods only."

They had a leisurely breakfast of grapes from the terrace, followed by quark cake cereal, dowsed with a substance of white herbal liquid. Then they made their way down to the marina. A friendly man greeted them. He introduced himself as Paulo, a fisherman and boat facilitator. He said they could take select any boat they wished, provided they remembered to say a word of appreciation to the great one, who provides all. Jill asked the man if he had been out in any of the Quantum storms. He said he had once been caught, just before entering the marina and had nearly perished. He explained that he did not mean being killed in the human sense, he meant being thrown about and filled with water and diverted to another location, perhaps light years from here and being faced with a very complicated return journey! He added that it had been worse than his worst memories of a storm he experienced on the Aegean Sea. He assured them that there would be no Quantum activity for the rest of the day but the lake had become very active recently. As they spoke quite a number of people gathered and began to make ready their boats.

Jill selected a sleek craft a bit larger than a laser. It had a mix-lock coloured hull - a colour tone that was quite popular. To describe it in earth language is impossible, as it altered between gold, pink and lime green in that order. However the style of rigging looked quite familiar. As soon as they were on board, Jill began releasing lines and preparing for cast off. Then she instructed Hiroshi to man the oars, and row out of the harbour, as there was not enough wind. Once outside she began to pick up the breeze, and swung the boat head on. Then called out to Hiroshi,

"Pull up the main halyard." Hiroshi called back,

"Jill - I don't know which that is!" Jill bounced forward and thrust him the rope.

"There, flex your muscles, and haul up the sail."

So as a fit Astronaut, tennis player and obedient servant, he jumped to it, and had no difficulty carrying out the chore. They were now setting out on their voyage in a new life; and already they were finding how to compensate for each other's strengths or weaknesses. Within minutes the sail was up, secured and with Jill at the helm, the tiny boat glided across the glistening lake.

---

(1) Chinooks are the warm air that flows over the Rocky Mountains from the Pacific Ocean.

Chapter 33

On their return to the Uclidia, both Captains Dave and Laura outlined the group's next destination. They pointed upwards towards the misty zone where the seams of the void appeared to come together. Dave displayed a blown up navigation chart based an EM/SPEC composite of what they knew already and Kuhn's mural. The reason for this was because there were no such charts in Purgosia. No one travelled upwards by any other route except through the Logo Optic tunnel that connect the above with the red triangle and eventually the Chasms of Yahweh. However that facility was not permitted to visitors and city management had said reluctantly, they must go through the void. They should stay as close as possible to this triangle and then follow the logo optic tunnel (1) upwards.

There was also a disturbing report that while they were away there had been an accident, and the Callisto had been damaged. Some of the more unsociable crew had attempted to borrow the ship. They say it was to learn more about the district. It seems Hamish and Raphael had been the culprits, and in their haste to depart they had caused damage. The event had also been observed by the intelligence of the all-seeing triangle which in turn had sounded the alarm. The triangle exerted enormous energy at that time and Larry reckoned that was what caused the storm on 'Lake Mutnauq'.

The offenders were then retained in the Callisto for questioning by the ships officers. Though the ship has been damaged no repairs could be carried out until the Captain received a damage report from Ernst and his team. When the report was received it highlighted the dangers posed by a return trip and re-inversion because the ship's laser gravity-system and rear thrusters were also out of order.

On a more serious note, the oxygen pumps, needed for the return journey, had also been damaged as well as some of the asbestos plates that formed the outer skin when they tried to force entrance. A few of the town's engineers were sent to assist the visitors but they were not used to the nuts and bolts of earthly mechanics and therefore acted as advisors.

Activity began immediately, but it was Ernst and his engineers that finally did the job. While they worked some of the city folk gathered to watch the mortals toil a task long forgotten. Eventually the repairs were concluded in a make-shift manner using various pieces of material from other parts of the ship. This was necessary as inverted substance from the triangles could not be guaranteed to revert when the ship returned to the universe. Ernst then reported to the Captain that the job was done, but that there was still only a 50% chance of a successful re-entry.

Jill and Hiroshi returned from honeymoon, both looking very happy. They requested to be allowed join the expedition on the next stage. The matter was passed to the city fathers for consideration, but was quickly rejected on the basis that despite Jill's good record she will have to finish her full term in the city before being permitted above. Hiroshi, on the other hand, because of his strange circumstances had a choice. The loving two were quite disturbed by this ruling, yet Jill in her wisdom accepted her fate and also encouraged Hiroshi to carry on without her. Without hesitation Hiroshi said he would remain with Jill for the moment and consider the return question later. Then without intending it to be so, he became saddened and sank into a sultry mood.

The Captain and an officers who formed a council, met the hijackers and their representatives. After some deliberation it was decided that the events had been so demanding on the mind and so taxing on the metabolism of individuals, that the laws governing behaviour could not legally be upheld if tested when they return. As a result of this event the Captain ordered that an emergency post inversion code of conduct be drafted with a view to implementation. This should take into account the good of the ship and that it is a sole ambassador of the human race faced with exceptional circumstances. It would also have to encapsulate the moral values and attitudes of the nations from whence they were dispatched. The laws would impose disciplinary action to be taken in the event of any of several offences. These included hijacking or causing deliberate damage to ship or persons on board or to any of the populations with whom they might visit. The rules were lengthy and finished with a note of caution. They stated that because of the telepathic powers endowed on the host nation it is inadvisable to fantasise or entertain any thoughts that could be construed as being immoral or aggressive. Crew should concentrate on their immediate activities and all strategic discussions are only to take place in structured meetings. It was recognised that all records of offences might become erased as this ship returned back through time, therefore any penalties had to be imposed immediate. The penalty for continued breach of the code would include being locked in the ships hold to be released on return. In the case of attempted murder or sabotage one could be simply ejected from the ship and face the consequences!

---

(1) The logo optic tunnel connects the two creation triangles with the omega gateway into paradise. This is however not in evidence in the painting on the back cover but it is meant to be there!

Chapter 34

A rather official looking automobile bearing a pennant made its way down from the town and headed for the Callisto. The crowd drew back to make way. The Callisto group were back wearing their RP suits having left their formal wear with the Uclidia. The vehicle stopped beside the open door and out from within jumped several military type people. Two of them were of the familiar Jet Packer variety, another was a female dressed in a smart business suit. There was a pause and then with a grunt, a rather odd character immerged. He was a large fellow with a broad grin and a twinkle in his eye. He sported a bushy beard and wore the cloths of an ancient mariner - this was confirmed by a bundle of charts that he carried in his arms. Around his head was a red bandana that gripped his flowing hair keeping it in some semblance of order.

Jill and Hiroshi recognised him from their honeymoon and called out excitedly,

"Hello Paulo!"

Paulo smiled and waved back and continued. The Captain greeted them though not knowing what to expect! The female introduced herself as Zelda Tallings from City Management. Dave remembered meeting her at the welcome function in the Euclidia. Zelda said that she needed a private word. Dave brought her into his conference room and summoned Laura Bingley and offered a seat. Laura was at hand and promptly came into the room. Dave introduced his vice-captain to Zelda, who smiled and made a gesture towards the tall man who she introduced,

"This is Paulo originally from Galilee, and he is an official navigator. He lives at 'Lake Mutnauq' where he keeps sail boats. You see, up to now you have been conveyed everywhere close to the land masses. Now for the first time you will be obliged to fly in the void."

Dave raised his eyebrows and looked at Paulo who just smiled back, and so Zelda continued,

"Trans-voidular navigation is a tricky business. A wrong move could allow chaos escalate into vibrational destruction. Also there is Thormentus, Diva and Zahtienne, fearful creatures who you may already know about! They are constantly directing trouble in the direction of the universe, being bent on its destruction. Basically they are old enemies of our state but if they choose to become aggressive once again, we could be in big trouble. Our target is that blurred area. It is not unlike the umbilical that was your earlier passport to this dimension. This time it is the final frontier and the pearly gate to paradise. We call it the Omega, because it is shaped that way. It is not the Omega that you know in mathematics but is the ultimate point of all mathematics and of proportions beyond human imagination. Even if you reach this area, your problems are not over. The very approach to the entrance that is the Omega, is perilous. Because of all this you will need the services of Paulo as your navigator."

Laura spoke up immediately looking at Dave as she spoke and taking encouragement from his slow nodding in agreement,

"Ms Tanning we are indebted to you for this care and consideration. When will Paulo be ready for departure?"

Paulo responded in a melodious voice,

"As soon as you familiarise me with your navigation system and allow me talk you people through some basic flight rules - I will be ready to depart."

Zelda shook hands and left with her team. Dave called for the navigators and flight group to assemble at the EM/SPEC. Paulo in the mean time was shown over the ship and by the time he returned the group had gathered. He was shown the Electro Magnetic Spectrum in a fully turned on mode. He saw how it analysed the components in the surrounding fields, how it gave scientific readings and also how by diagnostic imaging it could peer in any direction. The mapping of the Mandala and mural also impressed him. He was astonished by the accuracy of the Dan and Kuhn's basic concept and how it fits the current needs so magnificently.

Then it was Paulo who took command,

"Captain and crew, you have a fine ship here, the jolly Callisto. It is a bit the worse for wear but it will serve our purpose to reach and enter the citadels of paradise."

People gasped. Though they had already encountered many extraordinary events it was still exciting when said to their face.

Outside the ship Mexican music was being played and there was loud laughter. Paulo continued speaking in a steady voice but with the turn of phrase of a Cornish a seafarer,

"Me hearties, the void is divided into Latitude and Longitude just like the great oceans of yer' world. I know from sailing in the Aegean Sea and indeed along the coast of Italy and Greece. I have met storms but they are nuthin' compared to what can blow up in this here void. You met Gravitational waves when you entered this domain, but in the void you could meet Anti-Gravitational Chaotic Waves. These are the opposite of what you experienced only instead of waves they are deep troughs; so deep that one might never emerge only to vaporise in body and spirit. Now this does not mean death for us as that's impossibility, but for you lot, it would be fatal! Until we reach the exterior of the void anything can happen."

People shifted with uneasiness.

"So in a nutshell, the void is divided in the old familiar 360 degree circle, thus navigation could be similar to earth, that is if we were to hug the perimeter. However, we are not going to do that because we are in the interior where those co-ordinates will not work. We are positioned roughly in the central zone at 60 degrees latitude and north zero longitude, which is the polar line through the middle of the sphere. The Logo Optic tunnel that connects with the Omega also matches this polar line. However, it is very flexible and shifts position depending on ebb and flow. However, all this can be combated as I have up to the minute charts that show the danger areas but only I can read them and that is one of the reasons why you need me! Have ye any questions?"

He smiled and raised his shaggy eyebrows. Lionel piped up,

"Paulo where did you get your Captain Blue Beard phrases?" Paulo responded promptly,

"I got it from my friend Blue Beard - who else? He lives up here! I also know Sinbad!"

Lionel laughed and then Ernst asked, if the oxygen system will be needed

"No need," Paulo answered.

Dave asked where there would be any other traffic travelling on the same route? To which Paulo replied laughing as he did so,

"I'm glad you asked about that. Except for Template Ships from our outreach, nothing can be out there. He winked and then said,

"As you know the void is so hostile that if it were not for the AMGOD even creation would not exist."

Lionel then asked,

"Paulo are we vulnerable to the weapons that Thormentus uses?" Paulo looked thoughtful and then answered slowly,

"I never thought much about that! Ye' see I'm a bit out of touch, living back in 'Mutnauq'. In the last great conflict they used brimstone, but since then I heard that they developed a psychological weapon that when fired, left some Jet Packers incapacitated.

"Neg. troughs are our immediate challenge! You know there could be trouble ahead!"

There were no further questions and the team got down to looking over Paulo's charts and plotting their course.

Luca came to the door of the Callisto and wished the group God speed. Then as he retreated back into the crowd, Larry noticed that he had the faintest sign of a glowing disc around his head giving the impression of a halo. He turned to Everina and with wide eyes asked,

"Is Luca the Italian for Luke?" Everina said,

"Yes, you yoyo, so why do you ask?"

Larry pointed out Luke to her and said,

"We have had a very important tour guide- perhaps a Saint!"

Amongst the well wishers, Jill was surprised to meet an old friend Lynda with her Australian husband. There were lots of children and among them were Janette and Rico. Then a tall fellow pushed through the crowd. He had a broad Slavic face and pale blue eyes. His hair was straight and brown and oily in appearance. He diligently kept brushing it back from his face but it made no difference as the locks fell back immediately. As he approached the ship Dan, let out a loud whop,

"Jurek!" He shouted,

"Where have you been since the Institute?" Referring to the Institute of Applied Physics where they both had studied.

"I didn't know you were here!"

Jurek responded as usual with a broad smile and began to explain that he was on an archaeological expedition at the triangles rim measuring Negative Troughs from the deeper interior of the void and Gravitation Anomalies.

Dan looked impressed and then thought of something. He ushered him over to the door of the ship and said,

"Hey here is my son Larry, Larry meet Jurek. Larry is also covering does the same physics as you."

Larry responded with an outstretched hand,

"Nice meeting you Jurek, Dad often told me about you, and is it true you are a relation of James Joyce, Ulysses and all that?"

Jurek nodded and Dan added,

"That's what gives this guy the great imagination that he possesses. He is the one responsible for launching me into my physics fantasia world.

Everyone laughed and Jurek said in mock vanity,

"Ah shucks Dan you always say that!"

Then sensing the rising pressure to depart waved his hand and stepped back into the crowd. Dan rapidly took down his address for a future meeting. Out of curiosity some of the spectators had entered the ship. As departure was immanent they were escorted to the exits. Pat and her children while now quite upset; bravely waved Richard goodbye. Jill and Hiroshi looked on in silent contemplation. Then at a given command the doors were closed, names were checked off, and people went to their posts awaiting instructions.

There was a cheer from the crowd outside, good-bye kisses and waving. Then with out using engine power the ship floated high in the ether, and began to glide forward, gathering speed as it went. Richard had to hide his face for he could not look down at his receding family. Larry did look down and was fascinated to see Purgosia and its vibrant population shrink in size. In moments, the Sangrias were just red marks on the landscape.

The Logo Optic channel or tunnel could easily be seen winding its way upward. It was among other things, the navigational reference for the empire. It would not be difficult to see because it had a dazzling array of effervescent colours illuminating its presence. The outer rim was swirling with a 'Mandelbrots' designs (1) where as its inner regions were pulsating with ever changing colour. Also it was semi transparent and traffic could be seen moving inside.

Paulo who was still at the helm was intent on fine-tuning the flight path. He was engrossed in conversation with Dave and Lionel spelling out the finer points of extra-voidular navigation. Then he said unrepentantly,

"One thing puzzles me Dave! What in the name of all that is good and beautiful is that empty bird cage doing in the board room?"

Dave explained and Paulo responded with a huge bellow of laughter. Luckily Laura was not present at the time.

Since there was still an enormous distance to be travelled everyone remained absorbed with his or her duties However as the motors were now seldom used the team in the engine pit were redundant for the time being, but were on stand by for any emergency. While waiting, Ernst was busy checking and rechecking the oxygen system and other areas that had been damaged in Pergosia. He had to improvise and re design equipment to fit his needs and from the sound of his whistling while he worked, people reckoned that he must be satisfied with progress. Larry took a peek at what he was doing and noticed plastic canteen cups, empty biros and scotch tape were being used in his unique design.

Dave then told his management team that while in Purgosia he had met someone from the EUSARUSS flight centre who was present on earth when the Callisto disappeared. The story had made headlines and several rescue missions had been attempted. It seems they did not have a ship to match the capabilities of the Callisto that could cover the distance but also they were unsure where to look. Someone suggested that perhaps the area became more heavily shrouded after the Callisto had passed through!

Richard knew that a void as it appeared raised serious questions and therefore took out a philosophy book of his, and went to talk with Travis,

Hi Don, more questions!

"I'll bet you do." said Don and Richard questioned,

"How do we get our heads around this infinity question?

Don tried,

"As far as we have seen there appears to be one universe and one void surrounding it, isn't that right?"

Richard nodded slowly.

"Well there is another view called the 'Syncategorematic' view which gives us any number of finite Universes but will go on for ever! But where does that get us, no where as it is just beyond reason!"

Richard nodded again.

"Well," said Don with conviction,

"This sort of continuously multiplying magnitude is contiguous and unable to relate to one another they say – a God with his head in the sand. Of course the good God could produce, as many voids and universes as he pleases just like children in a large family- each one can be finite but with infinite potential. Therefore is our universe one of those! As we said, we cannot see any others, and if one believes that God has only one begotten son it follows that our universe is the only one so far! On a smaller scale, at one time there was speculation that there was a void within our universe, one million light years across in the constellation of 'Eridanus' that possessed another universe, but that has been disproven!"

He paused,

"As you have guessed, this void is in a state of repulsion but that may be good or bad, I do not know! However a possible absence of divine presence could be a clue!

Richard said cautiously,

"The Paradox is that Pierre Durham contradicts that even a void exists. This is in my book reference (1)."

He showed the text to Travis saying,

"I cannot comprehend that despite such compelling arguments in support of a void that they would deny its existence!

Richards was depressed and when Don went his way, he peered again around the extremity of the void. It did not look like going on for ever; it looked quite finite and looked like it could easily tolerate a much larger and expanded universe if it wished!

Richards Philosophy Book stated;

(1) This view was forwarded by a Franciscan, called Peter Lombard, (Ref Pierre Duhem,' Medieval Cosmology; The University College Press, Chicago and London) when he said - quote, God can produce endlessly a dimension that is larger and larger yet, but on the condition that at each instant the magnitude at that instant is finite unquote. The brothers of Purity and Sincerity adopted the Peripatetic teachings about the void. The Arabic philosopher al-Farabi, formulated the following arguments; in the fifteenth treatise of their encyclopaedia, they asserted that - the world void designates a free place in which there is nothing, but place is a property of bodies, which cannot reside except in a body and which cannot be found except with a body. Hence the existence of a void is absurd.....This rational demonstration proves that there is no void either inside or outside the universe -unquote."

Chapter 35

By now they were much closer to the Omega but still a long way to go. With the mist now thinning it stood out large and foreboding.

Then Paulo gave another commentary,

"Look my friends you are about to see the gates, the gates to the dynasty – the Great Omega! As we approach there will be chaotic turbulence and it will only be with their assistance that we will get landed safely."

The mist now cleared completely giving a new and uninterrupted view. People gasped. There like the entrance to Reno or Vegas was a great glowing horseshoe shaped arch with a smaller 'A' shaped gate within.

The upper circular area of this omega appeared to be made of dark reflective material; maybe glass! The Logo optic channel and all its transportation tunnels converged and linked with the area through the lower portion of the 'A'. This was also the launching pad for the torus of gravitation, the force that acts from afar and sweeps through all existence; the force that had caused waves when they originally arrived.

Paulo again said,

"My friends; that canal being so bright is the sole lifeline that keeps the machinery of creation intact! The gravitation we now possess is 'random grav' and is derived from the Omega and all masses in the vicinity."

It was then that the Lionel called out,

"Paulo, Skipper, Larry. Please look at the EM/SPEC. There are severe gravitation anomalies!"

There before their very eyes were buckled lines approaching from the South East!

Paulo bellowed,

"That's 'em. They are the 'Neg Troughs' I warned ye 'bout! Captain Dave let me now take command."

Dave nodded and Paulo bellowed once more,

"Sound red alert and action stations. Ernst, stand by with team in engine pit. Cadets stand by for damage control."

A siren sounded, the crew already in RP gear went into action as all unnecessary lighting was cut. Bathed in a blue glow, Larry stayed with the Navigator at the EM/SPEC. Paulo pointed to the distortions that were closing at a velocity far greater than their own. Pointing at the lines he said in an aggravated tone,

"Rats, they are being directed at us from you know who!"

Richard noticed that a black mist accompanied the Troughs. Everina began to shiver. Paulo called out,

"Ignite engines."

There was a roar and the ship shuddered. Then in an apologetic voice Paulo said,

"Ernst, apply one third velocity but in reverse!"

People looked at each other in dismay. Ernst was startled - what was happening? The reverse pods were immediately extended and on Ernst's command they began to fire. Paulo cried out,

"Turn about - 320 degrees to starboard prepare to roll ship. Communication, please issue an immediate distress call and state 'Neg. Troughs' of seven on the 'Trichter Scale' - approaching at five o'clock to our position at 82.78 longitude north to zero central to 01 east. Do this as if you are on earth – It will be picked up."

The Callisto went about and rolled to face the opposite direction. It was heading towards the waves but upside down, and moving backwards. Ernst was amazed at the acceleration. It was enormous and much more than they got when trying to evade the draw from the tunnel.

"I cannot believe it we are achieving greater velocity backwards than forwards!"

Paulo shouted down the intercom,

"Yes Ernst, this void does everything the wrong way around, did you never notice before?"

The first wave bent everything in its path, while the trough behind looked even more threatening. As the first hit the Callisto was lifted up stern first. To everyone's amazement they plunged through the surface of the wave and rode on the inside. Larry froze, he thought of Gasper the wave in his imagination. But he had never dreamed of riding the inside of a swell! The world around was now warped in every direction. The interior of the wave was not black and eerie as expected. Instead it was bright like daytime!

Again Paulo shouted,

"Bend the surfaces in the black void and you get the opposite effect."

Within moments, they reached the crest and dangled from the inside of the peak. Paulo bellowed,

"Ernst, engines full throttle forward I repeat, forward."

This time they would ride down the back of the wave nose first. The transition was instantaneous and effortless. Downwards they slid on a roller coaster into an almost bottomless valley. Ernst could not see what was happening from inside the engine pit and was shivering with fear yet he maintained perfect control. The ship gathered speed and the 'G force' became unbearable. As they hit the bottom of the trough the Callisto had almost approached the speed of light outside a vacuum's vacuum!

Then Paulo shouted,

"As before roll ships, engines full reverse, attain maximum velocity."

With a roar and a sickening roll the Callisto did a turn that would make a ballet dancer envious. Several computers were wrenched from their fittings and smacked into the ceiling. Some pots and pans hit the walls and Mantz who was not strapped down was flung against the EM/SPEC. The nuclear pack exploded into life again. The ship under extreme acceleration began a new ascent using all the positive gravitational energy it had attained in the drop - plus the energy of the engines. Once more the ship began riding backwards up the inside. Someone shouted,

"Neg' troughs from Hell!"

Though they had accumulated gravitational energy in their favour it seemed not sufficient to make the crest. Though the Callisto rocketed bravely upwards its speed reduced dramatically. Everyone gasped as they realised that was happening. The communications operator could be heard calling out repeatedly,

"Callisto to Omega, May Day, SOS under attack from negative troughs - position Latitude 82.78 North Longitude to Zero Central to 01 east."

Ernst's concern was one of fuel supply and the strength of the ships superstructure - he hoped it could take the stress. If there were many more waves to come he would be cleaned out of energy and worse still- the ship likely to crack open.

Now at about two thirds way up the wave, the ship ground to a stop. There was a groan and it immediately it began to slide back. Several people let out a scream. Everina thought she heard a child cry. How could that be there were no children on the ship! Hamish shouted an obscenity and a sense of horror took over. It was at that critical moment that there was a thunderous roar. A violet light illuminated the ship. It illuminated the waves outside. Then it systematically burned a track of light across the face of the wave. For a moment there was no result, but then slowly the Negative Troughs evaporated.

Everina felt the ship drop and then with a calamitous crash, all loose items flew in every direction – but at least the ship had landed on something! This was self evident when Paulo shouted,

"Praise the lord we are back on terra firma, known as good old black vacuum packed fabric!"

Through the windows a great piercing light was sweeping the ether in their vicinity. The light was coming from the Omega. It was like the beam from a lighthouse or a beacon at sea showing sailors the way. Then as quick as a blink it disappeared and the black abyss became calmed. The silence was shattered by Paulo's melodious voice,

"Well me buccaneers, you are all sea dogs now! Ye' did very well indeed but if it were not for that laser artillery from the omega we would not be here now. Oh by the way we all owe a word of thanks to the radio operator and to Ernst and of course to each other. Now time to clean up."

There was a round of applause and people heaved a sigh of relief. However the relief was short come by as a cadet burst on the scene dragging two small figures. It was none other than Janette and Rico. Everina let out a gasp! The children wriggled free and rushed towards her crying out,

"Please la madre don't be angry, we are sorry but we just had to come!"

Paulo's eyes widened and he bellowed,

"Now we are in a fine mess, they are forbidden to enter, as they are still Purgosians like Jill. We will have to declare them I don't know what will happen!"

Chapter 36

The Ω was now so large it filled the horizon. To an onlooker the ship would be just a dot in the face of the enormous orb. Now at close range Larry could see the glass structure in some detail. It was so enormous that it reflected the panorama of creation on its surface. To his bewilderment there were great faces peering down from behind the structure. Perhaps they were just magnified or could they really be gigantic!

In the centre of the glass expanse there was a large machine on wheels with a gun like object pointing downwards in their direction, while nearby there were several smaller versions of the same machinery. Maybe these were the lasers the miracle makers that had been spoken about and that had saved them from those dreadful waves, thought Larry. There was a rush of turbulence and the ship lurched just as Paulo had said. Then there was a sound like a Gregorian chant. Paulo said,

That is the sound of incoming prayers. They all rise here regardless. All we can do about the turbulence is to stay steady and wait."

"So this is Paradise?" Everina said. She was nursing a sprained wrist from the earlier impact. All of a sudden another shaft of light streamed down from the omega. This time it was emitted from a crack at the top of the A shape as which was opening. There was a hush within the ship and the EM/SPEC began to click,

"Total unification of natural forces achieved. Ultimate singularity realised. Time 111101.0005x times universal time. The Temperature is now registering 111101.0005 degrees Kelvinity."

Jean and Manz studied the readings evidently puzzled by the last term Kelvinity?

Richard mumbled under his breath,

"Open Sesame!"

Then as if answering his command, the crack opened wide allowing the light to become even more intense. Now the interior of the ship was stark white with no shadows for definition. The light penetrated into every crevice to the extent of making the people become almost invisible. The children covered their eyes and held fast to Everina. Then there was the sound of voices that echoed about the ship causing the crew to jump. However, Ernst and several of his team were not to be caught unawares and produced some dome halos that they had been given in Purgosia. Several people put on the domes and immediately nodded their heads in satisfaction. The voices could be heard to say,

"Ventilator Abel, Tango, Five, Niner, Probe Permission at 30 Trillion 0685 - √ of 1,111,011.001 Align."

Then there was silence followed by a scraping sound and then cough. After a moment, more dialogue,

"Supply 10 x27 mags of Surfactant. Lower CPAP – Vorsich Caperello. Validation authorised via Pedro@ Zero One x Com Saint – Enter."

There was another cough, just like a human cough and a tiny laugh. The sound was amplified so acutely that it vibrated off objects in the ship. There was a clank like something had fallen on a floor. Then someone said something like,

"Let it down now."

A long silver object like a forceps descended from above. It was accompanied by another object shaped like a dentist's mirror, which was directed beneath the ship. However with the turbulence there were several a severe bumps. Then the forceps clamped on both sides of the Callisto and stabilised the situation and immediately the ship was drawn upwards. There was a rush of cold ether that seemed to chill the inside of the ship. While ascending they infringed on part of the torus spilling out from the same opening. For a brief moment, it penetrated one side of the ship causing small objects to be drawn to it, just like a magnet. There was consternation as spoons, pens, pins, tins and screws went flying to hit the port side at enormous speed. Two of the team got badly nicked with the flying metal, but did not bleed. Fortunately this was only the source of the torus; its gravitation was in its infancy and by now the Callisto by comparison was quite a monstrous object in its own right.

The Ship continued to be carried aloft, while everyone sat in silent contemplation and the accident and emergency crews remained on full alert. With a jolt they cleared the entrance and continued upwards. From their perch they could see the blackness from whence they had come; and the lights of creation slowly minimising as the crack began to close.

They were now in an enormous chamber. White clad people were directing their ship to a safe landing. Giant hands were working controls and pressing buttons. Rico and Janette had slipped from their seats and buy now had managed to crawl to a window. The crew stared in awe as the shadows of several giants spread over the ship. Rico and Janette let out a scream. A cadet rushed to calm them.

Someone said,

"Paulo, you know the score, who are those monsters, are we their supper?"

Paulo let out a very loud laugh,

"Oh I should have told you or maybe you should have guessed – this is a giant world. But trust it!"

They were lowered onto a smooth floor still facing north. Before them was a glass wall through which they could see enormous sized greenery, a large orchard and gigantic tropical palms. Though the view was still obscured it looked as if beyond the land sloped upwards and was covered in fields of white roses. Flying craft of all shapes and sizes could be seen arriving and departing somewhere behind the greenery.

The ship groaned like it was being stretched and the temperature returned to normal. The giants stood back and could be seen more clearly. Some wore facemasks and some wore sound disks on their heads others looked quite informal. Paulo spoke rapidly to the crew,

"In a moment we will have normalised which means; grown to their proportions. Then we will be ready to exit."

Then there was a jolt, and the Callisto again increased in size. From within the ship there was a sound of groaning metal. The EM/SPEC had grown without and complaint and was now checking magnitude. Then its numerals began adding more zeros than it had ever done before. Most of the crew opened their safety harnesses and for some reason or other clustered in the centre of the ship. Some stretched out their hands as if watching to see would they grow. People watched each other and one fellow said that his friend was growing quicker than he!

No one wanted to be first to alight. Rico and Janette let out a whimper, which reminded Paulo to insist that they do not leave the ship until told so. Everina had now moved close to Larry gripping his arm as usual. Then the expansion process finished! At that moment she whispered,

"I wonder which one is Caperello?"

Richard moved to a wide portal and observed that the dentists mirror shaped object and the forceps were now quite small, just like at home and they were laid neatly on a table and what's more, the medical team had departed.

Larry looked over his own body to see had it all grown in proportion. The other members of the group looked okay! The floor where the ship was sitting upon was divided into three sections correspond with the triangles. These divisions ran right through other parts of the building like territorial divides, they were in fact the same rose lines they had observed from below. The enclosure and contents were made of fine white material, though the walls were filled with holes like a Swiss cheese. A least they were decorative, and enabled one to see what lay beyond.

Now from their higher position they could see what lay outside with more clarity. A river of many colours wound its way down from the territory of white roses and joined two others before descending through an opening. There was a very large fruit tree standing at that same opening and the rivers seemed to filter away through its roots on their journey to Purgosia.

Chapter 37

Just then the doors of the ship opened of its own accord. There was a burst of intoxicating atmosphere and an amazing freshness from the ether - a giddy perfume with a hint of lilac. In the background there was the sound of harps and other string instruments playing gentle relaxing chords mixed with the sound of humming machinery. Paulo ushered them towards the door. They began to alight, squinting in the extra brightness. Larry turned in a complete circle, stopping to survey the area around him in more detail. The chamber was enormous and in its centre was what resembled a black transparent lake but was actually glass. It was raised shoulder high above the floor level with people and computers around its horseshoe shaped perimeter. The people were normal toned and not blue and pink like in Purgosia. They were very intent on work and did not even look their direction. The black glass acted as a window on the world, a road map to everything.

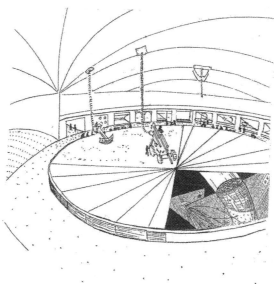

The ceiling was smooth and white and very high. This was evidently the flipside of what they had seen from below. There were offices or anti-chambers encircling most of the rotunda and there was a steps leading in from outside and up to other floors. Mounted in the Glass panel was that same enormous laser on wheels? The contraption pointed downwards aimed at co-ordinates etched on the glass. In addition to this there were several smaller versions also pointing downwards. They all had large white wheels and were connected to the ceiling with loose power lines. It looked like someone had written the 'Kahn Opener' in Arabic style writing on the side of the largest unit. This was meta-humour at its best. The ceiling though lofty was filled with information screens giving multi media coverage of everything outside - it was a den of cosmological information.

Turning back towards the orchard he noticed more medical equipment. It was difficult to figure out why this was so prevalent - perhaps this was a sort of cosmic-maternity delivery area!

Paulo being a saint was no longer blue and pink. He went forward picked up a phone-like contraption, and said,

"Greetings Pedro, this is Paulo here, we are home and dry, has the Lord ship arrived?"

There was an immediate response,

"Welcome ol'man, nice to see you still doing things the hard way! Yes, the Lord Ship is on the way."

Paulo turned back and put his finger to his lips and said, "Shush."

The group stood still, transfixed with the excitement of the moment. In the distance there was the sound of voices and an approaching crowd. Then a group of about fifteen people appeared coming up the steps from outside and being led by a man who preceded four figures; three of which were enormously tall. There was a blare of organ music like they had heard in the Chasms. Paulo went down on one knee and the group copied his pose. Then he rose as did the group but he stepped forward and outstretched his arm to greet the forbearer, a man called Antonio.

"Ah Paulo, we have found you at last!"

Paulo responded,

"Yes Antonio you are good at finding things!" They both laughed. Antonio neat and slender stood facing the group, and then swept one arm towards the four figures, and said,

"Behold your makers," and then stepped aside.

The group was overwhelmed by the impact of such a message. They felt light headed and inclined towards fainting. Everina began to shake from head to foot and with sheer loss of breath clung on to Larry for assistance. Several other people were overpowered, unable to remain and therefore staggered back towards the ship.

There standing before the visitors were four exotic people with Arabic features. Three were extremely tall, perhaps eight foot and dressed in loose cloths. One was average human height. As they moved, they caused a distortion in the surroundings, much like when they witnessed the son welcoming the mortals in the chasms. These movements caused a sound like chimes in a breeze, and perfume like lavender prevailed in the atmosphere. They possessed disks that floated just above their heads shimmering and flashing as if receiving messages. They also had no blue and pink colouring and neither did their entourage. They looked otherwise just like the people of Pugosia in clothing of their choice.

The most senior of the four, was male with golden hair and a short beard. He wore a burgundy cape over white clothing with loose pants tucked into soft brown boots. He strode forward, stretched out a hand. The first contact was Dave who instinctively responded by genuflecting. They both clasped hands, and as they did so Dave rose up and there was applause from around the whole enclosure. The operational crew now took notice and stood up at their computers to join the occasion. The great figure then said, in a booming voice that echoed in the chamber,

"Let me introduce myself, I am the Father of all Creation and you are very welcome!"

He swept his hand backwards towards another saying,

"My Son has spoken of you and argued your case incisively. Please realise that you are in a state of mild Ecstasy and Rapture. You are only being permitted to vaguely experiencing our world. This was made possible by bringing you gently through the process that prepared you for this visit. What you see is an approximation of what this state is really about. We permitted you to see as much as your minds could cope with – but there is much that you will not see or even be able to comprehend. However, let me tell you that you are doing well as no other mortal has trodden this path so far but with one exception! "

Then he smiled again and continued - only now letting go of Dave's hand.

"Well you may not know me, but I know all of you, this is Dave, and hello Ernst, I was glad to know that your niece who was very ill before your departure; has since made a full recovery. I could go on but will have you ask Antonio about any earthly concerns you may have – he will bring you up to date."

Antonio smiled and covered his head as if hiding. There was a big outburst of laughter and immediately the atmosphere became less tense.

He continued in a very serious voice,

"Before I go and leave you to enjoy our pastures, I must tell you that we live in what you will call territories. Despite this we are free to move in or out as we wish, just like our visit here today. It is difficult to understand how we can be hybrid of both physical people also land mass and at the same time, metaphysical beings who are immanent to all situations in as far away places as Doradus in the Pictor constellation or even your earth. However you will grasp all this as you journey through our realms."

There was little else that could be said. There was a murmur and several people looked out at his rose laden golden coloured territory that loomed above. Then he swept around his left arm and pointed to a young man saying,

"Behold my beloved Son, in whom I am well pleased."

The Father turned waved with his right hand and departed with most of his entourage. The Son stepped forward for all to see. Again everyone went down on one knee. He was the same handsome person they had already seen and at closer range wore just a white shirt and loose white pants, had black hair that shone with a tinge of navy blue. He also had a swarthy look found often in middle easterners. One of the female cadets let out an involuntary sigh. She immediately turned red faced while one of her friends began to giggle. The son smiled broadly as his white clothes swished with the movement and the surroundings shimmered. He indicated with the open palms of his hands for everyone to stand up.

"I want to welcome you all. Our tour basically will bring you to experience the three territories of which my Father spoke. They lie in a circle and mine is positioned over to the left side. You will see it soon enough!"

He then gestured in the direction of two more people, both females. One was very young, and the other more mature. They both stepped forward. He pointed to the younger of the two women and said,

"This is Spirinda, the Parakeet who spoke to you in her triangle."

Everyone exclaimed in a mixture of joy and surprise. It was wonderful to actually see her and to meet. Everyone clapped their hands in glee.

Then he continued,

"I see Spirinda has impressed you so far, and why not she is the mother of all mothers; of Gaia, Danu, Kilima, Aymare, of the universe and its galaxies, 10K-1, Messier 83, Centaurus A and all else you can see! Up here she possesses the third and last territory – the one that is abundant in oceans and gentle breezes and song."

People remained standing this time they may have been because they felt the sense of family and peace that transcends from the spirit.

All eyes gazed on Spirinda as she stood tall and slim resembling a Polynesian God. She was also in simple white and had long flowing black hair with a large orchid attached. Her eyes were a glistening brown and her skin was amber. She looked shy because of the attention, and appeared to bite her lip as she stepped backwards. It was amazing how one who is alleged to have spawned reality could also be bashful in its presence! Because of her radiant beauty, Larry squeezed Everina's hand, just to show her that she was still his number one. Her hand went limp and then squeezed back.

Then he introduced the second female,

"This is the Queen of Heaven - Miriam my earth mother. She is the exception that my Father spoke about. She is whole and entire in every sense the honorary person of this world. She does not possess a territory or a triangle but she is the mother of all inventions, and intercedes for all your needs even without you knowing."

All eyes focused on Miriam a majestic lady with golden hair, and dark brown eyes. She was gentle and graceful while generating the warmth of a real mother. She was dressed in a pale blue wrap that was worn partly over her head. Underneath the wrap, she wore a straight cut white dress with a thin golden belt that dipped in the centre as it was attached to a golden medallion. She was quite in keeping with the traditional image that many people have in mind.

Miriam stepped gracefully forward and glided into the crowd. She moved from person to person-shaking hands, embracing and addressing everyone by first name. She inquired about private aspects of their lives and demonstrated an intimate knowledge about each and every member of the crew - this included the non-believers. Hamish and the fainter hearted people soon got brave and pushed forward to be able to meet this Queen of Eternity.

At this point Paulo confessed to the Son about the stowaway children in the ship. The Son froze for a moment and looked towards his mother. She came too him knowing that there was a problem. He spoke to her and she moved aside, nodding her head. He then ushered Paulo, Dave and Laura to one side. Then he said quietly,

"This causes a massive violation of our nature, and my tribes could be very upset, not to mention Pedro our key holder."

Paulo quickly replied,

"Lord these children would have been here long ago but their parents are lost in Purgosia and they must wait to be reunited with them to complete the hex."

"Okay" said the Son,

"I will make a case but if not accepted they will all have to leave immediately which means the whole tour might have to be cut short.

Then he turned to Miriam and said,

"We will have to chaperone them at all times so will you arrange a guardian at night but during the day you will have to keep them as close as possible to your corporality. Is that okay with you?"

Miriam looked as if she felt trapped in the situation. Then she smiled and said, "That's okay my bennie elohim."

Paulo took Miriam to the ship to meet the stowaways Paulo then shuffled through the group saying goodbye - giving the odd bear hug and saying that he would catch up later to skipper their return trip.

The Son said in a deliberately pompous tone,

"Let the tour begin."

The Captain, Ernst, Mantz, Bakhr Jean, Ivan and some others tagged close to the Son as he led the way around the enclosure. He stopped at one of the computers where a man was working. He introduced him as Thomas Aquinas. Thomas welcomed them and then said,

I once demonstrated the existence of the soul but also I'm afraid I agreed with Aristotle that knowledge is only acquired by sensory experience. However what I missed was that there is a hereditary cognitive template in each being. That is the logo we infused at the creation of every soul. You saw all this in the Chasms of Yahweh. The template is pre-prompted and has an appetite to acquire knowledge. This cognitively independent state then makes way for sensory experience to flourish along with all its corporal phantasms. The rivers flow naturally from these territories like the movement in a body bringing the sap of goodness with it!"

The son said,

"Thanks Thomas, you've said it all and a bit more than I expected."

Then he recited from memory a verse from Revelation 21:22:

"The angel also showed me the river of the water of life, sparkling like crystal, and coming from the throne of God and of the Lamb and flowing down the middle of the city's street."

Everina and some of the Cadets had different ambitions as they talked with the lady Spirit who reminded them just to call her Spirinda. They asked with respect how could she look so young yet have delivered creation. She laughed and said,

"That is why I'm here and you are there. I'm a God in labour yet I'm as free as a bird. My world does not impose labour beyond endurance and its yoke is not a burdened. The process is achieved through mutual meta physical co-operation."

She told Everina that a group of the angels had made Jill's wedding dress the one she bought in Purgosia. The material was called Corncreen - a weave of fibre that grows in the pastures within her territory.

The Son then said with conviction,

"Look you are now in the most powerful citadel in existence. Our Lasers are energized by fusing inverted deuterium using pyroelectric crystal, inverted of course! This 'Zapper' is the cutting edge of our cosmo-medicalisation defence and control. This is the observation centre called Godhead One. Three more Godheads exist but at a higher level, as you will soon find. From here we can monitor everything everywhere within the void - though we cannot see into the pit!"

Mantz looked lost for a moment. The Son realised that was the case,

"Oh, the pit is the very bottom of the void, where the forces of Thormentus dwell. We try not to disturb them, since ions ago they lost word war one, and were expelled from the Deity."

They periodically direct negative wave troughs towards us but worse still, they have developed cosmo-psychic viruses known as screeches – which they direct into our vast communications network. The screeches home in on this control area and can eventually explode a 'compeglius' or a computer in your language. This can cause major damage so we counter it with regular virus dialysis, now a whole time job."

No one asked any more questions yet they were fascinated.

There was a pause and then Dave exclaimed aloud,

"This is the Captains Bridge of the greatest vessel anyone could ever command."

Larry wished he had a camera to record the moment at the same time humming to him self,

"I'm on top of the world and looking down on creation, and the only conclusion I can find is the love that we have."

Chapter 38

"At last, now let me introduce you to Pedro, not Paulo, but our OMCOM, the omega migration control manager."

The Son pointed to a tall man standing at a double door chamber with glass walls. The chamber stretched along a large portion of the east side of the enclosure. It commanded an overview of all the activities perhaps confirmed by what was written over the door '*hhh. com/saint@omega-controlcentre.amgod* .

Pedro said he was team administer over all traffic in and out of the deities. That he alone holds the codes that facilitated this movement. One person asked if many are rejected. Pedro showed a fain grin, thought for a moment and then said cautiously,

"All races and creeds, believers or non believers are welcome here. You will be glad to know we do not reject many. It applies only to a small percentage, most of who are well known for their unsavoury deeds. They leave their living state full of defiance and actually reject themselves. They never get this far and are stopped well before reaching Purgosia. The only way to come here is with credentials that I get from the Son everyone goes through him. Once Purgosia people are retained awaiting mass transfer in the last epoch - 'Pierre Chardin's Amorisation' followed by the day of General Judgement. It will be then and only then that you will understand the full ramifications of our glory!"

Then he lowered his voice and smiled helplessly,

"Now there still is the case of Janette and Rico that complicates matters. It defies nature and could blow our system by causing structural corrosion. However Miriam has literally assimilated the two into her corporality to avert this difficulty. In your case there are too many for this to be done, so we just have to take a chance! That's why we are here it keeps us in a job. We are always dealing with exceptions!"

He smiled again, and took a deep breath. People sighed with relief and Pedro looked at Larry gave wink and said,

"Larry you will appreciate this. Saint Patrick said that the shamrock is an ideal simile of the Trinity, Eammus v 33.

"Think of the Father as a spring of life begetting the Son like a river and the Holy Spirit like a sea, for the spring and the river and the sea are all one nature. Think of the Father as a root, of the Son as a branch, and the Holy Spirit as a fruit, for the substance in these three is one."

After this impressive rendering, all eyes were turned on what lay below. They now saw the triangles in a different light, swaying like a plant in the seabed with its roots firmly implanted in the Omega; where they now stood.

Pedro then added,

"It was a pleasure to meet you all but now I must be excused, and we will meet again."

There were about a hundred operators sitting around the oval enclosure yet much of the equipment was unmanned. The Son who had been quiet then said that there is a festival in Purgosia and they are short handed as many have gone below. He then said with a serious look on his face,

"We harvest all the prayers here you would have heard them as you arrived. They are acted upon immediately but sometimes the results don't get through for years because of distance, other times it happens right away. Atmospherics have a lot to do with it. That is how many humans become frustrated and can fail in fidelity. The residue of prayers and all good acts, or loving pursuits fuel the advancement of our dynasty. This energy is converted into a divine form of currency. I will show you all this shortly. In the mean time it is here that we monitor and grant requests. Of course often things are passed to me or Com Saint for a second opinion!"

Hiroshi said to Larry,

"Remember the PQ's in the Uclidia?"

Larry said that he did and turned to the computer bank. Every now and then, one of the consuls would emit a beeping sound. The operator then clicked on an illuminated blemish enlarging it for analysis. Having decided on what remedy was needed he or she would use a 'felucca' to click on different people on earth or elsewhere to inspire them towards a local solution. On the other hand where major problems like dangerous asteroids or eruptions were imminent they could evoke an antidote from a set of co-ordinates down the side of each monitor. These options in turn correspond to the large map on the central glass floor. Then on command the lasers would focus and with a loud purring sound direct a beam downward. The light though almost invisible could be seen as is zoomed towards a target.

The Son swept his hand across the glass and said,

"There is my Achilles heel. I have been human like you and experienced hunger, thirst and pain and I shiver from the experience. However, I fear if things go badly in the universe, I will be asked to return and I really cannot refuse a second coming."

The listeners suddenly felt a wave of pity, for the Son and guilt for being part responsible for his plight. How could humans have caused such a predicament to exist? However he seemed to read their minds saying,

"Please it is not for you to pity me. It is because of my pity for you that you stand here today. That is what redemption is all about!"

He led them to an adjoining room or theatre. Inside was divided into sections with people working in theatre gear. Each of the sections was dedicated to different medical disciplines. He turned,

"This is where we control the inverted biological aspects of the domain. This is where the Hazard Analysis of all Critical Control Points of the whole system are Monitored. Now bear with me for a moment. Here we go!"

"There is Anaesthesia, which is preformed by the lasers you saw outside. It is vital that we monitor the Volcanoes in Purgosia for time pressure per arc revolution known to you as blood pressure. Coupled with this there is occupational therapy related to the triangular alignment and configuration. As you can imagine there are ferocious hauling and tugging at the triangles all the time. If it were to drift something might rip apart. Then there is Orthopaedic Trauma which is psychological support for the cosmos on a continuous basis."

He looked around and people still looked interested.

"Next there is Dermatology, Endocrinology, Haematology, Microbiology and also Neuropathology as in Gravitational resonance. The areas of Inverted Pharmaceutical and Chemistry are needed for dealing with unsuspected virus in far away places. Then we have Neurology, as in corona outreach. Neurosurgical and Obstetrics combined and this odd combination is related to eventual deliverance; when ever it happens!" Then he coughed.

"Over on the right there is Otolaryngology, related to head and neck and then Pathology, Psychiatric, and Pulmonary Research areas that are in high demand with the activities of the arc and the ventilation from the blue triangle. Radiology is tied in with the holographs and then a Renal Medicine which is rarely needed but necessary. Though I have missed a few, there is also Rheumatology and lastly Surgical. The surgical laser teams have been trying to cut clear blockages that cause the universe to be ectopic. So far we have not succeeded and if not then the deliverance will prove difficult."

Then he said with curiosity,

"Would you like to see the operation theatre?"

Without waiting for a response he took them into an observation chamber where they could look down on the performance of the surgeons. There was a team of ten who were clustered around a circular operating table on which was a shimmering galaxy. The guests gasped and Larry questioned in confusion,

"Sir, is that a Galaxy?"

The Son smiled and said,

"Yes, that is a Galaxy extracted from an anaesthetised section of the Universe for repair. You have learned already that through the medium of my arc of time from Purgosia I can halt rotation and thus freeze time temporary."

As he spoke one of the surgeons extended a pointed object close to one side of the substance and directed a beam into its interior. The Son then added,

"Any observer in your cosmos will say that they saw an unidentified flying object and you know they would not be far wrong!"

Some of the group smiled. On closer inspection, Larry noticed that the object was encased in a film of plastic like material or membrane. The surgeons appeared to be reaching inside through the film and that the film stretched down through a gap in the floor. The Son then said,

"The film stretches back to the universe from whence the Galaxy has been withdrawn. The reason is that it allows us to work without having it expand or invert its substance. It was drawn up protected from 'Negative Troughs' inside a hollow laser beam that still protects it. By this means Thormentus and co. cannot claim that we broke any natural laws. We could have done that with you but you had already expanded too much by the time you arrived on the blue triangle."

As they left the theatre Larry had a last look at the non-inverted organic object shimmering like a giant jellyfish glowing and pulsating as it was miraculously undergoing divine surgery by an Unidentified Friendly

Organisation. He sighed and put his arm around Everina and followed the Son on the next stage of the orientation.

Then he opened a set of double doors to an inner chamber that was quite large. Inside was what looked like a massive roulette table. On top of it were a dozen or so raised columns, each having spokes that slowly rotated. As they did so small pieces of shining material were falling out of them on to the table. Attendants with long brush-shaped implements were scooping the material into containers and then onto trolleys. There were other dedicated helpers with unusual hand held calculators who appeared to be adding up the value of each consignment, before rolling it away for storage.

"This is our mint." The Son announced with a smile,

"Praque is our honey pot and with it one can buy prayer bonds or Praque futures. On average we receive a billion Praque per light minute when things are going well, at the moment we are only doing a third of that amount. This reduces the Praque value slowing down speculation and our ultimate expansion. However we have been through this sort of decline before and managed our way out."

He picked up a shoulder bag and led the way.

Chapter 39

Now it was time to leave the ground floor and go outside. The Son said with respect,

"There are many mansions in my Fathers house!"

The door of the complex was then thrown back, to reveal their exact position. They were in a crater made up of three land masses and in its centre was an enormous round structure where they had been. It was so dazzling that they did not attempt to look too far upwards. The whole area was steeped in a blue haze that was drifting from the east. This territory was Spirinda's and it looked quite different from the other two. It was very ecologically developed and was probably responsible for the eco system of the dynasties. The group now had a chance to look back and see the massive centre that they had been in and read a sign over the door that said the Omega Centre. It was a circular structure with a separate building even greater still, sitting on top but elevated above it. The upper building was suspended by eight enormous curved legs that housed escalators.

Quite a few people were already ascending ahead of them. The group followed the throng to the moving stairs. When they reached the top there was a balcony and then to their disbelief they entered an enormous hall that resembled a busy stock market.

A sign read "PC/TT/PM."

"This is our Pan-Creational Territorial, Telepathies, Prayer Market, which to be correct is the PC/TT/PM.- but some wise guys named it the Poor Credit Time and Temptation Post Mortem." Everyone laughed. The Son added,

"It is also aptly called the Praydaq, need I say more?"

Inside there were people dashing around with strips of paper while talking frantically with each other. Some of them had coloured tabards as if to denote their trade. In one corner there were coat hooks on which coats, jet packs and visors were hanging. Everyone was focused on texts and numbers that moved on central screens. There were several columns that looked like they carried up power and information from the theatre below.

The Son spoke, raising his voice above the din,

"As I told you earlier we trade in prayer. Did you know that prayer is the fifth dimension for the Universe, just as time is considered to be the fourth dimension? We produce Praque by fusing it with crystal and alloys from the golden territory. This in turn is currency which signals us to allow more and more expansion into the outreach. The expansion is proportional to the volume of Praque produced multiplied by the Quaternal ratio which is running at 4.5% at the moment."

He looked at people's amazed faces and smiled,

"One can also buy bonds which allow a stake in both the expansion in the outreach but also in territories below the Omega. Basically where a population is generated - prayer follows, and if one knows where the next colony will occur, the value of their bonds can soar. However if you bet on a territory that does not materialize, this causes Praque bubble that we have to deflate or it could cause a paralysis to further investment. Most of what happens up here seeps down through the systems even to the ends of the earth."

He continued,

"Lastly, one can buy Praque Futures, based on a guess at what the Quaternal ration will be at a given time. This is shaky business but it is popular. Wealth, however, does not mean that existence changes in any way; it is a game of achievement and an opportunity to assist the Deity."

Suddenly Hamish, one of the sullen three piped up.

"Is this a Democracy or what?" The Son replied,

"It is a 'Freeocracy'. What I mean is that one can do whatever one likes but within parameters. Those who are here are void of malice and only capable of getting total enjoyment from compliance."

"But Sir, could they revolt like in <u>Word</u> war one?" The Son answered with reluctance,

"Yes there is always that possibility!"

Hamish then said,

"You know all this King and Queen talk is not healthy. Why can there not be a Republic?"

The Son was about to answer but Dave intervened,

"Please excuse us my Lord but these questions are for another time and place."

The Son raised his hand,

"No, it is in order for Hamish to have such questions, but remember if we elect a Godot (1) for the want of a better name the real Father will still be there and cannot to be ignored. In effect you would only have a puppet Republic!"

A crowd of the investors had gathered as they overheard Hamish's questions and began discussing what had been said amongst them selves. The Son now wishing to defuse the situation took his group to see more of what was happening in the market yet a disturbing question had been asked!

Though people retained their paradise dignity, it did wear thin in some instances. A couple of fellows trying to purchase bonds from* Calcutta actually tripped and fell over. Of course, they were unhurt but looked foolish and caused some laughter from other traders. A newcomer to the game was sold a lemon because he bought bonds from Uranus which turned out to have no population and therefore no value! A woman had bonds for the Andromida Galaxy that she had bought ages ago. But since then it became colonised - she had just sold them for enormous profit and was celebrating with her colleagues. In this instance the profit will automatically go towards outreach expansion. One of the traders passing was asked by the Son to tell the group what the economic outlook was. He was a small plump fellow with tight cut hair. He said in a flustered voice,

"No, the outlook is not good, trade down 8.5% because of the festival in Purgosia, but also because of threats from the Pit!"

He smiled and went on his way. Just then a gong rang, if it had been a bell it would have been good news, but a gong was bad! Then he put his finger to his lips and in a loud whisper said,

"Oh by the way, before we leave finance, you should know the antithesis of Praque is called 'Draiks'. It is what fuels the Anti-trinity, the forces of blackness in the void. You have already felt its effect – Neg. Troughs and all that."

The Son looked at the group with wide serious eyes. He slowly moved his gaze across the faces of the group and as he did a dozen people cast their eyes downwards. What did that mean!

The Son then said the tropical garden was called Eden, and almost everything here is mimicked on earth. He opened his shoulder bag and issued dark glasses to the group and said nothing but pointed sky wards. There were three great roads radiating to wind their way up the territories. It was like being in the centre of an enormous tricolour bowl with something extraordinary at the top. It was something that they had not yet been even able to see or examine. It consisted of three enormous blinding suns each one was at the top of each of the three territories - shining immense light upon them as they stood like minions in centre of the heavenly super bowl! The Son watched in amusement as they reacted with such surprise saying,

"Common, surly by now you are ready for anything!"

Some of them began to laugh at their own foolishness. The Son also laughed and stood looking upwards at the Fathers territory the one that had white roses and lots of gold coloured land. And said,

"I'm sure you require an explanation!"

People nodded.

"Now at the zenith of each land is a sun. That sun is our very thinking self-beaming down on our subjects. Our warmth gives life to life, and keeps the whole system flowing. From these Godheads our energies expand outwards in thought coronas fuelling our eternal imagination. Our knowledge transmutes nothingness into something which we then take on board. In the first place, the structure of this nothingness is our cognitive selves yet in the notional form of cubes; which we hold behind all that you see. This nexus has an almost static time structure of its own; its seconds equivalent to a millennium on earth. Now as we talk the crystal shores of our imaginations is expanding in all directions into what we call that the outreach. Praque then enables all this to become paradised, excavated, formatted and fertilised. Let's call Prayer - our food for thought!"

People erupted into a chorus of chatter. Then one person spoke up,

"Sir, does that mean I could hurt you by digging in the ground?" "Yes you could – if I let you!"

One person still laughing at the kidding asked what is behind the territories and was told,

"There is nothing there, only the imagination that I have just mentioned. You may be glad to be told again, that you are vaguely composed in our image and likeness."

Then he stopped and looked at the expressions of disbelief. And continued,

"Your equivalent of the blue triangle is the lower part of your body, the maroon triangle is your heart and gravitation is your head. Then comes your thinking process which is a wretched version of ours, yet in a metaphysical way it works the same as it can inspire and lead you to us - where you belong, Capiche?"

The Son smiled and then he quickly pointed upwards towards the distant hills on that same golden territory. There nestled in the haze was what looked like a Muslim city covered in tall Byzantine Domes.

"Many of our subjects call the dweller in this territory - Father, Yahweh, Allah, Jehova or Muhammad and why not, because that is who he is. The Qur'an is held in high esteem in this land and Muhammad and Gabriel are in charge of our angel population and have used them to save your world on many occasions. Since he left you a half hour ago he is now in Iraq and later will visit many colonised planets and view the ectopic area before returning. The city you see in the Territory of the Father is called Mecca-nova. But alas we will not visit there yet; it is the good wine being kept till last!"

Navine and several others could not control her emotions as a tear rolled down her cheeks.

He pivoted and instead pointed to the west and to his own territory saying,

"That is where I am gong to take you!"

There before them was the second territory of the Trinitivity configuration. It swept upwards just like the others and was also topped with a brilliant Sun. In contrast this land had ochre toned wheat fields. On higher ground there were vineyards and beyond that there were rolling hills, and of course, at the very top was a blazing sun. Richard thought that the lower area reminded him of Tuscany. Then he made out the sight of a distant city – it seemed now that each territory has a city of its own. With that the Son again vocalised,

"Come visit the New Jerusalem, the capital of my territory."

He pointed to tow Aircrafts parked nearby. Hamish, Raphael and some others declined the invitation and stayed at the centre as they did not want to travel any further.

Just then there was a shout. It was Janette and Rico wearing small sun glasses and arriving with Miriam. They ran towards Everina and the other cadets, but were directed back to stay close to their mentor. They therefore held hands with Miriam as they all strode out onto the runaway. The aircrafts were shaped like birds. They had a broad transparent fuselage with wings like a sea gull – white and swept back and the symbol of a lamb on the fuselage. Pilots named John and Valentino were at the controls. Val was very caring asked Larry and Everina how were they getting on as friends while being on such a daunting trip, and then presented Everina and the other girls with garlands of grape vines and roses. They were happy to travel in his craft. John on the other hand was a rough diamond like Paulo, wore a bandana with Arizona Indian print along with a navy tee shirt and blue jeans. He had no gimmicks and introduced himself and without asking for any safety belts to be worn simply clicked his 'felucca' and in moments they were flying. A stewardess moved through the passengers and issued them with wrist dials as had been promised. On close inspection, the face of the dial was illuminated in four colours. It was explained that eventually the lights will become extinguished. By then they should be on their way back to earth.

They flew the crafts quite low over the wheat fields that resembled Manitoba and seemed to stretch for miles in all directions – concave of course! They were being harvested by teams of young people who waved as the craft passed overhead. Then a large track of bright full blooming red roses came into focus, adding contrast to the panorama. Soon all that thinned and terraces of vines appeared. These were laden with exquisite fruit ripened by long spells of sunshine. The Son remained quiet throughout the trip obviously enjoying the experience.

Then the city of New Jerusalem came into view. From the distance the first sighting was of massive skyscrapers their golden glass glistening with reflections even brighter than day. These stood in the core of the metropolis while around them was an older city with sand coloured ramparts. In this old encirclement there were countless domes and turrets giving it the appearance of a cross between Avila and Ancient Babylon. It was also strangely illuminated by more points of light shining from its walls even though it was day. The sight was awe-inspiring, people let out gasps. John spoke telling them what was written in Revelations 3,

"The city was divided into seven sections, each part with a name of its own," Ephesus, Smyrna, Pergamum, Thyatira, Sardis, Philadelphia, and Laodicea. The city shone like a precious stone, like jasper, clear as crystal. It had a great high wall with twelve gates and with twenty people in charge of the gates. On the gates were written the names of the twelve tribes of people of Israel. There were three gates on each side; three on the east three on the south, three on the north, and three on the west. The city's wall was built on twelve foundation-stones, on which were written the names of the twelve apostles of the Lamb."

The craft swept over the city and landed in a flat area designated for that purpose. There was a moving pavement that quickly took them to the nearest of three south city gates. On close examination, one could see that the city walls were really made of jasper, and the city itself was built with pure gold tinted crystal, as were the streets. One peculiarity was a lack of people. Then as if answering the question, John said that the city was prepared and awaiting for the many of the people from Purgosia.

Larry suddenly had a question of his own. He moved up to John and the Son and asked,

"Who was the prime mover behind the destruction of the Twin Towers in New York back in 2002 and the beginning of our subsequent space wars?"

The Son closed his eyes then slowly opened them and developed a grin. He looked at Miriam and John and cleared his throat.

"Larry m' boy - that's a chance question in a place like this. I know it would be cool to get the inside scoop, but I cannot!"

Then he turned his head as if listening to a something in the atmosphere. "Sorry, but there is a situation and I am needed. I will have to go but will be back soon."

Then he turned to Miriam and said,

"It's the Diablo syndrome again."

Miriam nodded as if fully understanding. He departing somewhat in haste accompanied by John.

---

(1) Godot, a name borrowed from the play "Waiting for Godot" by Samuel Beckett.

Chapter 40

Now with the Son having departed, the earthly visitors entered the City of New Jerusalem. As they did so there was the sound of revelry heralding their arrival. The welcome was generated by figures with golden trumpets standing like statues on the city walls. There were many flags and banners, fluttering and flapping like great sails on a ship. Some people stood in the streets waving in welcome but there were no crowds. Miriam said the breeze emanated in the third territory just across the way; just as the breeze of the blue triangle aerates the Chasms. Many of the banners bore coats of arms and pictures of places unknown to the visitors. Some showed great leaders with arms outstretched in triumph; others showed the meek feeding the poor.

On closed examination there were large highways that curved up in the sky and entered the city at roof top level. These roads were transparent and despite the lack of population there was plenty of traffic coming and going. Under the heat of the eternal sun, the group was conveyed along a road lined with tall Cypress pines and alighted at an archway in front of a very Italian-looking house. Although the material at this building was pinkish in colour, the shadows from the building were like rainbows. Miriam ushered the group inside and across a marble floored room and out to an open-air enclosure.

There were five men standing awaiting their arrival. Miriam introduced the first as Joseph her husband, and the others as James, Jose, Judas and Simon all being earth brothers of the Son. There was a display of food and drink laid out for the travellers. The menu consisted of grapes accompanied with cheese, which was called zallion and tasted of mint. There was quite a variety of bread that included the now familiar Quark Cakes. The wine on this occasion was Rose. Just as they were about to begin, the Son arrived back. He had been away about the equivalent of half an earth hour. He was smiling and said out quite loud,

"Thank you all for your patience: My task is complete, for the moment."

Richard leaned over to Larry and whispered,

"That was quick - Flash Harry."

Larry had to conceal his laughter, because of the funny way Richard had spoke.

The Son blessed the food and said grace. But then he added.

"Father, this won't take long. We'll be finished in a flash."

With that, Richard and Larry erupted into uncontrolled laughter, while the Son looked at them and winked.

Miriam then took the two children to an adjoining room filled with the family's original soft toys - where they fell asleep almost immediately.

The group then selected their food and sat on Arabic style cushions. Miriam began to talk of cherished moments of her life.

"I will never forget what a rascal my son was."

"No more blarney mom," the Son responded.

Miriam asked,

"What's blarney?" Larry piped up fun 'craig' pronounced like crack."

Everyone laughed and Miriam just put her arms in the air. A harpist began to play soft music and the atmosphere became quite enchanted. One of the guests asked about the miracle of Lanciano in Italy, when in the 8th century A.D. during mass the host was changed into real flesh and the wine became blood. It has been analysed and retained to this day, and has been diagnosed as being that of muscular tissue of the heart and Blood of the human species. They asked if it were true. The Son replied,

"Yes why not?" If people really believed my Father said their faith could move mountains. Bless the people of Lanciano! They deserved such a miracle to have happened. Now while on that subject, you saw how the circulation system through the heart in Purgosia sustains the world. Body and blood are very important constituents in the living experience."

The same guest asked how come a cosmic dialysis sweeps everything in is path, not only humans, but also raw material, into the loop? To which the Son answered,

"You are all made of star dust and all that material must live if you are to live so everything is treated the same."

Richard asked cautiously,

"If creation has a heart, then does the universe also possess one?"

"No there is only one heart that sustains everything in the universe – the same heart that you saw in the Chasms. However the Chasms will eventually close down as the Universe will not need sustaining when it enters Paradise. If I were to continue to connect it would be deemed as

Pan-en-theism. My arc at the moment is only performing an emergency circulation. The universe is ectopic and in dire need of dialysis and that is what my rotating heart is doing from its base in the Sangrias. If a Father was asked to give his dying child blood would he not contribute litres or even go on dialysis until the child was cured. So it is with me. You all have hearts because you are so small, but not the universe."

As he spoke he held his glass of wine up so that it caught the light. It seemed to shimmer and add weight to the words he had just uttered. Then Miriam was asked about her miracles and she confirmed each and every one. When asked about her last days on earth she told of the bittersweet memories after her son had ascended. How she had stayed in Meryem Ana, her little house that was near Seljuk and Ephesus. It is now a place of pilgrimages and she would dearly like to return to see it again.

Jean who had been quiet for hours, asked if our feeble minds were being tricked by what they were seeing?

"Your minds are not feeble, though your passions defeat your judgment all too often. We are showing the truth in principle but not in detail, and trust that you will trust us in return. If you had been complete unbelievers or cynics you will see us in different lights. For example the forces of darkness see creation as a machine, a 'Parousia Mechanica'. In it I am mistaken for a sort of pump and the universe a hornet's nest. The omega is a sluice gate and the triangles are electric elements that give out shocks. Everything is eventually flushed through the gate and devoured to fuel the machine. No matter how we demonstrate they cannot comprehend because they do not trust."

Then he got quite serious and said,

"With respect to our company of mixed beliefs but if it is claimed that after death the spirit is dissolved think again. That is what did happen eons before and despite that look what has emerged. Even if thought to be from a random fluctuation never the less human form has emerged and matter has become re organised and gripped by the spirit. Therefore why worry about the next stage, the hard work is already done! If one believes the theory that creation was no more than a random fluctuation, then by the same argument we have a right to be a Random Fluctuating God! That being the case during adversary and when needed; we may not be available to help because we are random and have just fluctuated! How'd you like that?"

The excitement of the day and the accumulation of events took its toll and in no time some of the group went asleep in their chairs. Miriam was not caught unprepared, and therefore said that she had accommodation ready for all. They were shown to rooms and soon silence descended.

On tip toes and moving with stealth, both Larry and Everina wandered out into the city. They saw steps that took them up to a battlement. From there whey had a panoramic view looking into the bowl of Paradise and Eden where they had been earlier.

They could now see the three suns that had shone so brilliantly. They were now barely glowing and the whole place was in semi darkness. However the land had absorbed the light during the day and it was still glowing. The great bowl of Paradise was shimmering with a perfusion of dark and light hues. Now that the sun heads had dulled one could see what lay beyond them. The sky was a mass of silver tubes or tunnels that radiating outwards like roots of a tree. Where the roots of one-being crossed with another there was a vibrant exchange of colour and activity. It all appeared to be one great thinking process.

Larry was quite overcome. He whispered sweet nothings in Everina's ear, and she responded with a kiss. He mumbled,

"Are we the only ones in love here or is everyone that way?"

Chapter 41

In the depths of the abyss and in the blackness of the pit that made up the innards of the void - there was a movement! It was followed by vibration that spread sending 'negative troughs' in all directions. The sound was like the throbbing of a distant warriors running into battle. Something in Tartarus (1) was awakening. This something was a being that was pitched against the divine dynasty and held it in distain. This was a colossus comprised of three beings that were the antithesis of the Gods. There was Diva the anti- spirit and one befitting of a female. Her strength and weakness was in her insomnia - she never slept! She had been on the prowl, observing all that had been happening in the above. What she learned had her quite alarmed and thus awakened Zahtienne who was the anti-Son. He was quite a warlike being also quite specialised in shooting laser fire, brimstone and ashes at the universe - his favourite pastime! All this was laser propelled but had in recent times being perfecting new more deadly weaponry called 'shock ray' but this was not yet ready for use.

She quickly explained the scandal about mortals who were permitted to visit the great citadel. She watched as his tiny eyes grew in disbelief. Together they slid across the hot slippery membrane at the base of the void. They entered one of many bee hive shaped dwellings and in the faint light awakened the occupant; their leader!

Thormentus slowly opened one red eye and surveyed the almost colourless world in which it lived. Everything appeared as usual in black white and tinged with crimson. He felt a flush of anger and shouted,

"Hell what are you doing to me?"

He rolled over and looked at his two companions. Even at this early hour Diva with her slim figure appealed to him and he therefore snapped fully alert.

"What my dear do you people want and why are you so pent up?"

Zahtienne attempted to explain but Diva cut in. She knew how to handle him when necessary. She began by putting her shining face close to his bearded silhouette. Then she narrowed her piercing eyes till they looked like slits. With a sly cat smile she exaggerated a twist of her lips and said out the side of her mouth,

"Snap out of it 'Thor' baby. Get back to the real world. You told us that you would never let a mortal outdo our fine regime. You said that humans would become extinct from over protection, small print, insurance, health and safety and all sorts of red tape that would strangle them out of existence You said that if they did per chance not self illuminate then you would hit them with the hammers of hell isn't that correct? Zahtienne don't you agree?"

Zahtenne a little embarrassed nodded his black shiny head quite vigorously. Thormentus responded,

"Yes my dear, that is what I said, but why are you reminding me?"

Diva shrieked her response,

"Because you old mutt, that is exactly what is not happening while you slumber valuable time away. Humans are alive and well and living in the God Damn Paradise!"

Thormentus, raised his voice,

"Tell me quick what happened?"

Diva blurted out the news adding details that would tantalise Thormentus. She made as big an issue as possible about the arrival of mortals in this higher world not alone alive but still in their inverted bodies! She added about the two children and that they had been able to enter the system where all others had been denied. Then she stopped and folded her black leathery arms and awaited his response.

Slowly Thormentus's slovenly senses switched from gazing at Diva to thinking about what she had said. Suddenly his black blood began to boil and a sense of rage took over. His blank features took on crevices and valleys rarely seen before. With an enormous roar her bellowed,

"That means war! These events present an opportunity that might not present itself again. Assemble the war cabinet. Don't just gape, do something, get moving!"

Diva pulled an ugly face and spun around, whipping him with her long black tail as she went.

Thormentus stood up and called for transport. Like a whirlwind a black triangular micro ship descended and a door opened. Thormentus stepped inside and demanded to be taken to the Father Ship which was called the Reaper and which was docked in the sky above. In fact the reaper was only one of the hideous ships the other two being owned by Diva and Zahtienne.

On board the Reaper troops poured out of their billets for the unexpected arrival of the great Thormentus. Communications were now springing into life sending messages of the disaster to their troops scattered about the void. Incoming messages were received on the prow of the Reaper via two antennas and transmitted down a central spine to the command centre. This is where Diva, Thormentus and senior officers were gathering. Micro ships and Blade fighter triangles were busily delivering officers to the Reapers deck.

Though these creatures stood erect they were all similarly clad in black and also possessing long tails like Diva. They also had antennas on their pointed heads - it was indeed the Beetle era in that part of the void. The surface of each triangle was busy with thousands of crewmembers going about their duties. Each one was wearing black headgear and a cape because this garb helped ward off the heat.

The terrible three who were the leaders had serious misgivings. They were grieved because they were incapable of having twin dimensional capabilities like the Gods. They could not retain several events indefinitely, while other events were going on. The Gods could do that with ease. They could only practice being in several places at once when they enter the universe - but not in the void. Finally they must remain on the same scale as the Purgosians and use their triangles as ships but not as their bodies; like the Gods can do! All this was a difficult aspect of reality to accept!

A bell made a dull clang. It was a call for meeting to commence. Thirty-one senior officers had by now assembled in the meeting chamber. The conference table was zee shaped and at the top were three Anti-Gods represented by three dark angels. These were a rare commodity but they had the bitter sweetness needed for such a ritual. The three sat at the top, the officers sat on the stem, and at the opposite end were three white knights used as the devil's advocates. They were ones who argued in favour of the opposite side, so that all eventualities would be taken into account. Word had it that their function was useless as Thormentus's opinions always held sway.

The meeting began with the arrival of Thormentus who liked to be last as this way he would intermingle and scare those who might be running late. He took his place half way down the table signalling that there would be no interference. Diva who was Chairperson introduced the current problems. She asked for intelligence report on events in the Citadel to date.

Clannad Deznog an analyst of the big brother section in Hada confirmed everything down to the latest New Jerusalem visitation. He said the infidels would be soon taken to visit Spirinda's Territory but not to visit that of the Father. He added that the whole exercise would be wasted on them anyhow. This caused loud laughter and amused Thormentus.

The advocates attempted to do their part and advise that soon the mortals would be gone and it would be better to wait till then to complain. However this did not cut ice with most people and the Dark Angels began to murmur to each other culminating in a rising chant. Everyone hushed and looked their direction. After several minutes they stopped and spoke in one voice,

"The spirit of this pit has spoken to us and demands confrontation. The humans are to be taken and fragmented into ozone's. This has been prophesised by Hammel, so let its word be done."

The meeting applaud. The White Knights called for order so they might make a counter argument but Diva did not comply. At this point Thormentus could not be contained and therefore roared,

"How in Job's name had a group of meagre mortals been able to visit where no living person has ever trod before? Just how did this happen and how did we not anticipate such an accident? Now that the damage has been done I say it is time for intervention; it is time to assert our right to fair play. What's more if this detestable universe is going to have its people given privileged treatment then we can be sure that it's very self will also be assumed totality to the very highest stratum. It will then occupy the last remaining place in the Heavens that rightfully should be ours! It is time for confrontation!"

Zahtienne's triangle was reflecting his emotions as it was beginning to show flame around the edges. Therefore in a pent up state he shouted,

"At last master you are seeing things our way. Your wishes will be fulfilled."

Three great black shadows slid from the depths; the last to rise was the Reaper, the flagship of the inferno and chariot of Thormentos. This ship as large as half of Purgosia and had a great picture of its master painted over its decks as if to mimic the corporality of the territories of the Gods!

As they gathered momentum there were shouts of approval from the crew who were anxious to settle a long outstanding score with the regime beyond the omega. Gunners manned the thousands of laser guns that were embedded around the edges of each ship. In the hold of the three ships alterations to all this artillery was being worked upon. Fighters flew on and off the decks and the activity grew to fever pitch. Diva's triangle led the way followed by Zahtienne who was an ideal second as he could provide the strongest artillery support. Then for one and all to see; the triangles rose like a swimming fish, their outer edges swirling as if propelling them forward. In its own right this was a spectacle of splendour!

---

(1) A Greek name for a place furthermost from Heaven

Chapter 42

The population at strata seven were quite aware that negative forces were adopting an aggressive posture. The Omega operators possessed the inside story as could see the activity being responsible for defence. In a conference chamber the council was meeting. The Son was in the chair but his Father also attended. Already the territories were being put on code orange and an automatic response was taking place. A squadron of Angel jet packers had been dispatched to hover at the blue triangle so as to be available on call. All attention was turned in the direction of the rising challenge. Since word war one nothing on this scale had ever occurred before. There was a common belief in the heavens that nothing could match the powers of the Almighty, but also an acknowledgement that one had to be careful!

The Son presented a case for negotiation, to which the council agreed unanimously. Negotiations would be the best way to combat the aggression. There were a dozen senior officers and advisers around a transparent table. In its centre was a lighted picture of the void with latitude and longitude markings around the edges. The commander and of all defence operations was Michael but Pedro was in charge of the Territories of the AMGOD as well as being the Omega Key Master.

Then the son addressed the group again briefly – not being sure that they grasped the full implications of what was happening,

"Gentle People of the Stratum, today history is being made. How we respond will affect the future in no uncertain way. Therefore we will have to show determent resolve but at the same time be prepared to compromise. You all know that these creatures that were once part of our regime want to return to power. They are making an issue out of the visiting humans but the nub of the problem is that they want to share power! Perhaps peace will not be maintained till that is done! However we will have to manage that change. We will have to fight our corner yet give them little by little hope and show them a path by which they will fulfil their ideals. On the long term we will have to temper them out of their dilemma. In the short term we will have to meet them head on and if necessary be prepared to give them grief so as to stimulate even better results!"

The officers again seemed to agree, but Pedro was the one to respond. This was because he was a very experienced warrior who not only knew the ways of the void but also had been a soldier while on earth. He reminded the group of the power of his veto.

"Do not forget that in all instances I have the final say about who enters here so with all due respect remember that my conditions for entry will have to be satisfied. Compromises will only come with conditions. Lastly we will have to consider that if we shake hands with the joker, no one should know until we have adjusted our Praydaq to a revised monitory valuation."

The Son replied that his conditions were reasonable.

The first two alien masses had by now risen dangerously near the blue triangle and there was no guarantee that they would stop there! The plan devised by the Omega force was that all primary discussions would be handled from the blue triangle zone so as to keep the enemy as far away as possible. A group of negotiators headed by Stephen a trusted servant of the deity along with the one called Antonio who was brilliant at finding solutions, were all dispatched to the triangle. They selected a delta winged transporter and flew down through the chasms and travelling south east till they crossed over the edge of the blue triangle and pushed out a little into the void. The Angel brigade came up from behind and spread out to rear. If there was going to be trouble let it be in the void.

Diva's advancing triangle began to make clanking sounds as it ground to a halt. Stephen spoke quietly to his negotiating team,

"Our task is to get as close as possible and challenge their intentions. I know that no one likes being in the void under any circumstances. So bear with me and we will see this through! However we must be aware of Diva for she is jealous of the universe as she had tried to conceive one for herself, but could not! This failure is a compelling reason for her aggression."

It was now time to 'pow-wow' with Diva who stood motionless on the point of her own triangle! Stephen and Antonio also put on telepathy helmets and stepped out on the flat surface of their delta winged craft. Dive also wore a helmet and gave them a supercilious glare. Within moments she became engaged in conversation with the divine negotiator. Both parties also had hand screens so as to have visual contact during the negotiations which would be carried out over an intercom. Diva opened the discussion with a list of demands,

"It has come to the notice of our majestic forces that you have allowed a breach of nature. This is therefore favouritism and distorts the law that banished us from our rightful place. Here are our demands;

One, that we may have representation on the Presidium in Stratum Seven and that free elections are held pan-universally and into infinity and that candidates may be elected from the four corners of the void, areas that had not yet been included in your so called 'Freeocracy'. That the future of the universal child be put on the agenda for discussion. This universal child if given birth will be in defiance of us who were banished into your void.

There were further sounds of chains being drawn. Then Diva continued,

"Two. That the human visitors who are in violation of divine nature be expelled and punished if necessary. Remember this is not the first time that this has occurred. Take the example of the one called Miriam. She, just like the Son also ascended with her body intact. All this was as much violation as your recent visitors from earth. Is all this to become a habit, might we expect hundreds more we ask? Now please answer that?"

Three, that the great Thormentus, Zahtenne and I, are cleared of all charges of inciting the revolution in Paradise - at the dawn of creation. We have served our time and the slate must be wiped clean."

Another Pause and then Diva spoke again,

"Four, at an administrative level, we want that we can send people to visit your world, because the son of the Highest Magnitude made a visit to our realm eons ago and now it should be our turn."

"Five, there is a product that you have accumulated. You call it Prayque. We understand it is the residue from what you call prayers. You use it as a currency. Our equivalent is Draiks but this is very weak. We therefore would like our finances linked together to improve life for our subjects."

Then Diva was heard to add a final two condition. In a shrill voice she said,

"Sixth, we want a Republic in Paradise. We want a legitimately elected God!"

Then she repeated with emphases,

"A legitimately elected - G o d!"

Then a pause,

"We believe the Trinity should be replaced with new candidates voted in by the people. The new Trinity to have members elected from the four corners of the worlds and that includes representatives from our beloved Hada."

Stephen could not contain himself.

"The People!" he said,

Diva cut in with rage,

"Let me finish. Seventh and last there should be a democratically elected Queen of Heaven. The Virgin called you call Miriam, should take her place in this contest as she has no right to hold sway on such an unelected position. Now I 'm finished you may have your turn - S t e p h e n."

Then she twisted her antenna to receive incoming jargon and Stephen's reply. There was a deadly silence broken only the sound of ocean waves on the blue triangle and a distant hum from the ominous black triangles. Stephen took a deep breath to calm his nerves derived from being exasperated.

Then in a calm voice he spoke,

"Greetings Diva. It's been a long time since we last talked. The last time it was on a one to one basis that broke down in disagreement. To begin we are appalled at the show of strength that you have presented on this occasion. It has come without warning and in our opinion is unjustified. First a few observations, the incursion of the humans that you take so seriously also includes humans who may have allegiance to you yet in true democratic spirit we have received them without discrimination. Your list of demands will be treated with respect and relayed to the heads in the omega. However I will tell you in advance what I expect the response will be!"

A Pause, then,

"I must remind you that God will never negotiate with you and that is written in scripture by my good friends Matthew and Mark. However that is not to say that God will not supply you with assistance as an aide to recover your trust. Now if you insist, and if your representative is to be re-instated on the governing body, it will first have to do away with death. Death is evil is a price that you extract from us as a price we must pay to buy back the souls of our people. Death will eventually be overcome but it need not have ever existed in the first place but you are prolonging its presence. These souls have been redeemed yet you extract suffering just for your own gratification - why must that be? It is yourself who created repulsion and broken symmetry causing the formation of the void and no doubt your demise. You have the power to rid creation of this terrible disease. You will no doubt be asked to demonstrate an act of dissolvent of death as proof of you sincerely."

Stephen paused again and then spoke quietly to Antonio who appeared to find him the answer.

Stephen continued,

"It is quite unrealistic for you to ask that we turn away from our endeavour that is to bring the universe into our family. Creation is enjoying opportunities that might also be open to you, now that you ask! Yet you are negotiating a major change at the expense of the universe - that does not make sense. Finally we have certain information that in secret you have developed weapons of mass psychological and spiritual destruction. They must firstly be declared along with their capabilities - and deployment agreed between us as otherwise fruitful negotiations are impossible."

Now Diva was getting impatient. Stephen went on,

"In sixth place you have put in a request for a Republic. To our team this sounds next to impossible. No matter how many people one elects they cannot physically, metaphysically or territorially replace the trinity. These candidates would only be puppet representatives and in such a case still subject to the natural immensity of the trinity in which they dwell. Now I think the root of this problem is that you have forgotten how the heavens are structured and that they surround everything that is."

Diva showed her displeasure by turning her back and tapping her foot. Then Stephen, turned and looked at his companions, took another breath and said,

"Lastly point number seven, be prepared you may be asked to put forward a list of worthy people as candidates for Queen of Heaven. Thormentus must surely have a mother who is worthy, or perhaps you Diva, who would you suggest? "

Stephen got no more said before Diva and her whole triangle let out a loud shriek. It was lucky that sound did not travel in the void in the same way as in the atmosphere, for if it did it would have rocked creation off its hinges. She shouted back at Stephen to say he was condescending and also that they did not have weapons of mass psychological destruction. Then she quoted scripture for her own purposes.

"1 Corinthians - The son said he would destroy his last enemy – death!"

"Now let's see can he do that!"

She laughed openly and swung her right arm towards the blue triangle and her left towards the universe shouting,

"Zahtienne let them have it."

Instantly there was an enormous barrage of negative psychic energy in the form of hail and brimstone that swept in. The Angel carriers responded by calling laser fire from the omega in an attempt to block the deluge. The Omega instantly combated the enemy fire but not before several hits bounced around the retreating negotiators. However as usual, the universe though very far away took the full impact of the aggression. The battle ended as quickly as it began with Diva's triangle pulling back to a position that was still menacing yet just far enough back to avoid further confrontation.

Chapter 43

While all this was happening high up in infinity and well beyond the Omega the crew of the Callisto were still in the New Jerusalem but planning a visiting the territory of Spirinda. They were quite unaware of the political events that had just taken place.

By contrast very far below in the tormented universe, life was going on as usual. No one could have known the threat that was posed. Hail and brimstone was quite invisible and even if it caused war, famine, economic property bubbles and strife no one could prove how, by whom or why! Perhaps at that moment people who leaned to the dark side may have experienced the devil's own luck. Politicians might find that their cravings for war under a pretext of establishing democracy achieved a landslide victory. Their opposition crumbled and their media spin wins the hearts and minds of the population. They can ignore world opinion and do what they choose. They would have found things that day were going their way and life was a bowl of cherries!

Back up in the lap of the Gods where war and peace were monitored closely there was still much activity. Now with the retreat of the black triangles, there was a stand down. The Omega centre became like a railway station with groups of saints and jet packers arriving for duty but being sent to temporary stand by accommodation. Word had it that the festival in Purgosia might be temporary called off.

Stephen and Antonio arrived horridly from the front line. They addressed the gathering in Com/Saint and reported in detail. It was agreed that there were serious legalities that would have to be resolved before any reply was forthcoming. Stephen agreed but felt it would all take time to unravel and he must hurry. He then left like lightning for Purgosia to examine the archives that were enshrouded in the vaults below the Chasms. He would have to examine it all line by line and converse with the best legal minds in both strata. Then finally he would listen to the advice of the Son. He intended making little of the Republic proposal but on advice from Antonio he prepared a detailed report on the matter just in case!

The only dilatory people in the Omega were the remnants of the Callisto crew who had refused to go on the grand tour. They had remained in accommodation on board the Callisto, which was still sitting where it had been placed near the omega entrance. Looking the opposite direction they could see the control arena and the glass floor of the Omega Centre. They were puzzled by the sudden burst of activity that had erupted and the display of fire power by the lasers. Raphael had watched with intent and followed every move the gun operators had performed.

There were seven in the group and that day after the others left they had relaxed in the garden reading or playing cards and enjoying the rays of three suns. Dalia suggested that they should sample some fruit from the trees, though they had been told it was only for the inhabitants. She plucked three that resembled wheels that had a texture like an orange but oddly, without skin. Along with two others she devoured the fruit and found it pleasant. The effect was nothing other than it satisfied their curiosity. On the other hand they all agreed that they shared the same ambition and that they now felt disposed to carry them out. On the second evening two of those who devoured fruit, Raphael Ulleman and Hamish Cauldron were about to turn in when Raphael called out to Hamish,

"Ham, don't turn in yet, I have something to say."

Ham who was very tall and thin turned and scowled.

"Come on Rap, what is it?"

Rap pulled Ham by the arm and said, "Shush."

Then in a whisper he said,

"Look I've been doing some thinking since today. We could make a name for ourselves because this here utopia is not what it's cracked up to be. It is already out moulded and out of date. I have overheard some of the operators talk and they said that they were under threat from black triangles. They mentioned Thormentus and we all know that he is the one who shoots psychological fire and brimstone at the universe – we saw him with our own eyes. Those black triangles out there are new age technology. They will overrun here and when they do our lives will be a misery unless we join them here and now. You see when we go back down to earth nothing will go our way unless we show our metal. Are you with me so far?"

Ham replied, with some interest,

"No Rap, oh I mean – Yeh!"

"Okay then have a listen to this. To begin with the worst-case scenario for doing something wrong up here, and that is we will be sent back to earth so that we can die just to satisfy their system. Then we will either end up in Purgosia or be sent to the Black Triangles. It's a no loose situation and all we have to do is improve our lot. If we impress Thormentus not only will we improve things but also we will be guaranteed a fortune while on earth. Therefore let's sabotage the Omega defences and cause an unholy row."

Ham was appalled and shook his head but Rap cut in quickly,

"Look Ham you miss the point. There is a stash of currency up here called Praque. It is so strong it would make the Dollar and the Yen look like monopoly money. If we can knock off a few million just for ourselves, and then some for the so called enemy; we could buy some respect from that Thor' fellow – what ye' say now?"

Already Ham had changed his mind and began nodding in agreement while a large smile crossed his long face. However he did have a question,

"Rap, you know-like, we are supposed to be inside Utopia, Paradise and all that. Do you think they are reading our minds and watching everything we do, so if we try something they will jump us?"

Rap said coolly,

"If that were the case I would have been ejected from here ages ago for the thoughts I have been entertaining. Therefore I think not, they rely on trust and leave one another to their own devices. However maybe after we have pulled a stroke they will get wise but then it will be too late."

Ham looked reassured. Rap went on,

"I've been taking stock of things around here and find that when night falls the place empties out. They don't need many to watch what goes on in the void, they are distracted and concentrate on the void and our planet because of all the mess that we cause them. Up here is psyco-medical and administered by a guy called Raphael, my namesake. They seem to be repairing structures and listening to incoming calls from the universe. It is also the main administration centre but most of all it is a trading area that stores large quantities of beautiful P-r-a-q-u-e."

By now Hamish was becoming excited and began pulling on his shoes.

Rap had a bit more to add,

"Those laser guns on that glass panel are only used on occasions. They are usually unmanned and provide us with an opportunity that should not be missed."

Just then a female voice cut in. It was Dalia Kozinda.

"Okay boys I've heard all you said will you count me in? If not I will split on you!"

She was a small fit looking girl, with cropped hair and icy cold eyes. She never smiled but right now she was laughing as she spoke. Rap replied,

"Okay Dal, you're in but you better do exactly as I tell or I'll break every bone in you body when we get back down that is if I don't toss you into the void before then."

She nodded her head though still laughing as she did so.

"So as I was about to say, all we have to do is, nick the loot, store it on the ship, find the power switch for the Lasers and fire them at everything we can. Then turn the beam to short range take, out the floor and the whole of their artillery defence will fall into the void and we will follow making our escape in the ship."

Ham began to clap his hands in delight. Rap hissed at him to shut up, and smacked him over the head with roll of paper that he grabbed from a desk. Rap then said,

"Tonight at 0.300 we will begin our activity. Dal, your assignment is to lock the resting chambers on the ship so none of them do good-ers and those two kids can get out and mess our plans. Then get down to the engine bay and turn on the main power and follow the manual at the console. I've read it and it is ABC stuff for idiots."

Dalia responded to this by sticking out her tongue at Rap who was so intent the he hardly noticed the provocation.

"However don't turn the activation key till after we begin shooting. Make sure the main door is wide open and stand by." Then he said to Ham,

"Your job is to examine the lasers, find the power switch; I think it is just left of the drivers console I mentioned - but don't turn them on. If anyone asks you what you are doing just say you couldn't sleep and even ask how the things work! That would be a natural question and we might learn something that way. Understand?"

Ham said "Yeh Rap, yes of course." Rap continued,

"I've been watching the movement around here for quite some time and I've concluded that most of the place is on a sort of automatic system. It is like the very walls are alive but most of the focus is on what's happening below. So that gives us an opportunity and if all goes well the whole place will come apart at the seams."

Then Rap growled,

"Oh! I just remembered Miriam has left the two kids in the rest area with the others, we don't want them screaming and kicking up a fuss so Dalia be careful."

Dalia again gestured with annoyance and walked away.

Rap said, "That's an affirmative, it's as good as we'll get and really she will comply."

Ham then said, "How are we going to locate the Praque?"

Rap gave a crooked smile and said,

"That's where I come in!"

He turned and began to study a map he had already prepared.

Chapter 44

That morning Miriam and the Son had bade the group farewell as they climbed on board their flights. To their surprise Paulo the navigator had returned as their guide. It seemed he had been asked to do so but the reasons were undisclosed. They greeted him like a long lost brother even though it had only been for a day and a half. Janette and Rico were returned to the Omega Complex with Miriam, who was to look in on them frequently. However they said they were bored and wanted to go back to Purgosia. She immediately arranged that games and cyber pets be delivered to the Callisto - and this eased the problem.

Soon the group bade goodbye the New Jerusalem and flew across the territory of the Father; by passing it, crossing over the omega centre and landing at the foot of the third territory - which was Spirinda's. Just then there was a beeping sound. People looked at their watches to find that the maroon section and half of the Golden section were already fully aglow. Paulo had not seen the devices before and looked at them with interest, the crow's feet lines at the side of his eyes and face stretched in a smile. It was amazing that these features had accompanied him from this life to his eternal life.

Remaining in their seats they were spellbound by the sheer extent of this new segment. To begin, with it was covered in a blue mist which seemed to clear as they approached. From top to bottom it was bathed in sunlight from another brilliant Sun-head- its own. They began their trip from the base of this new segment. They slowly journeyed upwards over fields of blue flowers while a gentle breeze disturbed their blooms emitting lavender perfume and spilling blossoms. It was from here that the blue haze originated with its delicious aromas sweeping across the other segments and lingering in the valley of the Omega.

The only missing element was the sound of bees or the swarming of birds, to make it like home. There was however one exception and that was that familiar sight of a host of white doves, just like they had seen on the blue triangle – this confirmed they were now in the true land of the Paraklete.

Next they flew up through meadows giving away to grasslands and the beginning of tropical regions. They looked down on breadfruit trees dotted everywhere like the Mekong Delta. Tall waving eucalyptus was also growing in sprawling woodlands sparkling as their leaves turned in the wind. Then at grass root level the picture grew even more interesting.

Paulo pointed down and told them,

"See, below there is sago swamps, fronds of shade acacias, flaming yellow cannas, white calophyllums and tall bamboo and even great Mango trees. See also, their fruit is purplish or yellow under their large leaves."

Then they approached a great body of water which just like the other territories was concave. This was an immense ocean, sand dunes, headlands and bays. As the segments were gently curved it meant that the sea looked oddly different with a bent horizon. Then the vegetation thinned, and they came across more sand duns, this time very large and with a landing strip at back. John and Valentino clicked their 'feluccas' and the crafts gently set down.

"This is Punto Espiritu, and you know who that is!" said Paulo.

They walked through the dunes to the sea shore. There was an elaborate beach house made of palm logs and platted leaves and with wide decks facing out to sea. There was a luxurious scent of flowers and fruit and lots of interesting vegetation. There were spider orchids and magnificent herbaceous epiphytes, shade trees with pink and white frostings of thick blossoms.

They were alerted by the sound of rumbling surf breaking on the shore line. They assembled on the deck and look in awe at the ocean before them. It was full of impressive waves that were breaking at least a half an earth mile from the shore. They were each and every one, waves of perfection - moving ever so slow yet taller than anyone had ever seen before. Their texture must have been denser than water perhaps like the liquid in the blue triangle! The smaller shore breaks were equivalent to a very large earth wave of about fifteen feet. As they did so they raced up the strand for hundreds of meters. Then needless to say the outside waves were four times higher than the shore breaks. Each outside wave broke on a rocky point, spilling mainly to their left like tumbling skyscrapers. Every now and then there were even larger sets perhaps six times higher than the shore breaks that rose like icebergs on the horizon. These came in with such force that they almost engulfed the deck as they raced up the beach in their dying moments.

Paulo put on some beach music and he and the some volunteers began to dish out containers of fruit drink. It tasted like papaya and mandarin. He laced them with a secret liquor of his own making which he called grand mariner. There were pictures of past events fixed to the walls. These had taken place in this vicinity some time in the equatorial past. They were quite old and showed groups of youth standing with oars and paddles and some of people receiving trophies.

People began to stretch out in the sun and relaxed. The palms around the house heaved in the breeze and creepers rustled with the strain. Then Paul pointed seawards, and in an excited voice shouted,

"Look, look, this is why we are here!"

There was a dot sighted at about a half-mile out. It disappeared from sight for quite some time and then reappeared, only to go again. Larry studied the scene and declared that the waves were at three-minute intervals, the longest he had ever seen. Everina nipped Larry's shoulder to get his full attention. She peered into his face and yelled,

"Wow Larry, wouldn't you like to be out there? Can we get you a board?"

She turned and looked around as if hoping to find one. Richard bounded over whistling through teeth and saying,

"Larry wake up, this is your country!"

Larry said nothing, he was transfixed by the scene but did not think that on this occasion it was his prerogative to surf nor could he handle the size. Then Paulo pulled a lever and a glass screen came down in front of the group. It was an image enlarger he said. Immediately a close-up of the boat filled the screen. It was an outrigger canoe, and there were three males and one female on board. Three of them were teen-agers while the female was none other than the Spirit with whom they had an earlier encounter. She was poised at the stern of the craft and was calling out orders to her comrades. She was very tall and was dressed in floral pattern beachwear, a garland around her neck and an orchid in her jet black hair. The others were clad in floral print shorts like they lived forever in this tropical fantasia of the spirit world! As the craft came into view, it was perched on a peak from one of the outside monsters. Larry looked over the screen and glimpsed them, a dot in the distance - gathering speed amidst walls of sapphire blue sea. He ducked back down for a closer up. The canoe had now gained speed and was pointing straight down a massive wall of water – just like Gasper the wave in Larry's dream.

The surface of the sea was now sparking with electric energy which must also have been a lubricant, as the craft seemed to slide so fast to its left that it outpaced the wave break and planed merrily across its giant unbroken wall. Then with a thundering explosion, the crest tipped over and rolled sideways as if to devour the riders. It tumbled in syrupy swirls and even electric flashes as it went. Despite the threats the spirit was kneeling upright and tall. Her face was set like flint while her long black hair flowed behind her glistening like stars in the night. The craft kept hard to the left as the crest was propelled by the rocky shallows of the 'Punto Espititu'. The massive curl caught up and encased them in a great cathedral of cascading liquid. For a long minute the tip of the canoe was all that could be seen. Then like a cannon shot it broke clear to make a spectacular turn straight for inwards.

The challenge was all but over and it was time for some moments of pure joy. Their happy faces filled the screen. The sound of their laughter and hooting could be heard over the din of the ocean. Having beaten the torrent, they were now riding the white water victoriously to shore.

Just then several youths with surfboards raced down the beach trying to get to the sea before the next surge. They flung them selves on their boards and glided up the face of the next shore break. Immediately they seemed to thump their decks and some extraordinary power gave them instant thrust. As the wave approached, they increased velocity bouncing over and out with ease. Once beyond the break where Spirinda had been they turned and again thumped their decks. Immediately they shot forward each one on a wave of their choice - surfing to shore like a swarm of bees.

At this sight Richard said,

"Larry this is your chance for an agency!"

Larry grinned, and shrugged, it was all too much.

As the canoe arrived, a beach vehicle and trolley appeared from the trees and rushed to the waters edge. In moments the barque was hitched and drawn out of the sea and speedily taken up the beach before the next deluge. Then the crew dashed towards the beach house and slowed to a walking pace when they knew they were safe.

The Spirit stood taller than the males and despite the turmoil still wore the garland and a flower in her hair. People stood back as she arrived. She smiled and immediately spoke.

"Aloha, my friends you did not recognise me at that distance!"

Paulo did the decent thing and shouted,

"Aloha my princess, you are Spirinda or Maya filled with shakti energy all of which you needed today. We enjoyed the spectacle!"

Everyone clapped enthusiastically.

Then she began to shake hands and mingle with the guests. When she got to Larry, Everina was about to ask about dolphins and all sorts of animals, but did not get the opportunity.

Spirinda looked at her and smiled, and said softly,

"You are Everina we met in the omega. I wish I was you so young and human and an earth life ahead of you hopefully having a family and all that goes with it or even no family and just drinking in the simplicity of life. You are so lucky you must cherish every day! Oh by the way, once again, call me Spirinda it will come easier."

Everina was speechless. Then she gathered her senses and said,

"Spirit, excuse me, Spirinda are you lonely?"

The Spirinda replied with a wink,

"No Everina, No I am ever so happy, I have all you people eventually coming here as friends and I love my spiritual family. But you see no matter what wealth of Godliness I possess, I cannot be you in your time and in your place, so just love it while you have it! You will come here eventually but you can never go back to where you are now. So love it and love him!"

She glanced towards Larry and back to peer into Everina's dark brown eyes. Everina gazed at her transfixed as if seeing an apparition and with that a tear rolled down her cheek. At that the spirit raised her voice,

"Now I read that you ask in your heart about animals. Well Luca already told you that animals are not yet released from the Universe and that is where they remain in proximity after passing and will stay there in their phylon and noosphere - that Pierre Thillard de Cardin calls - a state above earth where souls dwell. Now I am – qualifying that these will be animal souls waiting the day of deliverance. They are being saved to eventually fill the heavens. They will inherit what we have prepared for them; those poor wretches deserve it! You know I will fill this ocean with dolphins, and the trees with birds and the flowers with bees. They will be no longer dumb but will speak to us in their own way. Their singing and humming will be as sweet as the angel's finest song."

One of the young canoeists looked at her with glaring eyes, and she responded with a giggle and said,

"Oh sorry Lancius - a l m o s t - as sweet as the angel's finest song."

Lancius looked relieved.

She moved on through the crowd speaking personally to one and all.

Larry was curious about something. He walked onto the beach and directly to the boat, which was still dripping with foam. Great globules had fallen on the sand leaving a residue of large bubbles. He bent down and looked closely, just as he had done in his dream about Tramahon. There looking up at him were what appeared to be similar eyes. He recoiled in fright and at the same time he heard echoing laughter emitted from the foam. Despite his temporary divinity he flinched like a human would and backed away. Then the bubbles dissolved and all that remained was the sound of wind and the strains of island music the background. He reached into the water and it felt like glycerine.

Chapter 45

"Now we will take you to visit the city of Paradiso. It is way up north on the other side of the ocean and close to my sun head. So let us be off" said Spirinda.

They said good bye to John and Valentino who said they would return later for them in Paradiso. From here they were transported by vehicle to a sheltered inlet with a large wooden jetty. They were driven directly on to a ferryboat with a much curved prow. The vehicles were chained in place. The group were told to remain seated and to clip on their seat belts. Larry and Everina avoided such restrictions and instead made their way to the bow of the craft!

"Titanic," - said Everina as she spread out her arms. Larry followed suite, hoping that the others would not notice. However the fun did not last for long because at the mouth of the channel the boat met the full onslaught of the sea. The first wave to hit was small yet it was so ferocious because of the weight of the thick liquid that they were almost thrown across the deck. They hurriedly returned to their vehicle and obediently buckled up for the trip. Paulo greeted them on their return,

"Now you young sea dogs, ye have not yet got yer sea legs."

Then he gave a roar of laughter, he was his old self – he was back at sea.

The boat built up enormous speed. In a few moments it was moving so fast that it began to plane from crest to crest, avoiding the troughs and never dipping down even once. It was like being in a low flying helicopter over snow capped mountains.

Needless to say the city of Paradiso appeared within moments nestled inside a bay with headlands at both ends. As they entered the bay the wind and waves died out. The first impression was of a city bearing every architectural style possible. At the waterfront it looked like Venice with a Cathedral and Official buildings and more doves flying about the enclosures. There were also a series of canals penetrating inwards in all directions.

Then the skyline rose to withering heights, bearing yellow brick skyscrapers and even greater glass geometrical buildings twisted and stretched ever upwards in artistic forms. They ranged all the way from triangles to spheres, helixes and multi connected structures. At the top of every building flags and pennants were drifting gently. There was a central building that was taller and wider than all the others and it had an enormous dish like a radio telescope on top and every flag that ever existed in rows around its highest point. There were spheres floating like multi coloured bubbles floating all about the roof tops and they in turn seemed to reflect coloured sunlight about the city. The effect was uplifting.

The city was surrounded and with deciduous and coniferous vegetation and even more eucalyptus. Then to one side of the bay there were hundreds of tent type structures comprising of great canvases. They were draped and fixed at odd angles thus creating enclosures and coverings for activities such as sports grounds and meeting places. Some were so large that they covered the area of a city block. Each of the tent canvases stopped about four meters short of the ground making it possible for one to see inside.

The bay was filled with pleasure craft bearing every conceivable sail imaginable. Some were from ten to two hundred feet in height, some transparent double sheeted and filled inside with gas while others were solar models tilted upwards so radiation pushed over their surface causing propulsion. There were also small pleasure craft and paddle boards with the silhouettes of individuals gently stroking the sea as they went.

They steered to one side of New Venice as the locality was called. They entered a wide river with white sand banks and then to a crystal clear lake at the back of the city. Then the craft docked and they had their first opportunity to see the natives of the Paradiso. Most of the locals were wearing casual gear, like plaid lumber jackets of various shades while many others had ski wear or just warm looking fancy gear - and as expected some were carrying jet packs. The reason for the heavy clothing was obviously because they were now at quite a high altitude and the temperature was low and it was not yet summer.

Ernst the chief mechanic was interested in the docking arrangement. The craft had literally glided up out of the water and onto a boat slip and stopped. A gangway had risen to connect with the exit door. Ernst therefore asked one of the land crew how all this had been made possible? He turned, smiled and said,

"Ernst it is done by 'displonics'. The ship lets us know the electro magnetic ratio to its mass in advance and we input that information in the harbour compegulus - computer in your language. It is like a cut and paste exercise that you people used to do. When the craft arrives it clicks displace, and then Paste and 'zap' it's done!"

With a curious look on his face Ernst said,

"How did you know my name?"

The man smiled again pressed a button on and his wristwatch. The dial got larger and displayed a tiny TV screen. Then there was the sound of music and news and even commercials of various sorts. One example was,

"Paradiso community invite you to Ski in the Himmel Ice range. Stay at the Buff Springs Complex - the price is either two weeks voluntary or 285 Praque per person. Dial sss.himice.paradiso."

The man then said,

"Praque is hard currency but Voluntary means voluntary work as an alternative, the work can be what ever the Praydaq admin requests. People enjoy that sort of challenge as it often takes them to far off places. So that's how I knew your name; I read it in the bulletins that we receive. So have a great time in Paradiso Ernst."

Ernst thanked him at the same time noticing several artists painting scenery by the inlet the scene they had chosen was well worth the trouble. Then he joined the group and they departed for the city. Spirinda travelled in Larry's Transporter which he noted was much the same design as in Purgosia. Amazingly her voice could be heard in the other vehicle. They left the docks and turned on to Via Magnificat, the city main thoroughfare. It had all the hallmarks of a busy metropolis – people moving about trading goods and wares. There were beverage stands and live music was being played to the listening crowds. The aroma of fresh brewed coffee style dankus in the pine laden atmosphere reminded Richard of Seattle. From there it turned into an eight lane highway and they began to gain speed.

Spirinda began a commentary,

Then Via Magnificat got larger and took on a new meaning.

"This now my friends, is know as the Milton Freeway it intersects the City. It is in honour of a man who believed he would never ever get to visit here. We honour his dream because this was his chosen utopia. It is his business as to whether he did reach here, not for us to comment. On your right is the city sports centre, it comprises of fifty-seven tents that offer every sport that ever existed. The area is proportionally as large as your Disney World. Tomorrow will be our City Marathon Day and that includes one for children. People from the three segments will compete and if I may say that comprises of more people than you can imagine."

They got a glimpse a soccer field, and then an enormous swimming pool, and then what looked like a golf club and clubhouse. When the reached the city centre there was the huge central building with the roof top dish that they had seen from the sea. However there was also a vast central park with an enormous monument in the middle. It consisted of three moving staircases that rose up about two hundred feet to a platform. This was where people could enter a sphere, which would become elevated some five hundred feet in the ether. From this position people could look at the panorama. They could also get an image-enhanced view of the Smiling Sun Heads. Looking back they discovered that the roof of every building was adorned with flowering gardens. Amongst a great perfusion of colours were hosts Trinitivias just like what had been used for Jill's wedding in Purgosia. There was a fine Hotel at the Park called the El Dorado and that is where Paulo said they will be staying.

Chapter 46

There was no noise from the continuous city traffic. The only sound was that of chimes and of people laughing heartily. There were no fumes but instead there was the scent of many perfumes lingering over the whole metropolis while a great feeling of laziness prevailed. Then Paulo and Spirinda said there was just one more thing to be done. As their last port and call the group would fly to the highest point possible and visit Spirinda's Sunhead. Travis was taken aback saying several times over,

"Paulo, we never expected to be privileged to such an extent."

The group became equally excited by the daunting prospects. In preparation for their journey they were given extra clothing like parkas and more protective sun glasses of a great thickness. Then Paulo doled out halo communication disks and belts with wires and soft lining called 'enegynos' to prevent weakness or fainting.

They travelled due north and just like in Purgosia their transport left the highway and became airborne. They flew up and into the snow clad mountains at the equivalent of 4,000 earth meters. The mountain range was the highest in the territory and called the 'Himmel-Ice'.

They were told that the mountains were taking on a new meaning in Paradiso. It seems that a great number of Saints had discovered a love for skiing. So it was no surprise when they came across an elaborate resort that commanded a majestic view of the slopes. They landed near by and watched the activity with interest. There was a great number of people ascending or descending the valley. Their skis were short and quite transparent just like most commodities in this part of the outer world. The standard of skiing was amazing as due to many of them wearing jet packs, they could jump and fly and spin like real 'hot doggers' but never fall. Others were conveyed to even higher elevations on snowy version of lighted pavements that resembled chilly versions of those in Purgosia.

Richard saw snow on the wing and it was like powdered plastic, if one could imagine such. The snowflakes were enormous and looked like tiny triangles all linked together in a circular pattern. Then Larry almost wept saying,

"Oh my God this is Paradise Lost for me, If only I had my skis!"

"Don't worry Mr Milton you can come back later."

Everina laughed but added,

"I think poor old Hiroshi would be impressed."

Larry lamented,

"Hope the poor sod is okay!"

Chapter 47

Soon after that they reached the summit of the third state of the union. The great body had been broadening as they journeyed upwards. The area was aptly called the 'Shoulder Territory'. Dominating all this was the ever increasing Sun Head beaming down on them and now filling half the sky above. They were in fact now gazing at the true yet enormous face of Spirinda - the source of magnetic power and love. The flying craft landed in a wide parking area, filled with cars and milling people They appeared to be taking the same trip, some on foot with back packs and others in vehicles. Paulo said,

"These are saints going for an adventure in the notion land. Up there they will learn more and more about our being and visit exotic places, towns and villages with real people who will give them hospitality. They come home with incredible stories, why not, its fun!"

The group alighted and clambered into a large waiting vehicle and then Spirinda who was still faithfully with them, instructed,

"If you first want to see the notional template, the continuous rubix cube that lies beyond this mass, you must be wearing your glasses. You are permitted to visit my Sunhead, but not that of the Son or the Father. As I am the closest to you in more ways than one, I'm sure mine will do just fine! Now put on your glasses and come into our imagination!"

They did what she suggested and were agog with what the close up effect. There before their very eyes was a Carona of tubes radiating outwards in every direction like spokes in a wheel.

Spirinda explained,

"These are shafts or tunnels that spread out but naturally collided with each others. When that happens, and does happen all the time, it is our sharing of minds and the essence of the mystery of our three being one. Where I meet those of the Father and the Son there are dynamic consequences with wonderful life results! We are like three trees with our leaves inwards and our roots outwards. Our roots are like the human brain.

However we are not confined like you and thus enjoy the ever outward expansion in harmonious union.

The template though static becomes a difficult phenomena the further one moves from our warmth the more it becomes crystallised with globules of nothingness. Our sun heads are constantly on the move slowly sliding further and further out bringing the territories with them. We have our agents out there clearing the way as we go. These are volunteers who travel to the extremity of the tunnels. At that point they cut and hack at the nothingness that plagues the template – even sometimes receiving serious suck bites as their body surfaces are drawn by the emptiness. They wear protective clothing, but sometimes that is not enough. Our outreach forces are led by a king ship, a link ship, six sub links and fifty-three battle wagons. This configuration was suggested by Miriam who is quite a tactician."

At that Travis began to count something on his fingers, said nothing but could not conceal a broad smile across his face and he mumble,

"Peyton would be delighted with this!"

Then Spirinda finished by saying,

"These soldiers are the cutting edge of the extended states of Paradise. They mann the battle wagons of a republic that may soon come into being! Now come let me show you more!"

The group who did not understand her remark about a republic, shrugged and continued onwards. The road led to a car park at the summit. As they landed some vehicles were actually driving in and out of the sun. Larry noticed that as they drove inwards they seemed to turn upside down and grow in size till they filled the sky and then disappear. Returning vehicles had the opposite effect. Larry's only explanation was that the zone was concave.

"Spirinda, are you coming with us, it will mean that you will journey into yourself, is that possible?" said one of the group.

"Yes my dear, we do it all the time."

Without hesitation Paulo drove straight into the orb. As they entered the inferno it became apparent that they would travel along its surface; and this was amazing. It was like driving in a flaming meadow if such a peculiarity were possible. There was no heat but a sound like a roaring river. Every now and then there was a clear gap when the sky above showed an opening like a sunspot. Through the gap they would see the panorama below 'a Gods-eye view' of the world. At a glance they could see across the bowl to the other territories and down to the Praydaq and again down through the Omega and to the fibre-optic channel, the maroon triangle, Pergosia, the blue triangle and finally their tiny Universe!

"Richard said that there was no doubt they must have extra-enhanced vision to able to see so far. They then came to the first of the tunnel entrance of the nearest corona. It was like an enormous circle of gold shimmering like a holograph. It was at least a Kilometre in diameter and it carried traffic moving in both directions. They immediately drove through and onto a roadway stretching before them. With a jolt they were connected and sucked along at very high speed. The countryside was green, blue, orange with many red fields, and lime coloured trees and then the quaint villages that had been mentioned. Spirinda had them slow at the second village and allowed them see the people milling about evidently at a market. Some turned and waved quite unconcerned that all this inhabitancy and countryside was stretched around the cylinder.

Spirinda explained,

"The physics just in this Corona only is dominated by template transmitted electro magnetic gravitation, which works in strange ways. It automatically leans towards propagating femininity in the Logo, why not!"

In the distance they could see lakes of and oceans of pink and even a silver aircraft flying towards them. Sunlight shone down the Cylinder from her Sunhead, illuminating the complete interior making it possible for people to swim and laze in the divine rays.

Then the Spirit spoke again,

"Now to explain about the 'dynamic consequences' I mentioned. As the other two adjacent suns are also part of the scheme our thought channels intersect at various points along the way. Where this occurs it creates what we call Neuron Arenas and Synapse-Kopf Arenas (Intersecting terminals in the human brain where thoughts originate). In these compartments a female logo with ingrained intellect is released and transmitted back through the system and down to Purgosia. The same applies to the Son and the Father, but theirs will all be masculine! So what we are saying is that the gender is decided long before it becomes implanted – this will of course not be accepted by your medical profession." Then she laughed.

Mantz was fascinated, and said so, but Spirinda went on,

"We sometimes create invert thought substance, which is in fact material, as you know it. We use this type of peculiarity as a training area for our voluntary medics so they can laser test on real matter. As you know we are working with your substance all the time. The neuron and scnaps kopf arenas are ideal for psycho- medical laser experimentation. However, when they work on this I hear a buzzing that drives me mad."

As she was speaking they were rocketing at hyper speed through the web of channels. Suddenly they seemed to be in the interior of a meta-nova star. They could see nuclear fission but luckily could not feel the results. Next they saw the planet like earth. It was enveloped in blue parcels of protective shield. Spirinda said,

"That's the Orion aurora, shielded against the solar radiation pouring in earth's direction."

Then they glided across a thought duplicate of the Andromeda galaxy and with a gasp they were plunged into a dormant black hole that exists at its centre. They experienced what it means to journey through a zone that has the total absence of light. The amazing thing was that in the absence of light they still could see, but not with their eyes, it was with their senses. They knew that everything around them was though distorted beyond recognition. Then they were plucked from that predicament and landed in a room bathed in sunlight and in which a woman was kneeling and evidently in prayer. Moments later they were at the bedside of a very sick person. As they arrived the person opened their eyes and cried out. A nurse arrived and gazed at a monitor and called out loudly for assistance. There was a commotion at the bedside. Some one had evidently awoken from a coma. Everina felt tears in her eyes, no less Larry.

"We have just one more difficult experience for you."

They were propelled to where a dark thin man was lying at the side of a dusty road. He was so devastated that he must be dying. A figure approached and bent over him and began to offer him water. The person then began to bandage his wounds with a handkerchief and a linen scarf. The beneficiary was a woman gowned in a white shawl with a broad blue band around its edge. It seems Paulo knew her personally.

"Now back to adventure."

They were then shown a galaxy that existed very much in the future. It had a population who had developed connecting bridges or tubes, between its planets. On their arrival the tubes began to vibrate making a sound like chimes that grew into a galactic melody, which gradually died out. As they retreated the music re-commenced. Then a stream of numbers appeared. There was mathematics of every sort flashing before them. In a blink there were equations of all sorts, streams of algebra, trigonometry and a deluge of geometry displaying every shape imaginable. "Here comes the limit of our journey!"

Up ahead were three large olive drab template ships and one link ship which was even more enormous. The crew was dispersed over a strange blank wall of grey ice that filled the end of the tunnel. One of the ships had long cables linked to a power box on one side of the tunnel and other cables attached to the link ship. It was firing its lasers straight-ahead each blast extending the deity. Others were in smaller open top craft and were cutting residue material from template mesh.

Spirinda then said,

"Sometimes when they really get going and hit a good light patch; the thought bubbles propel them so fast that they glide from bubble space to bubble and effortlessly cut through the nothingness. This as you see is a tough section as dense as earth rock and resembling grey styrofoam. Many of these people who qualify to be on the template team have already had seismic experience before coming here. Their good works usually increase the territory by about the equivalent of 100,000 earth Kilometres per thought second, but of course that is not so great at this magnitude. Our long-term ambition is to democratize all the nothingness by way of our osmosis. We know that this must be done because from time to time we discovered pockets of substance that was not completely a nothing. Now if this seeded emptiness fell into the wrong hands it could yield an enemy! Also the waste from our digging is melted and injected into the void as a cooling agent. Wait till your physicists get a hold of that. You know by then they can have it, it won't matter because we will have moved on to new pastures!"

Everina drew a breath and squeezed Larry's hand. He almost got a fright as he was lost in the divine and she really earthed him with the electric reminder of her presence. He pulled her close and squeezed.

Spirinda then said,

"On our way back you will visit one more 'thought pocket' before we return. This thought is generated at the synapse intersection of the Son and myself. The event reflects on a piece of history written about by Plato in both Timaeus and Critias."

As she spoke they swept over a blue ocean and approached land. A huge rock like Gibraltar appeared and they glided out beyond it into a darker deeper ocean. Then they turned and dove downwards. Then with an almighty splash they ploughed beneath the surface. As the bubbles cleared they began to make out the outline of dwellings on the seabed. It was a city and was laid out in concentric lines. In its centre was a hill on which stood a temple containing a golden statue of Poseidon driving six winged horses.

Now even closer they saw that the houses had walls covered in gold and the roofs though in the abyss still sparkled with gems. Then they came to the surface and the experiences were concluded.

It had been a pleasant note to finish and so with that they returned to where they began at the car park outside the Sunhead. Everyone in the group was feeling dizzy from the experience but delighted with the generosity of the spirit.

Chapter 48

It was Nadine who brought about the groups' next experience. They were tired and ready for rest in the Dorado but she inspired drama of the third kind. She had been pondering many bold assertions about amorization and the final Judgment and therefore asked Spirinda,

"Will the Universe converge? What will it be like when it arrives, and how will it fit?"

The Spirit bit her lip and squinted her dark brown eyes and looked at Paulo, who shrugged his shoulders and smiled back helplessly.

"You really want to know?"

The others unenthusiastically agreed.

She said that she would try and simulate what will happen but as usual they will only see what they can understand not its entirety. She moved aside and seemed to speak into a handheld phone or perhaps just spoke into the palm of her hand! It seemed to do the trick because she returned and said,

"Look to the east to where my territorial left shoulder touches that of the son's right shoulder. Look, see, there is a natural border a rose line that runs all the way down to the omega centre and further."

People looked and identified the intersecting line one of several that they had seen in the sky when in Purgosia. Then an amazing thing happened. The line began to become an opening between the two territories exposing the void and the universe that was now much enlarged. It was even growing while at the same time travelling towards the opening. It had now swung the full circle and was poised as if to enter the territories.

Vehicles passing at the time did not stop or even notice the phenomena because the show was only visible to the visitors.

Then there was a throbbing that grew louder by the moment. By now the gap was so large that anything could enter the heavens.

At that moment Spirinda spoke again,

"Just about now the obstetricians are preparing for the great convergence. This is a moment when the fruit of centuries comes to bloom. Right now the people in the Universe have just experienced the second coming of the Son, of Mohammed, of Isaac, of Jacob and Elisa and all other adorable beings that have lived."

Then she quoted scripture,

(Matt 24.29; Mark 13.24-27) "There will be strange things happening to the sun, the moon, and the stars. On earth whole countries will be in despair, afraid of the roar of the sea and the raging tides. People will faint from fear as they wait for what is coming over the whole earth, for the powers in space will be driven from their courses. Then the Son of Man will appear, coming in a cloud with great power and glory. When these things begin to happen, stand up and raise your heads, because your salvation is near."

While all this was being related the Universe had already reached its point of maximum three-dimensional expansion. It had attained equilibrium and the correct ratio of dark matter to matter in its make up. The maroon triangle now revolved and under laid the blue triangle. This new configuration resembled the Star of David. They were pallets that will deliver the great cosmic birth. The onlookers could see all this with great clarity and exclaimed in awe at the wondrous spectacle. The Universe had become one with Purgosia bringing with it all the inhabitants who had been waiting the final day. All this activity signalled that the time was right for Eschatological birth! It was time for human resurrection to begin. The people of Purgosia would at last become at one with their remains. The rabbit was about to be drawn out of the hat!

To make room for this cosmological birth the Praydaq Complex had moved to one side thus exposing the omega through which this mighty guest would arrive. The blue triangle gently delivered the universe through the opening. There was a blast of trumpeting that echoed around the whole enclosure and this was combined with the music from a billion harps. The Universe, now free, did not need to be sustained any longer – it was unhitched from the arc and all other dependencies. It had inherited the fullness of its own time and had no reason to be shy about this well earned embellishment.

Then, as per the metaphysical rules of this stratum it began to grow. It extended until it filled all of the available open space now looking almost as large as the other three territories. Now after ions of colonisation it had become fully personalised and spiritualised. It had lost its space-like transparency and appeared as one body. It now completely filled the space between the Son and the Spirit so making the trinity into a new Quaternity! Then in crowning glory, a shaft of golden light sprang from its highest point – it was to be a new sun head in the heavens!

As they watched, this new being took on facial features and peered down on the onlookers. They were transfixed in its gaze, too overpowered to even feel uncomfortable. The body of this novice AMGOD had deep blue seas and was otherwise completely green and wooded. It had hills and dales and was teeming with animal life, the first such life that paradise had experienced. Then to Everina's joy the first birds, entered into heaven! They went flying around in swarms. They wheeled in circles, chirping and squawking but none the less forming tiny words. The doves belonging to Spirinda appeared out of nowhere and raced to meet the new inhabitants, causing a swirling storm of feather and claw. In the distance, there was the sound of barking and the whining of stallions and the baying of wolves. Then African animals appeared in hundreds and lastly a great band of resurrected people. They came walking into the valley out of the woods, to relish their promised inheritance. The Universe and its people were now apotheosised. Millions accumulated in the valley curiously looking upwards in fascination.

The saintly inhabitants from the Territories and those in the Omega now came out to mingle. Paulo turned to Larry and Richard, who were nearest to him, and in a low voice said,

"John, who you met earlier, told me of this; but what we shall be in the future has not yet been revealed. However, this event will give you a good idea of what's to come!"

The work of redemption was now completed in the void. By now there was nothing left below, except those who still defied!

Paulo said,

"Now the Father will sit on a white throne and decree that those who are unworthy will remain in the void forever. The angels sing 'Hallelujah, praise be to God in the highest'. Thus the Omega will be sealed, perhaps forever! What remained below will stay below – c'est la vie! Now, just as there are the three cities of Mohammed, New Jerusalem and Paradiso, one for each territory. Now we will have Purgosia in the territory of our new and Blessed Off-spring!"

Bill Travis was by now feeling very proud because of his state in life was receiving vast re-affirmation. He had a perpetual smile and was laughing and pointing at various aspects of the extravaganza. He reminded the others near bye him that humans had been bought at an enormous cost, and that was why the value of life was so high and why each one had an original debt to repay!

Chapter 49

The group was still entranced by the immensity of the simulation, convergence and apparent final judgment! As they stood quite in rapture they heard the sound of tambourines echoing across the great valley. Every angel in creation, with their white side fins like wings began to rise in the centre. They erupted in a growing swirl of white and gold that filled the sky like a twisting tornado. With that the four segments, began to rotate. The new segment was carried along in the motion. Then harp and trumpet music grew in magnitude to a chorus of a million angels. They were singing 'Hallelujah praise to Hosanna in the highest'.

Then there was a shimmering across the four territories and the ghostly shapes of four people emerged. They were like the souls or the essences of the segments. They began to rise towards each other hold hands and slowly rotate. The angels travelled ever upwards while the coronas from the four suns revolved and shone into infinity like bacons in the night.

Then the blue haze, in the middle of the valley, became more pronounced and the sound of humming bees could be heard. Paulo whispered that he once had a rapturous vision when on earth. He then said that every time the essence is perceived it appears different. It drained him of energy yet he was elated in spirit. No one yet understood. Then there was the sound of hymns that grew ever louder. Then the ghosts like essences, took on very human shapes as their plasma bodies became free from the territories while glowing spiritual energy poured from their hearts.

The spirit of the newborn Universe also had released its spirit, to join the bonded circle. Oddly it seemed incredible because it had a limp! The shock of this disability caused gasps. The group was witnessing the pure presence of the AMGOD. Despite the size of the figures they did not damage or crush the Praydaq or any of the people. Their textures were like rainbows that do not damage the countryside. These giant figures were the sole source of light and thus glowed like phosphoresce. As the music increased in volume the figures rotated faster and faster. Their faces were now more visible and their eyes were gleaming with joy. The face of the Universe could just now be seen for the first time. This was the face of a very young person. It was impossible to identify gender because of flowing garments and long dark hair. They were pleased with one another, very much a family and that was no doubt the secret of their success! They were now in ecstasy and rapture, and the hypnotic effect was so compelling that it spilt over and affected the crowds.

As they turned, their garments swept over the valley causing people everywhere to cheer. No one wanted this enigmatic show to stop. The music was rhythmic, complex, melodious and haunting. It was like Beethoven, Bach and Bono yet different and was music that earth had never known. The heaving sound was profoundly electrical and filled with echoes from the void. It combined the sweet delicate flute notes with the sounds of a thousand strings.

While all this was going on, people were in a trance and receiving experiences of pure joy. They were waving their arms, as if at a rock concert, while some were applauding. People in the crowds began to produce musical instruments, guitars, mountain horns, saxophones and a host of other instruments. As if by magic they all began to play in harmony with the Gods. Their contribution was enormous and the fulfilment they got from accompanying such an important gathering was clearly written on their faces. Then with a loud crescendo, it all came to an end. The great figures turned to face outwards and then bowed to the audience. They were, of course, the now familiar Divine Family and, to everyone's surprise, Miriam was there now standing in the very centre; though she was only of lesser size, and did not possess a territory, nevertheless her spirit had risen to equal height as the others. Then the spirits slowly sank backwards into their territories and the suns began to blaze again. After some songs of praise and much merriment, the angels descended, the crowds became quiet and the blue haze faded. Then a booming voice echoed out over the valley. The Father spoke for all to hear,

"Come all ye now, and possess the kingdom that we have prepared for you!"

That is all that was said. The words were greeted with a great roar of approval that echoed around and around the bowl's mountains and valleys. Then as they watched, the whole process went into rewind; people departed and the animals left. The triangles repossessed the Universe, and slipped back into the void. The crack was sealed and just three territories remained. Miriam stood at the omega complex now fully contained and smiling up at the suns above. The visitors were both sad and dumbfounded, and Spirinda wept!

It was time to go - the group wiped perspiration from their brows and silently climbed back on board the transport and departed. By now it was getting late and as they descended they once again passed the ski area it was closed for the evening.

Everina asked Spirinda

"How come the Blessed Offspring had a bad limp?"

Spirinda said that the Blessed Offspring will always have a disability, because it will have an ectopic birth – due to an imbalance of matter to dark matter in the Universe. As a point of interest, the Blessed Offspring will choose to retain its disability as a testimony to all those who had lived with a disfigurement in universal life! If it were not for human efforts through Prayers and good acts like that of for example; Live Aid and other wondrous groups - it would have perished long ago. However despite that it will be a continuous unrelenting struggle for it to survive."

Nadine asked what will happen if does not survived?

Spirinda said,

"Then sadly humans will not belong to any territory. They will not have achieved unification – their spirits will not have united sufficiently to warrant ownership of the Universe. The Universe will not possess a whole and living soul and will therefore amount to nothing. They will have collectively failed yet not individually. They will be permitted here but will not share the joy of being one of four territories. This will just be a fragmented solution and humans will just be pitied. This is a barely satisfactory outcome leaving the way open for Creation to be attempted one more time. Remember the powers of darkness will gloat over such a failure!

After this word of warning there was silence for a while then they asked about the beautiful music they had heard in the valley, and were told that the deaf who had lived on earth who composed it.

Shortly after that, they returned to Paradiso and were brought to an attractive part of the town called the golden city. They were given rooms in that impressive hostelry named the El Dorado. Once again they experienced traditional 'zip to room' facilities only this time they knew what to expect. Then the spirit left them, and they turned in for the night. Larry and Everina were too excited to rest and went up to the top floor of the building to view the City. By now every tent and building had taken on a different colour, a feature that was caused by the interior lighting. The fountains in the Central Park were glowing and the Trinity Monument was ablaze with lights. Far below, the sea shimmered and the clank of the halliards hitting masts on boats could be heard. There was also the sound of music, singing and general merriment in the streets below. Everina slowly kissed Larry goodnight, rendering him speechless, and then before he knew it spun around and departed singing as she went,

"I'm a big, big girl in a big big world".

---

(1) Rapture and Ecstacy, a spiritual state of enlightenment. Ref; De Veritae 12.2 Summa Theologica 11-11-175.3 Aquinus, Platonism and the Knowledge of God by Paddy Quinn, 1996

Chapter 50

Down at the omega centre several of the crew who did not go on the Paradise trip were asleep in their Hybos - this included Janette and Rico. Miriam returned them to the ship that night, because as Queen of Nations she had other pressing matters for her attention.

Now in the tranquillity of nocturnal Paradise, things were not as they seem. At the equivalent of three a.m. two figures quietly left the Callisto and went towards the administration rooms. At this time of night, the lights were dimmed and not many saints were on duty. The few that were there would only have to deal with serious matters that could not be handled by the Jet Packers. Security cameras grouped around the perimeter of the enclosure were pointing down into the void and this meant their crews were quite preoccupied with that task.

The two silent figures were none other than Raphael and Hamish, both dressed in dark cloths and wearing scarves to cover their pasty white faces. First they walked cautiously to one of the medical rooms and located two trolleys. Then they tested for squeaky wheels, and were satisfied as there was no noise. With map in hand, Rap led the way to Com/Saint and pushed the door, which swung open. There was a large conference table of which the centre was filled with a large flat monitor. The tabletop screen was still turned its saver showing lazy pictures from around eternity and intermittingly showing one-liner prayers. One side of the room was lined with cupboards, but there was also a steel door.

Rap cautiously turned a handle on the door. To his satisfaction, it opened to reveal hundreds of boxes labelled "Praque – 5,000 Guinsks". At this sight, Ham let out a gasp. Rap reacted in a hissing voice,

"Shut up Ham, quiet, you sound like an amateur."

He punched Ham on the arm just to drive home his point. Ham scowled and began to open one of the boxes. Just as anticipated they discovered the contents to be filled with coins. They were quite transparent like ice but difficult to distinguish. Ham dug his hand into the contents and trickled them through his fingers while their reflections danced across his smiling face. Then Rap studied the boxes more closely and found, that it said in many languages, one of them English, that the weight was 6.3 million 'Gravs'. On lifting one of the boxes, Rap reckoned it weighed the equivalent of about 5 kg. Without a word, he returned to the table pressed any button he could see and instantly the screen became active. The void appeared showing what lay below but also it showed three black triangles that had not been there before!

"Rap, Look here comes our pay cheque!" he said pointing at the triangles.

"Let's get busy."

Rap could not understand the keyboard, but one key had an icon of a bird with a message in its beak. He pressed it and immediately he gained access to s-mail. The address boxes had twenty-three options. He spotted one named that read xxx.thormentus.void666, gave a grunt of satisfaction and typed in the following,

"Three disciples in the Citadel are about to cause major disaster and remove quantities of Praque. Are you interested exploiting the situation? Rewards expected! Reply to raphamdal@uuu.callisto.e/usaruss."

He signed their three names and pressed and pressed the bird button again. The address appeared and several arrows shot towards the text. Then several comments in strange language appeared, almost certainly meaning the message was sent. Then he was given an option of a bank house icon or a school kid eraser. He chose the Eraser and the message was deleted he hoped.

They hurriedly loaded twenty boxes on the two trolleys and speedily pushed them towards the Callisto. So far no one had looked up from the task or interrupted, luck was holding. Dalia was waiting and had the entrance lowered. In a few moments they had unloaded the boxes and they were hoisted on board. The two men lowered the boxes into a compartment below a floor section then heaved sighs of relief. Too late Dalia remembered that she had forgotten to lock in the people who were at rest. To their horror they heard two voices chirp,

"'Hola, what you doing wid ze' boxes misters?"

It was Janette and Rico. Dalia immediately fielded the situation,

"Janette, why are you not in your Hybos?"

"We not sleep. Are you having fun? May we also ride on ze' trolleys?"

"Shush kid!" said Rap, "You better not make noise or tell people what you saw here tonight or we will have you thrown out into the void."

Janette began to cry. Rico looked disillusioned and a fearful expression spread across his innocent face. Rap blurted out loud,

"Dal, lock them up in a chamber somewhere – pronto before they blow our cover, also get the sleeping quarters locked before more zombies interfere."

Dalia dragged the children to the Cadets locker room and pushed them inside. Then she keyed in a locking command on the digital box by the door. The two males then headed to the command centre of the ship. To their delight they found a reply to their message from one called Commander Wilma Darrell 3rd Division AVD (Army of Voidular Dynasties). It said,

"We are concerned that this might be a trap. Will advance to a strategic proximity and await evidence of your action. If it is favourable we will exploit and you will be rewarded."

Rap wrung his hands together in joy. He immediately printed a copy and then deleted the message, and also tried to remove it from any storage file where it might be retained. He just had to hope for the best that it had been deleted. Then they both slid into the shadows with combat in mind. They went to where the Lasers were situated, and both climbed into the controller's positions, one in a fixed base laser and the other on the mobile gun that stood near the centre of the glass floor. They tuned to short range and without hesitation opened fire. The first shot from Rap on the mobile, sounded like thunder. A streak of red light tore around the perimeter smashing computers and ripping out glass as it went. Rap was shocked by the awesome power he had unleashed. They both let out loud whoops and fired in full circles. This concluded with firing through the glass entrance and out towards the transport tunnels, flight pad and river that looked like honey. They wrecked several flying machines and caused a cascade of golden substance to shoot in every direction. However, being magnetised the particles reformed in an instant and seeped back into the river. Ham let out a roar of anger, and Rap fired again. The second attempt was no better, so they turned the laser upwards at the roof and floor of the Praydaq. The effect was spectacular as a complete section of the trading hall fell down cracking more glass beneath them. Ham, who had been slower to master the controls, was now becoming efficient. He was able to fire his gun in every direction and that included down at the glass floor. Rap followed suit, and in moments there was a massive hole and dangerous cracks. Ham let fly one more time and jumped clear just as his laser begun tumbling into the vacuum diminishing in size as it went. The mobile gun did not fall through, but became wedged on a sharp edge with its mechanism, jammed and firing all directions. The side effect of all this violation was a hurricane, like wind at the vacuum sucked at the environment. Everything was now being sucked into the void.

The children herd the noise and felt the ship lurch. Amidst sobs and shivers they began to climb up on top of the lockers made possible by a fixed wall bookshelf for literature on cadetship. It acted like a ladder for them to climb. At first Janette refused, but Rico reminded her about what the men had threatened her, so she changed her mind! Then once on top they crawled into an open air-duct that looked inviting.

The two terrorists stopped firing and with beaming grins and looks of guilt on their faces, struggled against the storm back to the ship. Sirens were sounding over the installation and voice recordings issuing automatic instructions could be heard. Dalia was prepared and as planned had the ships motors humming. The power packs were beginning to kick in one by one causing an ever-increasing din. The two threw themselves into the moving ship as it lurched towards the opening with its hull grinding on the floor. It was about then, that the first Angel defenders arrived, tumbling in from every direction. Flying craft buzzed overhead directing blue powder on to the flames. Ham was last in, and hastily closed the door. The three made their way to Captain Dave's control centre and on the EM/SPEC began to plot the direction of the ship. As the ship lumbered towards the open glass floor escape looked imminent. Rap was at the helm, shouting profanities as he steered towards the opening. Suddenly a buzzer sounded. Rap stared at the consul where a flashing light indicated – 'Urgent, door A1 releasing'. At that very moment, the power automatically reduced and the ship ground to a halt. Rap let out a bellow.

"Ham you idiot, you did not close the door properly!"

To which Ham replied with his eyes wide open in surprise,

"Honest Rap, I did close it right, I know I did."

With that they both scurried to the indicated area, where they discovered a dozen Jet Packers and Pedro standing inside the open entrance. To make matters worse Rico was standing with his finger jammed against the door control panel while Janette was leering at them with a look of revenge on her chubby brown face. The two froze in their tracks and frantically thought about excuses. Dalia saw what was happening, and went to unlock the resting area and slid into her Hybo and closed the lid.

Rap quickly regained composure and exclaimed to Pedro,

"Pedro, thank heavens you have come. What ever is happening, we thought we were lost. We were preparing to fly for our lives!"

Pedro gave a doubtful look and snapped back,

"Has anyone here been hurt?" – "No" said Rap.

"Do you know who fired the lasers?"

"We didn't see anything till the flames erupted. Are we under attack?" Ham blinked his eyes in apparent innocence.

"Senior Pedro" A tiny voice intervened. It was Janette. "Those men were out and when they came back they said they would kill us." She pointed at Ham and Rap who responded with,

"No not at all, we said to mind as they might get killed if they are not careful on the ship."

Janette had never told a lie and began to cry. Pedro beckoned a kindly female angel to comfort her saying,

"Do you gents realise just how dangerous it was to attempt a departure in the middle of such an attack? This whole event will be investigated, and we are taking charge of the ship till your Captain returns."

"That's great news," said Rap, biting his lip.

Pedro quickly turned and detailed three of his force to take charge and departed.

There was a sudden high-pitched whine. People stopped in their tracks and turned towards the entrance where a flying craft was descending. The sleek object though mostly transparent had an insignia of a Lamb and three white stars on its fuselage. Officers in combat gear alighted followed by the Son. He was visibly angry and his aura shone brighter than usual, while his surroundings warped as he passed. It was obvious that he was the supreme command in this time of crisis. His subjects fully understood the position and watched his reactions and awaited his orders. He firstly looked around and spoke to the nearest hurt person who was been attended by a corps person. He gave them his congratulations for being so courageous and immediately went into Com/Saint.

There were about thirty angel officers and saints waiting for his council. Though under enormous pressure he remained calm and spoke in an even voice. He asked Benedict about the psyco-medical situation and Pedro for a material damage report. Pedro said that there was a doubt that this was an attack from beyond, and it could have been an inside job. People looked amazed. He added that he would confirm all this soon when the all seeing visual wall panels are replayed. He reported the damaged floors and lasers and sounded happy that no one had been lost. However, on the deficit side one hundred and forty have been disabled so far, many of them had been night traders on the upper level. He added that the Praydaq had fallen several points but that this element of the report would come through the proper channels.

He thanked Benedict and then asked Gabriel and Michael who had arrived from the Corona, about the battle situation. They told him that there was now a real danger that since their defences were reduced the black triangles might take advantage of the situation. If they did not get the vacuum sealed the triangles could be penetrated and according to eschatological law the perpetrator would increase in size and become a threat to the whole domain.

A furious effort to shore up defences and seal the damage began. Architects and engineers, some specialists fresh up from Purgosia, began directing operations.

The breeze was like a tornado in reverse as papers and lighter objects went cascading in downwards spirals.

Chapter 51

Gabriel and Benedict then surveyed the audio visual lighted table with the flat computer terminal. It showed the position of the black triangles but now there was evidence of them making a dangerous advance. They were heading in three different directions. The first of their targets looked like being Purgosia - crammed with humans hoping for future ascent. By now the area was being evacuating many of its population going as per the national safety plan; through its subterranean system to the uninhabited reverse side of the triangle. Above that there was one heading towards the Logo Optic Canal and above that there was one heading for the Omega Complex.

Just then a voice from Purgosia blared through the console. It was from one of the city fathers called Alessio. He questioned in a voice marked with tension,

"Bless you Gabriel, but I am here with the mayor and several of your angel commanders and we would like to know what's going on? As far as we can see something erupted at your omega and we are being approached by one of Thormentus's ships from Hada. Our combined defence system has not kicked in and we are vulnerable. They are already dangerously near and time is running out. Are you already under attack? You know if you also have any problem we will get your left over's, so tell us!"

Gabriel quickly brought him up to date, and explained that he would have proper communications restored within about twenty-five minutes. He said the Son was ready to speak to them through the Chasms and that even as they speak the omega was being repaired. He asked if the safety shield at the Logo Optic Canal had been completed. Alessio said it was being extended but was also delayed with having to work on the safety shield for the city. Gabriel said he would see what help he could muster from Com Saint because they both agreed if the Logo-optic flow were damaged it would have a tumorous effect on everything. While this conversation was going on Gabriel could hear the sound of announcements and sirens in the background. He switched off communications now feeling quite worried.

Chapter 52

On the night of the sabotage, Hiroshi and Jill had been sitting on Dan and Maria's deck looking up at the night sky. They had been watching their triangle change, as usual, from maroon to rainbow as the sky turn opaque. They had seen the Omega glistening gold and beyond the membrane that enclosed the void they had even seen a hint of three suns glowing in the background. They never had been there and had only heard about it by word of mouth.

Hiroshi and Jill went to rest, but could not. There was much disturbance coupled with the fact that the Callisto and their friends were now so very far away. They both went out on the deck and gazed up at the heavens. Then in the stillness of the vault a gigantic flash occurred at the Omega. This was followed by red and yellow laser light dancing wildly in the sky. They both gazed in surprise and curiosity. Then another terrible eruption occurred. Streaks from lasers could be seen shooting in all directions. Some of their beams missed their targets and penetrated as far down as the Sangria's.

Sirens went off in Purgosia, as the authorities were alerted to danger. Then the deluge up above was followed by a loud hissing sound. There was an uncanny flow of ether causing a wind to blow that disturbed the composure of creation. It was like a tropical storm blowing and drawing across the land. It was so strong that is rocked the complete triangle making the ground shake under their feet. No doubt from a distance it would have resembled a decorated Christmas tree in a draught.

"Something has gone dreadfully wrong!" shouted Jill.

Hiroshi agreed and with that they wakened Maria and Dan to tell them about the event.

Chapter 53

Thormentus and his Diablo Control were situated on the Reaper, as it headed for Purgosia. Now it was his opportunity to get even; to dislodge the human visitors, to blast the brain of the AMGOD and to drive a spear into the heart at Purgosia. As commander and chief he was bent over a monitor that viewed the battle field through the nose cone. The information was then passed along its spinal column and into the nerve centre where it was analysed and disseminated to all concerned.

It was true to say that some of the unfortunates who made up his military did not agree with what he was doing. They had always been obedient and accepted their fate but; to go to war against the mighty one - was not their idea of fun. Also fighting a war diminished their chances of there ever being a solution to their isolation. After all, they had been tricked in life by Thormentus and therefore now felt quite despondent!

His armed forces had brigades who could fly like jet packers. They used the similar methods as their alleged enemy only they were clad in the darkest of colours contrasted by the crimson communication antennas that they bore on their heads. This feature helped add style to their otherwise mundane garb. They consisted of both male and female both of which were expected to fight side by side even in combat.

One time these creatures were individuals with different looks. Now on close inspection only vague traces of character remained. Collectively they were quite menacing with their hoods and capes. The ship was manned by 100,000 of these troops along with a thousand officers; who were answerable to a ten senior officers known as Centurions.

Thormentus looked up from the screen and turned to Lexentra his Aide, and said,

"Our battle plan is thus - Zahtienne will hit that dumb Logo Optic string, and we will smash the city of Purgosia and time will stand still! Diva will penetrate the damaged Omega Citadel and land in the lap of the Gods. It is now confirmed that the vacuum has burst wide open and we have a window of opportunity. Diva is not only moving towards the Omega, but is being drawn towards it by the principal of expanding magnitude and displacement. God does things in strange ways!"

Then he began uncontrolled laughter, almost looking happy by sheer accident.

There was a murmur of satisfaction from the officers. Thormentus continued,

"Some humans have caused this sabotage. Though I do not need their help - nevertheless I want their names so they can be rewarded. You never know we might use them in future!"

Lexentra replied,

"Sir, when you negotiated with Stephen and Gabriel you asked to sit on the world council. If we attack it will destroy our chances of achieving that aim."

Thormentus leered back at him and said triumphantly,

"Look if this opportunity is exploited we will be the world council. You may not realize this but we will become the owners of vast quantities of Praque and that will give us the same power as these Gods." Everyone was impressed.

"Now anyone with unworthy intentions, contrary to mine, better own up now!"

Chapter 54

Spirinda had also felt the effect of the violence at the Omega. Larry was jolted out of his slumbers by what he thought was an earthquake. He jumped to his feet and looked out the open veranda. He could see the town shudder while across the valley the other two territories also shook violently. He went to call Everina, but she was already at his door. They hurried to the Lobby where the whole group had assembled, everyone looking quite confused. Paulo arrived with a worried look on his face. Then Spirinda arrived just as there was another distant rumble. She put her hand to her head as if in pain or concentrating on her thoughts. A serious looked crossed her face usually smiling face. She spoke with emotion in her voice,

"My dear friends, this is the last I shall see of you for a long time. I want to wish you well, and to say that while you may not remember every detail of this journey, you will at least carry with you a template from heaven that will react to any good you do. It will help you remember the important aspects and to convey them to others. Now why has all this come to happen so quickly? Well I'm sorry to say that the Omega centre has been sabotaged!"

There was a gasp from the group and she continued,

"Even the smallest human contrived aggression hurts us and we feel pain. Thormentus is taking advantage and is moving in for an attack. Therefore look at your wristbands, they will by now be almost totally lit except for the golden area but you have seen much and would be leaving soon anyway. However, in view of the crisis we must hurry a bit more than anticipated."

Then she quoted from scripture: *Eph 5; 10;13.*

"Finally, build up your strength in union with the lord and by means of his mighty power. Put on all the armour that God gives you, so that you will be able to stand up against the Devil's evil tricks. For we are not fighting against human beings but against the wicked spiritual forces in the heavenly

world, the rulers, authorities, and the cosmic powers of this dark age. So put on God's armour now! Then when the evil day comes, you will be able to resist the enemy's attacks; and after fighting to the end, you will still hold your ground."

Then she said,
"May the power of al-hukm l'illah be with you!" and was gone.

John and Valentino had returned as planned. Paulo gathered the group on to a two hastily organized flights. With sad hearts they soared high above Paradiso over the ocean across the Punto Espiritu and then leaving the tropics they descended over fields of lavender and arrived at the Omega Landing strip. The Complex was in a state of chaos. People were milling about evidently with special tasks to perform. Many were now dressed in combat attire and most wore head communications discs. Their battle dress was of blue and grey camouflage with the pants tucked into thick soled valcro closed boots. Their helmets were 'Kevlar' shaped, transparent with a midnight blue tinge, and studded with star markings. A defence jockey was announcing com/saint messages much like this,

"Medic team AK101 required at bay 24 - Daniel Mezelupe of A company – Construction, report to Red sector etc."

There was an emergency field hospital set up on the flight landing area. It was already full of hurt inhabitants and as they looked even more arrived. The interior of the Omega Complex was now like a war zone. Machinery was being linked to emergency power units. Lasers were being repaired and the mobile gun that had tipped into a crack in the glass was being hauled back in place. The ceiling and floor of the Praydaq were being mended with a self-growing substance taken from the territories called 'Bodmat-A' (Body material A). The shattered oval glass was also receiving the same treatment but progress was slow. Richard overheard one of the senior controllers reporting,

"This is the Territorial Defence Commander, Defence Plan Red A1 now in effect."

Then the Defence Commander spoke again,

"Standby 5th 8th and 26th Angel Divisions this is a mobilisation command rendezvous 04000. Point Lomanda. Angel density now increased by 25 millard. A progress report on the Logo Optic defence shield is urgently required. There is a possibility of recalling outreach divisions, this is now being considered!"

The jargon went on and on. Because of the suction it was still a struggle to walk upright. The group were now almost bent double with the draught, as they hurriedly made their way to the Callisto. Dave and Laura did not get on board till they had firstly visited a meeting room in the Com / Saint area. They knew it was going to be an uncomfortable encounter. The Son and senior officials were there with a serious expression on each of their faces. The Son related the events and then said that several billion Praque had been stolen, and that on a replay of the interior monitoring showed it had been stacked on a trolley but moments later they saw a trolley falling into the void. Dave and Laura were shocked and asked if any of their people had caused such an accident. They were told that the night people on duty became so traumatised that they could not relate properly to what had happened.

Then Paulo arrived entered the meeting as he now had everyone on board and ready to go. Therefore with a feeling of guilt they both shook hands with the Son and his group, not forgetting to thank them profusely. They said they would be eternally indebted!

Then they followed Paulo and once on board they discussed the route back. Paulo said,

"Originally we had hoped that you would fly down the Logo Optic, and pick up Hiroshi, be placed on the gantry and sent earthwards with a time adjustment provided. Now in view of the danger you will have to make a dash for home across the blue triangle. However I assure you that we will do everything possible to provide as much assistance as possible."

Savouring that guarantee and with a feeling of anxiety the two Captains prepared to leave. Just then Miriam came to say good-bye to the Children and wish the group a safe flight. She told the children that the Father sent his good wishes and that he would help find their parent. Then she embraced everyone on board including Rap, Ham and Delia. She then promised that she would always be near by and as Queen of Nations and Angels would protect every car they drove and even cup from which they drank and will always intercede on behalf of their requests. With these words of consolation and with Paulo once again as skipper they prepared for embarkation. Everina and Larry were almost last arriving. Just then the theatre lighting turned blue like UV. Paulo looked out and said out loud that it is to protect our eyes from light loss as we drop into the void and please come in immediately.

Richard was even later arriving and therefore came at a running pace saying to Larry when he came,

"Buddy, as they feel so much pain up above, tell me, if there was a nuclear war anywhere in the Universe, would the heavenly atom become quantizised? Would it cause harm up here? I fear it might!"

Larry squinted at him and rubbed his chin and said,

"A profound thought, Professor Opelli, now stop it and just get on board."

Chapter 55

The 'Shrink Doctors' in their white coats gave them a welcome nod as they poured onto the Callisto and then made frantic preparations for their departure. Unknown to the people on board, this was because announcements began to warn of another attack now imminent – enemy closing rapidly. They must hurry to deminiturise the ship to fit the scaled down domain. One of the medical team was a woman, who had a distinct Russian accent while the others were men. However the controller was a young fellow who spoke with an impeccable an Oxford accent. He said,

"Attach the clamps."

There was a clang and then the shrinking process began with a microphone advising that people should fasten their seat belts immediately. Once again there was no need for turning on the power as lighting and computer power was drawn from the surroundings. Then the Oxford man stood at a console and called out some numbers, and with a jolt the shrink began. Everina watched the team grow larger by the moment. She turned to Larry and said,

"Oh Larry he is gorgeous, why didn't I talk to him before we left!"

Larry turned and gave her a half smile, sleepy, bored look, and said,

"His name is Bond, James Bond."

And then he rolled his eyes upwards.

The team was by now looked like great mammoths beaming down from above. They were gently lowered through the opening. Then just as they were being let go there was the same distinct sound of Gregorian chant echoed on their intercom. It was the same ascending prayers they had heard on arrival.

Now freed the Callisto and its precious contents began its decent. Several of the group left their seats and went to the stern of the ship to watch the retreating Omega. The forceps had by now been withdrawn and the Alpha opening closed. However, the beauty of the citadel was marred because of the shattered glass and the gaping holes not yet mended. For a fleeting moment, the brightness of the morning sun of the segments shone through the membrane that separated the void from above. The lines of the territories could again be seen spreading from the Omega and encircling all the way around the void emphasizing its container-like shape. Then because of the great distance all colour faded from sight and the blackness of the void prevailed. They were inside Adam's apple and sliding into its core and the time was near for 'Le Crunch'.

Chapter 56

Pedro informed the Callisto of the approaching enemy. Then he watched the ship shrink from sight. He heaved a sigh of relief, the whole hospitality undertaking had been a strain and anyway he was characteristically cross. It was at that moment that several of the Com/Saint Presidium members came running to his side. Their spokes person a mature lady with golden hair and an ebony coloured face, said in a quivering voice,

"Pedro, our Praque is on the Callisto. Our guards never checked the ship because they did not know about it in time. The monitors now show it being put on board!"

Pedro froze. He glanced down at the departing speck and then over at the approaching enemy. He drew his face into a crinkled mass and rolled his eyes upwards. Then he said in carefully tailored words,

"It's a paradox, it's too late they've gone! Late, yet we create time! No we cannot use too late as an excuse!"

The bearers of the bad news looked anxiously at him as if to say what next?

Then he snapped,

"We will have to bring back the ship. Issue a request immediately and I will explain to his Majesty."

On board the Callisto, Paulo and Captain Dave were beginning to sort themselves and the crew into some sort of order. Dave was keen to regain command and above all to interrogate Ham and Rap, and sort out the whole terrorist debacle. It was then that the ships conventional communications sprang into life. Com/Saint, Omega command was on the air,

"This is a confidential report for Captain Dave. Please confirm that we can continue!"

Dave went to his cabin with Laura and Mantz and responded with an affirmative and the report proceeded,

"This is Pedro to say we are now in possession of information about the serious theft of which you were made aware. It seems that the missing Praque has been stashed on board your ship!"

The three looked at each other in amazement. Then Pedro continued,

"We wish you to return immediately, but in the mean time no doubt you will begin a search. Also by returning you may be caught in the crossfire from an attack by enemy forces that now can be seen rising from the southeast. Therefore you are requested to come with great haste."

Lionel navigated the Callisto into a pivoted turn and headed back the way they had come. Dave ordered Laura to begin to have the ship searched – Jean, Ivan and Mantz were asked to assist. Dave gathered Paulo and his officers around the EM/SPEC and called a red alert. The dark triangles are moving quickly and might block their return.

Meanwhile, Laura mobilised the team of cadets to assist in the search. The task took them down to the engine room and it eventually back up to the Library, where Janette and Rico were reading. It was Janette, who spoke first,

"Allo Senorita," said Janette with a smile,

"Are you looking for ze' treasure?"

Laura was taken aback and nodded while saying,

"Why yes Janette dear, as a mater of fact we are and can you help?"

Janette followed by Rico curtly put down their books and briskly walked out to the corridor and towards the main exit. Then Janette stopped and pointed to the floor.

"It is there."

The Cadets quickly removed some tiles and uncovered the containers of precious bounty. Laura whistled in amazement saying out loudly,

Why Children, thank you so much, you will be rewarded for that, and by the way did you see who put it there? The response was definitive,

"Ham and Rap the funny men who frightened us!"

Almost breathless, Laura reported the discovery. Dave was relieved but it was also an embarrassment and an indictment of the frailty and untrustworthiness of the human species. The whole event was quite a mess and the only ones to gain were Janette and Rico who will be rewarded the promise of fresh made ice cream when ever they get nearer home.

Now with the Black Triangle dangerously close a group a company of courageous Jet Packers on Jet Skis emerged to escort them in. Each Jet Ski had two people on board armed with light weapons. No sooner had they began flight, than the Diva's ship almost as expected, began to fire.

Her forward most point had just come into range, and she now demanded quick and decisive action to shock and awe the enemy defences. There was an almighty barrage from at least a fifty guns of her forward section. The complete Omega became engulfed in explosions. Much of the barrage travelled into the interior and into the lap of the Gods, as the omega now lay open and vulnerable. The effect was amazing as any objects hit began to quiver and then turn blue and purple. Then they became transparent and erupted in a shower of violet fragments and pink vapour.

Dave immediately ordered the Callisto to stop.

Then to everyone's horror, Diva began to shoot down the Jet Packers one at a time. Yet despite this massacre, they still kept coming on.

Richard shouted,

"Just like the Battle of Midway, they just kept coming."

However, Diva's deadly fire had no respect for bravery and one by one they were cut to pieces - their stunned bodies left floating in the ether. Soon all that remained were two skis that gallantly moved in a circle and flew straight at the Diva's forces. This time they scored a hit with their pump action zappo's causing a large chunk of black material to fall from the triangle. However just like their companions they also were bowled over by Diva's gunners and was last seen unconscious and floating into the darkness.

Unfortunately the crew of the Callisto could see all that was happening and all these defeats did not help moral. To make matters worse not only was the war erupting above, but it was now affecting Purgosia far below. With a booming voice, Paulo said to Lionel, Dave and Larry,

"Captain me' thinks we are in a tight spot. Not a wing or a prayer will get us back inside the citadel without being damaged. Now if we do get hit, who will stop the attack on below? You know we might have to lend a hand!"

Dave radioed for permission to descend to Purgosia and Paulo reluctantly agreed.

Just then as another salvo was fired but this time the Callisto was the target. Paulo covered his ears and said,

"You know those guns are based on high sound frequency, that's why it hurts our ears. I can't look at the flashes either they can blind me. Actually if any of us spirit people get hit we are in trouble and they can just walk all over us. It will take our people a long time to locate those incapacitated floating in the void. You know the big three could call this war off if they wanted. One sweep of a hand is all it would take but they will never do that because freedom of choice and evolution would be retarded."

Dave said in curiosity,

"Paulo that is strange! I can see those flashes quite well also, but I can't hear anything."

"Neither can I," said the others.

As most of the divisions of the Omega army were dispersed across the empires of Eternity it fell on the home guard to defend the citadel. They had mended much of the damaged equipment and the smaller lasers were now beginning to fire. However this defence was not enough to slow Diva's advance.

The citadels incapacitated were numbering hundreds and most had been moved back to safer pastures. Anyone caught in such a barrage would had been deafened and dazzled to a state of temporary blindness. Diva had now fine-tuned her artillery to get maximum results.

The Son was in the Com/saint, which was now in the front line of resistance. He was covered in dust but was intent on monitoring the activity and was being constantly advised on the situation. He had emphasised to Pedro that it was critical that the Praque is not ceased by Diva, as in her hands it could finance a sub creation with incredible complications for all.

Chapter 57

If things looked bad up on seventh stratum, they were as bad, if not worse, in Purgosia. They were receiving the full brunt of another attack from the forces of Thormentus. It was quite a spectacle as the giant black mass of the Reaper filled the sky. All around the insidious object poured streaks of red light down on the almost helpless city. Each ray caused a large explosion of high luminosity accompanied with a deafening sound.

The population was not in a position to defend, as they were but dwellers in transit. They had never experienced an attack of any sort before. It was almost like being back on earth it was so bad. They were relying on the power of the AMGOD and the City's garrison for protection. As the attack was on such a broad front no extra help was available. Many of the Omega population who had been attending the festival could not get back as the Logo optic was temporary on shut down. All the Purgoians could contribute at best was to help put our fires, assist the wounded and that included fallen angels of their own.

Heavy traffic was filling the road out of town as designated vehicles took the stricken to safety in the Sangrias. The Angel Garrison who was providing the city with defence had mounted lasers on the top of buildings. They were also flying formations to draw fire from the city and to prepare against an invading army that could descend from Thormentus's triangle.

Another frightening aspect was that several battalions had already returned in tatters. By now the Euclidia had taken a bad hit and its associates were quelling vibrations that were spreading just as fire spreads on earth. The Chasms of Yahweh had closed their giant doors for safety. There were prepared to stop the arc if necessary. If this were to happen – universal time would be in suspension and everything would be crystallised in a frozen moment and would remain so until the flux returned. It would be like the human world going into a coma.

Hiroshi and Jill had decided to leave Dan and Maria's house and go back to the city to see if they could be of any help. They also expected that Hiroshi might have to make a speedy exit if the Callisto returned. As transport was disrupted they hitched a ride from a military vehicle filled with a group of Jet Packers who said they were part of the Screaming Angels' division. They were a nice bunch of people and the conversations developed around sailing, and hit tunes that had become popular there. Five of them had done service on earth one in Japan and another in Tibet. They said their families were all in Purgosia -no one had been lost. The third had served during the famine in Ireland and the fourth had been at Guadalcanal. The fifth earth visitor said that she was on duty as far back as the third century and that the person whom she was responsible for had an uneventful life and died early. She had not been sent back since then and was much happier here. Then a fellow leaned forward and said,

"I was not on earth but worked in another Galaxy; I was looking after a Doctor, who spent most of his life on missions in Andromeda where famine was rampant. He died of ill health derived from a life of hard work. He is not known on earth, but up here he is held in very high esteem."

Hiroshi looked amazed and asked,

"Does that mean you get the credit for his success?"

"No, he gets the credits, not us!"

There was a big laugh and a jeer from the others, who slapped him on the back and said,

"Shabib is so good at his job that he's been put with us Screamers."

There was another laugh. Shabib looked puzzled and one of the fellows nearest - ruffled his hair. Then Shabib also began to laugh.

Chapter 58

Diva had now somehow accelerated and had closed in on the Omega. Her deadly point was aimed at the gaping hole in the glass floor. Her guns on the forward section were blazing away at any targets they could indentify. Her beetle like army was riveted in lines prepared to disembark and fall into the fray. As the point struck there was an enormous shudder. Then according to the law of metaphysical equivalence the front, now inside the citadel began to grow just as all object do when they enter the higher stratum. The hideous black spear now growing in size - tore its way up wards through the Omega never stopping till it severed the Praydaque and stood defiantly in the middle of the valley of the Gods.

At that very moment Diva emerged from the nose of the ship. She was flanked with officers and assault troops who stood aghast from the intense sunlight. Slowly they began to focus on the valley and the amazing colourful splendour of it all. From her high vantage position they commanded a view of the whole interior all the way up. However unlike the humans they could see the splendour of the three dazzling sun heads. They picked up the aroma of smoking incense and lilac and bougainvillea and roses. This spectacle left them speechless, but not for long. With a high pitched voice she screamed,

"Where is that so called Virgin Queen and Mother of the Son? Come out and show yourself and fight me to the death!"

Miriam had made ready her house to accommodate the wounded. She was now in the frontline helping people on to the last remaining flights to safety bound for the New Jerusalem. She knew that the territory would protect her no matter how badly the war raged. She knew that Eternity would still be there when this war was passed. She therefore made no reply but continued with her work of tending to the wounded. Diva's piercing eyes quickly spotted Miriam in the distance and called on her gunner to get her in the sights.

Diva's triangle was not only an object of terror, but also in some ways it was a comical sight. The front was still growing to enormous proportions, but the rear was still in the void and was therefore quite small by comparison. If Diva could hold on long enough she could unload her invasion troops. She commanded that the doors be opened and troopers to disembark.

A defensive line had now been set up around the Omega. Most flying craft had withdrawn and were in formations circling above awaiting orders. Diva intended over running all this with three divisions of her very best troops. With the doors now open in the side of the ship the enemy hoards were poised to land. Then the forward gunners stopped firing. The din from the attacking troops ceased. The enemy had slowly been overcome by the splendour of the Stratum. They had never expected to see such beauty. They had forgotten what the sensation of love and harmony was all about. They had not seen colour or felt rays of the sun for decades. They could not believe there could be three enormous furnaces of sun light effortlessly heating the empire. They had expected an ugly machine that ruled its population with an iron mitre. They envisaged a God sitting on a throne bellowing warnings and demanding that Diva depart. But no! Maybe they had made a terrible mistake! They had forgotten what trust really was. But again they were shaken out of their trance by the voice of Diva sounding through out their ship,

"In the name of the great Thormentus what are you all doing? You are required to take advantage of this situation. Officers, land the landing force immediately. Gunners fire at everything in sight or face the consequences"

Then she spoke to the gun command centre,

"One of their principle celebrities is over there by the vehicle that landed. She is in a blue coloured garment and loading wounded enemy into the same transparent vehicle. Have you got her in your sights yet? She is to be annihilated and that is an order. Fire, Fire, Fire!"

Chapter 59

The Callisto was being followed by a swarm of Diva's flying demons. They began to fire small arms and throw chains at the stern of the retreating ship. As they were slower, soon they were left behind. Paulo had become delirious and collapsed due to the overbearing din and had been taken to sick bay. Lionel had taken weak and was in sick bay and so Dave asked Larry was asked to take the helm.

Rap and Ham had been handcuffed and locked in a small storeroom. They were desperate and began tapping a Morse code message on a pipe in a random effort to inform the enemy that there was bounty on board.

Then from below the booming voice of Paulo was heard to say,

"Jude where are you?"

Then as if Jude had answered his cry, things began to happen, but not as Paulo had expected. It was Don Travis who came up with a keen observation,

"I believe we mortals might be immune to all this demon artillery! None of our crew is affected - perhaps we live at a lower frequency! I think we might be immune to their powers."

Then Larry said,

"Therefore let's see if we can take a shot at Diva before we go!"

He interrupted Dave and asked for permission to attack Diva's flank just once.

Dave felt at this stage anything was possible and contra to his usual earth judgment, he agreed on a one hit basis.

Everina looked in amazement and pride. She felt a little envious but as it was Larry, she made allowance. Larry spoke to the engine room and requested some old fashioned atomic power. Ernst dashed to be of assistance. Then he sent cadets to man the upper communications laser to see if it could be used for defence. Three cadets scrambled up the ladder and swung the gun in the direction of the enemy.

With that there was a high-pitched hum, and the Callisto became fully self-motivating for the first time since facing the 'Neg troughs'. The crew let out a cheer. The cooks turned up the player and a CD played Yellow Submarine.

Observers above saw the Callisto turn about and begin a rapid approach. Diva's rear observers informed her that the ship was surrendering. However within moments that became evidently untrue. The Callisto was actually going to attack Diva's flank. Through a temporary observation area Pedro saw them coming. His eyes opened wide in astonishment and the Son was informed immediately. He responded with a wide smile and slowly nodded his head.

The effect on Diva was quite the opposite. Top side, she had a serious moral problem as the gunners had refused to fire into the interior of Paradise. No one would obey the command to shoot at Miriam it would be a perversion they said! Then below there was a new threat. With two thirds of her triangle still dangling in the void she was exposed to this new danger emerging. She screamed for the rear guns to fire immediately. Her commanders barked co ordinates and deadly accurate salvos were discharged instantaneously. A hundred red streaks homed in on the golden hull of the approaching Callisto. There was a shudder and a metallic sounding eruption and in an instant the streaks returned to source. There was a ghastly chain of eruptions around the lower side of the triangle as Diva's guns lit up in flames. Every gun that fired was destroyed by the rebound. They were not tuned to meet humble inverted substance of the human kind. Her rear artillery was now in ruins. The Callisto continued on course firing as it went. Diva though having a thousand guns could not fire any for fear of more rebounds.

"Cease all rear gun firing she yelled."

Now, too late for her, the vacuum took over, it began to pull her ship backwards and in the confusion she lost her grip. Her warriors now partly landed began to fall through the space now widening around the ship. With a great roar like a sinking liner the triangle slipped downward. Diva and the gunners at the point could only look helplessly; as they journeyed back to whence they had come. The defenders were relived but also looked on in amusement and in a comical moment they began to wave good bye as the enemy sank out of sight. As it went it gathered speed diminishing in size and made hasty retreat.

Pedro returned to the console and shouted,

"There she goes, 'hell bent for leather'. Please accept my congratulations. Perhaps humans have some use after all."

Larry said to the skipper,

"Captain, will we ask if we should try to get back inside the Omega now that the way is clear?"

Dave agreed. The intercom crackled and Pedro came on the air.

"Well done Callisto. The Son sends his good wishes and says all is forgiven. We are very grateful at what you have done, but don't attempt to return, it's even more hazardous then when you departed. Go with all haste to Purgosia and safe trip."

The Callisto went back on course and Larry turned his attention to the middle attack which was threatening to sever the logo optic tunnel. Again he called for Ernst to give him everything he had. The ship was now almost in free fall as it descended towards Zahtienne's Triangle with the deadly pointed nose.

Chapter 60

The Son stood amidst the cheering home guard and defenders of the omega He tensed for a moment as he received a message from the Father. As he expected it was time for a conference. He turned to his officers and said,

"I am the one in difficulty, yet I always do what pleases him. It's always the way!"

John listened and cherished the words. Then the Son continued,

"Please summon John, also Andrew, Elijah, Jeremiah, Mohammed, Abraham, Shirdi-Sai-Baba, Adi Shankara, Jacob, Gabriel, and also Michael, and bid them to go immediatly to the Father in his city of Mohammed. Pedro you should stay here and literally 'hold the fort' - you are like a 'rock' - stay until I return."

In a short space of time, they were flown to the City of Mohammed. This is the city that the humans had not visited. It was a city of golden turrets and long draping flags each one with a name from every family in the world. Its roofs and walls shone like crystal while cherubim and seraphim played music and sang from the trees that filled its parks and boulevards. It was there beside five pillars of Islam that the Father though in sombre mood, joined them, embracing each one in turn. They then flew north to the Sunhead of the Father's territory where Spirinda was awaiting them. They then stood in contemplation and surveyed maps and pictures of the war damage below.

Then the Father spoke solemnly asking,

"My colleagues, what do you think of the situation?"

Shirdi-Sai –Baba a dark bearded man spoke first,

"My Lord, the situation is bad and will get worse. Even though we, I mean the humans, blunted their attack, they will rebuild and come at us again. The concept of our safe heaven is shattered and the incentive to come here will soon disappear and that will stunt creation."

Then the Son spoke,

"I believe you should hear some of what was levelled at us by Diva."

He pointed to Andrew, who nodded his head in acknowledgment and said,

"I think we should move into emergency mode and recall some of the template ships, because this aggression is bottomless. They had very high handed requests such as to Replace Miriam as Queen of Heaven and to replace the Trinity, you my Lord included, with an elected group – a Republic!"

There was a deadly silence. All eyes were wide with surprise and instantly turned towards the Father. What would be his reaction? The Father looked solemnly ahead and then he threw up his hands and said,

Okay, now listen. As you know over the eons every time the humans advance and think they are close to us, what do we do? We retreat. We cannot let them get to grips with us directly as it would spoil the magic and the test that they must endure."

Everyone nodded in agreement.

"So what is wrong with a puppet group who could be go betweens? They would represent us and in doing so may prove to be even more understanding than we! They might well serve to bring harmony, a much needed commodity and above all they will be a screen behind which we can get on with our work and relaxation. So please say that this one is being looked into and then prepare for us to take a ballot at a future meeting."

People looked stunned but also relieved that they could have their say in the process and debate. They had not had time to ponder the matter or seek legal advice nor peoples opinions.

Then Andrew outlined the criticism of Marie as Queen of Heaven to which both the Father, Son and several of the attendance immediately cried out that - this one is not negotiable!

Andrew humbly took all this down on a note pad sized laptop computer. Then the Father stood tall and splendid his hair long and dark, he had a beard, a white blouse with pants loosely tucked into low cut brown boots. With a sense of ceremony, he donned a golden cloak and silently stepped backwards into the Sun Head. As he did this, the sun began to shine brighter than ever before. Its light illuminated the valley and poured through the cracks in the Omega down towards Purgosia, the Calisto and into creation. In moments, his bearded face filled the enormous orb and his lips began to move. A voice boomed out over the world below. It rolled like thunder vibrated into the void,

"My Son you have excelled. Your Spirit proceeded and surpasses all. My people you have fought hard. I will delay just a little longer but then will be forced to command this conflict to end!"

With that the other two suns joined in the illuminations as if going on high alert.

Then the sun and the whole valley shuddered perhaps as a demonstration of the incredible Love energy that was in store. At that point, the sounds abated and the Father stepped back out from the sun head. He rejoined the group and told Andrew that at the first opportunity he was to try everything to re-establish diplomacy but also they may recall a third of the template ships – and there is to be one more meeting like this in 20 hours time. Thus congress concluded and the icons returned to their pastures.

Chapter 61

The closest triangle to the Callisto was still that of Zahtienne and he was still intent on severing the logo-optic canal. He had heard of the weakness of Diva's lasers, and feared that the Logo optic might possess the same reflective qualities. He was therefore intent on slicing it with the razor edge of his triangle before it became shielded. He was aiming for a point about half way down. It was a race to the death. If the flow were to become severed they all well knew it would cause a fatal haemorrhage to reality and they would lose the day and a lot more!

The Callisto was now in a power dive, perhaps faster than any object has ever travelled before! This attracted Zahtienne who looked up and pondered what was about to happen.

Larry on the other hand, did not know how he could challenge such a big mass with their small ship. Everina left her post and seated herself beside Larry. Dave who was now back on the podium, looked at her, was about to say something but changed his mind and just winked. She ignored him and whispered to Larry,

"Larry I love you, you can do it, I don't know how, but you can do it!"

Larry flickered his eyes her direction for a split second though concentrating on the EM/SPEC. Then he gave a small grin in recognition and called out,

"Give me velocity boys - I need more mojo!"

There was an instant hint of increased engine power and the velocity indicator raised by one notch but not enough.

Then unexpectedly there was a bellow from Paulo,

"Jude, come in Jude, we need your help"

Then as if in answer to a prayer, Rico and Janette pushed forward before anyone could stop them. Rico piped up.

"Larry put out ze lights and computers and table and no shoot de laser. Throw out things."

Dave said,

"Ten Four"

Larry responded willingly over the intercom,

"Thank you Janette and Rico, now this is urgent; Jettison unnecessary items. Kill all electro usage, computers EM/SPEC. All energy needed for velocity purposes. Major Benson please tell the cooks that includes music."

Everina grabbed the children and pushed them into seats with belts. She was just in time as there was immediate blackout and deadly silence descended except of course, the whine of the atomic powered engines straining below and a few big 'swosh' sound as crates and boxes were jettisoned.

Larry said gallantly,

"We will now fly by the seat of our pants!"

The velocity needle rose two points. The controller then began to call out,

"One hundred and fifty seconds till 'black jack' hits the Logo Optic! Can we close on him before he severs?" Larry shouted back,

"Maybe with five seconds spare!"

There was the terrible possibility that the Callisto might hit Zahtienne at the wrong point. No one could even guess if that would happen. If it's a direct hit in the wider section, they could all be thrown into the void and undoubtedly perish. Below them and closing at great speed was the deadly black point – their target.

Just then the enormous power of the Sun Heads poured down from above. The inside of the ship turned luminous and there was a surge of new energy which meant – velocity! The controller barked,

"Contact!"

Then with a thunderous crack the Callisto hit the tip of Zahtienne's triangle. The point severed and shattered in all directions. The whole triangle shuddered, and began to crumble from the point backwards. It started to swivel off course, rise up in front and then to sink backwards - crumbling as it went. Vapour poured from all sides, and hundreds of its crew jumped to get away from its collapsing structure.

Then they saw it. The logo optic was intact. The crew let out a cheer, the lights came on and the music blared. Paulo had now found Larry's ray bans and covered his ears with ear warmers. He had been almost humanised.

Then he saw the desolation outside he shouted with relief,

"Well done Jude."

Then thought better and said,

"And that goes for Dave and Larry and all the crew. Your inverted human material has polluted the negative enemy structure just like a virus."

Everina butted in for she had gathered both Janette and Rico in her arms and was whirling them around shouting,

"Look Paulo these are the real heroes."

The scene outside resembled the Hindenberg airship disaster but even on a larger scale. By now Angel Jet Skis were rising up to take supportive action shooting at as many of the enemy as possible - rendering them temporarily incapacitated and allowing them sink into the depths of the void.

Everina now clutching Larry lamented,

"Oh this is like a very bad dream. Larry please tell me it's a dream!"

Larry looked at her and with all sincerity said,

"Yes, it is a dream I mean it, it is a dream."

She felt better having his assurance and gave a faint smile. Amidst congratulations from the crew Larry made a final request,

"Skipper may we do the same for Purgosia, see Thormentus is almost there?"

Dave and Laura both agreed and so the Callisto recommenced its dive gathering speed once again.

Meanwhile far below Jill pressed her face to the side of the Jet Packer's vehicle and looked up. Something had caught her eye. It was a golden star sweeping down from the heavens. She shouted,

"Hiroshi look up it's the Callisto, driver please stop the vehicle!"

They all stared upwards through the transparent ceiling in time to see what looked like a fireworks display. They witnessed the forward guns on Thormentus's triangle shoot upwards at the Callisto. Despite the danger of rebounds Thormentus felt invincible. There was an ear splitting crescendo as the barrage erupted. Streaks shot all about the Callisto but then in the blink of an eye they, rebounded tearing Thormentus's guns apart. The Reaper was seriously damaged and stopped moving towards the town. Then slowly it began to move backwards, to the sound of cheers from the inhabitants, saints and scholars below.

Thormentus could not believe his eyes and stormed about the control room shouting,

"Move you fools, get us out of here, retreat out of range."

A Demon communications officer named Otmo Fryke entered the control centre. Despite the chaos he boldly walked up to Thormentus, saluted and delivered some important news.

"I have a message from the earthling who caused the diversion. It has been received in Morse code."

Thormentus looked up from his situations chart which was covered with ash. The other officers of his team looked with interest. The communications officer continued,

"The message stated that there are ten thousand Praque on board the Callisto because he and his accomplices had stolen it from the omega centre."

Thormentus's face lit up with excitement. The whole ship began to vibrate from his emotions. He quickly re evaluated the position and said,

"You speak of the Praque. Is that definite?" The officer nodded and added a,

"Yes Sir."

"Good. Now if I can get a hold of that Praque, as I have often said, I will change the world and its rules of engagement and even make worlds of our own!"

The officer interjected,

"Sir I beg your pardon, but if we damage the Callisto we might loose the Praque in the depths of the wilderness!"

Thormentus turned to one of his other senior commanders and barked out an order,

"Quick Lyrnex, speed up our withdrawal. I repeat disengage and fall back to equatorial position 11,000."

Then he rubbed his hands together and said in a low voice,

"If they unload in Purgosia, we will renew our attack if not we will take them as they try to exit at the umbilical. At that point they will be most vulnerable. I now want the Callisto watched on magnified screen to ascertain if the Praque has been taken off the ship or otherwise!"

Then he added,

"Major Fryke, why are you not top side seeing to things?"

Fryke hurried out of the room his black face showing a deep red flush from his master's belittlement.

On board the Callisto, Larry turned to the command group and said,

"I do not recommend that we chase this enemy any further. We have won a considerable victory and if we get in over our heads, we might end up losing the day and even the war."

Captain Dave replied,

"We agree Larry. Does anyone remember Admiral Spruance at the battle of Midway? Richard quoted that battle already. The Admiral won the day by not chasing the retreating enemy for fear of suffering casualties that would diminish his limited success. That way he was hailed as the winner and that in turn had a big impact on his enemy."

Dave therefore said,

"Larry my boy, take her in!"

However before handing back control of the ship - Larry said,

"Skipper please permit this final request."

Dave nodded but regretted his agreement because Larry said,

"Stay buckled in we are going to perform a victory roll."

Then he took the liberty of flinging the ship into a three hundred and sixty degree turn as they approached the stricken city. People did as they were told and held on tight.

Down below, Hiroshi watched with baited breath and saw all that was happening and screamed with excitement,

"Look a victory roll in a space ship - they must be nuts!"

Jill and Hiroshi looked at the sky with pride and amazement. Immediately after that bells began to ring and the sense of terror abated

Chapter 62

An escort of Jet Packers rose to meet the arrival of the Callisto. One of the escort who introduced himself as commander spoke over radio He said that they could only be afforded a brief stop. He then gave a friendly salute and led them in to their landing place.

Hiroshi had already decided that he would return with the Callisto. It was a difficult decision but both he and Jill were fully reconciled to the choice. On the good side, Hiroshi told her he would reunite when back on earth and this prospect eased his departure. Jill hoped that her embodied self would be polite to Hiroshi, and not be prone to earthly whims that might spoil the sincerity of their meetings. She also hoped that earth Jill had not been approached by that awful Louis O'Meara who had pestered her for years. As far as she could remember, she did not marry him or anyone else, but for that he could not be sure! City hall did not have a record of any wedding but they had been known to make mistakes. Hiroshi also weighed up that if he did not return, he would be designated as a missing person and his whereabouts could not be explained. This would cause his friends lots of problems with E/USARUS. However, there was a disturbing side to it all - he could not know to what era he would return and would he even find Jill? That was the gamble he had to take! There was a group of singers in flowing gowns that appeared out of nowhere. This time around there was no official reception for the crew of the Callisto but their close relations had come to see them off. Amongst them were Dan, Maria, Patty and family, also there was Amy and Zachary and both Everina and Hiroshi's families. There was also a pretty dark skinned couple with an eager look on their faces. As the doors opened Larry alighted. He was feeling sad at the thought of leaving this exciting world and in his heart would like to stay. He just had no ambition to return to the hassle that the Universe had to offer. The war of the Gods was terrifying, but it did not include the spectre of death and this was a considerable advantage. So despite the war, he felt that he was about to leave pleasure-island after a vacation and did not want to go home. He envied what Dan, Maria, and also his two sisters, Jill and Amy had achieved. They were in Utopia or just on the brink of being there. Their very souls were on a new mission, learning how to accomplish things while remaining at rest in the Son.

Everina came out behind Larry along with Janette and Rico. Just then there was a shout that came from the dark skinned couple. They bounded forward saying,

"Are you Janette and Rico? Yes you are! You must be? We have found you. We have found you at last!"

The children looked in amazement holding on tightly to Everina. A tall woman, Zelda Tannings, who was with the couple said,

"Janette, Rico meet you parents."

Everina felt their tiny hands release their grip on her, perhaps for ever. Then they ran like gazelles throwing themselves into their parent's arms. For a few tender moments they all began to weep and hug. Dave came forward with two Callisto service medals for special performance over and above the call of duty. These were pinned on both their tiny blouses and a salute of was given by all present. Then one of the cooks came out with the ice cream that had been promised, he had made it when the power had been turned on. Everina wrote her address on a sheet of paper and gave it to the parents and said if ever you are on earth do look me up. The she giggled at her own gullibility and hugged them both good bye. With tears in her eyes she stared as the children waved and melting into the crowd.

Then the slim figures of Pepitra and Agnes Palcveska appeared. She was the girl who had helped Everina with her shopping. George Kuhn and Dan's old friend Jurek from the college of cosmic physics were also there. People hugged and exchanged gifts. Some gave their wrist timers as souvenirs as these made pretty gifts with their dials almost fully illuminated in the colours of the rainbow. However the golden segment was only slightly lit, because as already said; they would not be permitted to visit the Father's land of Mohammed.

Then Agnes came forward holding a gift. It was a magnificent Excalibur. It shone with a light so bright that people squinted. Its metal glistened like it was coated in crushed diamonds and the handle appeared to be made of material like ivory. Engraved in small writing, evidently in English, Latin, Hebrew and Arabic were the words, which Agnes read out,

"In appreciation the gallant action performed in the name of freedom by theCaptain and Crew of the good ship Callisto AK 171 - from the People of Purgosia and the Omega Presidium".

A list of crewmembers including the three terrorists was engraved in a line down the centre of both sides of the blade. Then Agnes sheathed the sword and handed it to Larry and said,

"Laurence Coughlin, Son of Daniel and Maria Coughlin-De Laundre, as you were commended by the Captain and crew for helming the ship during the recent crisis and for taking defensive action in time of need - you are here by bequeathed with this sword, to carry and to parry in times of need. Guard this with all your strength for it is made of the most precious 'de-material' known in this dynasty and that is called Prayque."

There was a gasp from the crowd. Then she presented the sword to Larry, who bent down on one knee and accepted it like he was a knight of old. His action was reflex, but it looked the part. He then stood up and raised the sword for all to see. Its sparkling texture glistened even more with the movement and the onlookers clapped with appreciation. Then smaller replica tie pin or broaches of the sword were presented to Captains and crew and some children came forward with a bouquet of "Trinitivias" for Vice Captain Laura. She was told that these flowers were eternal and will remain fresh forever and to keep them just for her home.

Larry turned to face the Captains and the group and held up the sword for all to see clearly and said,

"This comes as a great surprise. Thank you Agnes and the people of Pugosia for these gifts, but for my part I feel the Captain and the Callisto should have this sword and not me!"

There was an immediate outcry from the group en totale,

"No Larry it is now yours, keep the Excalibur, it's yours."

One of the military people approached the Captain, and said that they had removed the stolen Praque and would be transported aloft immediately. Then some of the families donated food saying that when they arrived in the Universe they will be very hungry. However, the ship did have dried ration on board to cover such an emergency but the extra food was welcome. The question was what would a reverted quark cake look like in reality? Would it just disappear in a stream of energy?

Hiroshi hugged and kissed his wife and with tears in his eyes boarded the ship. While this was happening, the sky was filled with activity. All of a sudden the ether was filled with a very loud buzzing sound. Some of the crew thought it sounded like a blitz from World War II. A monstrous dark green ship appeared bearing the insignia of a Maroon triangle with a lamb and a silver star. This was as large as the Uclidia and big enough to take on any black triangle. This was the first of the link ships, arriving to defend the city. Sirens went off in Purgosia and people could be seen cheering their arrival. It was exciting just to be there, Larry was sure he just did not want to leave. The giant ship circled the city and then took up a position above the Sangrias and in sight of the metropolis below. Word had it that the rest were on the way but were being delayed.

The city under the protective dome was not quite as enticing as when they had arrived. In a sense Larry consoled himself that they had already got the best out of heaven for the moment that is! They had been so well looked after and now it seemed a good a time to depart.

Just then the singers began a farewell lament. It was soft and alluring, and sounded like the Hawaiian wedding song. The words "Sweet Aloha" could be heard. They were given the all clear for departure. The doors closed Lionel was back to navigate once again. The Captain once again became a man of prominence - all hands awaiting his command.

"Ernst – all systems go,"

Then he smiled and barked out,

"Mr Benson, please check for stowaways."

With that the ships engines whined and it began to move. This time there would be no golden pallet it was to be a DIY journey. At first their departure was painfully slow. Paulo and their friends could be seen waving for quite some time. Then as the ship gained speed Purgosia shrank and all that remained was the vibrant maroon triangle and the shining arc rising from the Chasms.

Chapter 63

The interior of the ship was buzzing with activity. They quickly left the maroon triangle and slid over the apex of the blue. Now back in more familiar territory they were on the road for home give or take a few inconveniences one being the pursuing enemy with vengeance on their minds. With all that was happening there was no guarantee that Sprinda or the Citadel would be able to look after them any more!

As per usual meetings were called to discuss operations. There were maintenance reports and engine tests, and briefings with the crew. Having been so long out of touch with reality, there was a danger that they might not respond effectively on return. Dr Mantz and Dr Burnette were concerned that the crew's muscular strength might have dissipated due to different gravitational circumstances. All they could do was insist on exercise and leave it to chance!

Hiroshi was overcome with melancholy and retreated to his enclosure and sat with head in hands. Richard and Larry knowing his plight followed to make sure that he was not overcome with grief. When they arrived, Hiroshi was meditating evoking Buddha and imploring his return to life when they enter the umbilical. Perspiration gathered on his brow and a tear rolled down his cheek. Richard tried to cheer him up by reminding him that if things go wrong he will be caught in the flux and whisked back to the Chasms and to Jill. So either ways he was in a win-win situation. At that moment Everina arrived and immediately hastened to Hiroshi and caressed him. She wiped his brow with a paper napkin taken from her pocket and said with a smile,

"Jill is waiting for you at both ends of a rainbow. You will find her no matter what, so take control and live the stress; it's not bad, it's just a trial. We know you can do it because you have always been strong and determined so be that old Hiroshi we know. Take a lesson from above and trust that is what we have all been taught up there!"

She joked that he better look brave as Jill could be watching him now on some 'Purgosian gizmo' or other. Hiroshi began to smile and then to laugh at himself, and then he burst out,

"Sorry you guys, I guess the old fear is that I get back to earth and find that she has already married."

Larry giggled, saving the day. They all shared the humour and began to laugh. Hiroshi for one moment looked hurt, but then he too giggled but than began a bout of uncontrolled laughter. With that episode the worst was over for Hiroshi, and he departed with his friends chatting away and asking about what they had experienced up above in bright blue yonder.

Chapter 64

All seeing Thormentus now knew that the Praque had being removed from the Callisto. He also had heard about the Excalibur and replicas and realised they were made of Praque and therefore valuable beyond belief. Down in the work rooms of the Pit, Zahtienne's new guns were completed and many were already transported up to the damaged triangles. Even as repairs were being carried out, Thormentus called his officers conference - though it was most inconvenient for some. Diva and Zahtienne arrived, both in a state of agitation. The atmosphere was tense and no one spoke waiting for Thormentus's first words. He began quietly,

"Fellow warriors of the cause, need I tell you, your performance was disastrous." Then he raised his voice,

"Why in the first place did some blithering idiot advise me about the visitors? What did they expect from me - a miracle?"

He gave a fiendish grin,

"It was better that I slept and never knew about these perpetrators of the void. But ye had decided; we will tell the great Thormentus and he will put things right."

Then he roared,

"Well you were wrong I did not put things right and why not? It's because of you, and you and you!"

He pointed a crooked finger at Lyrnex, Fryke and in various directions but carefully avoiding both Diva or Zahtienne and continued his sentence,

"Have botched it up!"

The officers cowed in deadly silence. Then he said in a softer voice,

"Now you will methodically re-organize, and you will have an opportunity to regain my respect. Here I go again, the plan is as follows."

He sat back and looked at Diva for help as usual to read his mind and develop the strategy. Being well able to do so she promptly spoke in her usual shrill voice,

"The Reaper is to block the entrance to the umbilical. Our other two are more damaged and slower to repair so we will be used as shields. We will then follow and close in behind the Callisto and it will then be in a trap. Now there is one other aspect to consider. The blue triangle itself might cause us grief if we pass over – of this we are not yet sure! So we will close in at the last minute to minimize the time we are over that dangerous territory."

The Callisto was now travelling along the central spine of the triangle. This time around things looked quite different. The sea had taken on a grey blue hue and perhaps a great storm was in the making. There were already some large waves moving from north to south of which many will crash straight into the entrance of the umbilical. They had progressed nearly three quarters way when in an alarmed tone the navigator announced,

"Enemy sighted behind."

Two had risen from the depths and were closing in to port and starboard. Both these enemy objects were in tatters but still active and therefore a formidable obstacle not to be underestimated. To make matters worse Lionel had something else to say,

"Another ship is up ahead and attempting to block our exit!"

The Reaper had now appeared travelling towards the 11 o'clock position No sooner had they made that sighting then there was a broadside from the Reaper. Several of the shots hit them mid-ships. The effect was terrifying. The ship shuddered from bow to stern. Someone shouted,

"Why did that not rebound?"

All power was temporarily lost. They were plunged into blackness and an icy chill swept through the ship. The computers began to make a whining noise an officer reported excitedly,

"Captain we are also receiving what might be a screech attack!"

After some fast keyboard work the computers seemed to recover and slowly drag back to normal aided by their astro-virus scans which by now had become more active.

Then suddenly the ship became filled with what looked black hail followed by roaring hot brimstones that tore through the interior knocking the crew over. Richard had been flung against one of the walls receiving a severe bump from a fire extinguisher. Dire emergency alarms were sounding and fire crews were working to fever pitch. Ernst staggered to his store room and with his team had emergency foil sheeting rushed up to cover the perforations. He hastily mobilised the Cadets to help and with broad tape and they fixed the sheets in place. There where twenty four holes to be patched and there could be more to come! He then went to his engine room to retrieve some thicker metal sheets for welding in place at the first opportunity.

The din was overcome by the voice of Dave,

"Chief is there any casualties?"

"Chief Ryner reporting; Sir there is fourteen with lacerations and concussion cases. No fatalities but lots to clean up!"

The Skipper said,

Thanks for that Dave, now Lionel don't slow - retain maximum velocity and head straight for the target.

On board the flagship, Thormentus worried that he might not get to block their path; gave an order.

"Launch the hyper stealth fighters"

"Under the command of both Major Otmo Fryke the attack will penetrate the Callisto stun its crew and collect the Excalibur's large and small. Then destroy the navigation and direct the Ship down into our valley of tears. All this activity is to be done so fast that their help will not have time to rescue. I will also be with you in my blade the Amadeus. Now prepare to launch".

Fifty one wafer thin blades bristling with warheads, antennas and new complex weaponry roared off to tackle the advancing Callisto.

It was just at that crucial moment that Delia unlocked the hold that imprisoned Ham and Rap. She flung the door open and whispered,

"This is it Rap, you are free, let's take the ship!"

She led them out onto the lighted corridor. There was no one in sight so she led him to Larry's quarters. There beside his Hybo was the Excalibur in its leather scabbard. She thrust the treasure into Raps hands and said,

"This is you may have heard, is made of Praque!"

Raps eyes widened with anticipation and a grim spread across his long bony face. He grunted and said in a menacing voice,

"Are you sure? If that is true it means it can do untold damage if used correctly. Okay, let's take the ship then we can turn it over to Thormentus and collect his reward."

Dalia with a puzzled look on her face asked,

"How do you know there will be a reward?"

Rap made an impatient reply,

"Because Dalia, we will bargain beforehand. If they do not agree, we will threaten to fly through the umbilical where they cannot get it, or if all comes to the worst, we will detonate everything into smithereens; that is after we have departed in one of their emergency escape craft."

Dalia smiled because that was the sort of language that she liked to hear. Within a few moments, they entered the engine room and with the point of the Excalibur levelled at Ernst's throat demanded cooperation. Ernst put his hand to his chest to relieve a tightening that had suddenly occurred. There was little he could do but obey. He told the crew to do as bid and thus the culprits gained control!

Without hesitation Ham and Rap threw every switch in the opposite direction. There was a high-pitched screeching noise the immediately the engines shut down. Ernst covered his ears and began to cry saying,

"Mein Got, you 'vill destoy everyzing!"

Ham hit him hard and growled,

"Shut up old man, you won't be needed any more so look out!"

Then Dalia grabbed the intercom and shouted,

"Captain and crew I am your colleague Dalia and I speak on behalf of Thormentus. This ship is now under his command. You are to surrender immediately; if not we will kill Ernst and his crew one at a time till you do as we say. You have no choice as we have possession of the precious Excalibur that can sever your plasma body in one stroke."

Chapter 65

Back in Stratus Seven, the damage was rapidly being repaired. Miriam and even the Son were working flat out to help the injured. The Gods were flexing their territories to assist with movement. All transport was now receiving super-gravitational assistance to make the journey faster. The template ships had been delayed but were now on their way. Their great Sunheads were moving in consultation with each other and their thoughts and questions were being communicated directly to .com/saint. Pedro though it was time for another meeting of the giants.

This meeting was for the same Committee of the Most High as had met before. It would take place as before on the shoulder plateau adjacent to his great golden orb. The Father stood there waiting on their arrival. Beside him was a table with a cauldron and a crystal sphere and a map like a horoscope. He invited his Son to speak first.

The Son said that the attack had shaken the very core of their existence. Their old enemy had resurfaced and hit them hard. The questioned was why had they not addressed the problem sooner, rather than letting aggression break out? They must have known that the visitor's arrival had opened old wounds. If we had been vigilant we could have returned the visitors at Purgosia and not allowed them travel any higher. Now we have inadvertently been our own worst enemy! Now where do we go from here?

One person suggested that they fragment some of their territories into one massive triangle and sweep the void clean – an army that no one could defeat. Another said this might win the day but the reformation process would be long and tedious and full of unforeseen difficulties. What would happen if some part of their essence would not re-unite, then a whole new struggle would kindle in our midst?

Another option was to shrug it off and hope it would not re occur again. This was quickly rejected as derelict. Another option was more deadly. It suggested they withdraw the sacred triangles of nature thus severing the Universe and casting it adrift to its demise. The remaining humans would by then have lost their inheritance as blessed offspring which means they could not come into the fold as one body at convergence time. A pity, but instead they could be granted entry on an individual basis only. They could be withdrawn immediately and the void closed and crushed out of existence taking with it all the troublemakers. We would then have a secure citadel a fortress Paradise, an island haven that could not be harmed. We could then consider making a new void and consummating a new creation!

Spirinda sprang to the defence,

"I know I speak for the Son and myself when I say - how can you think like that, if termination were to happen the further development of humanity would be discontinued, and those who had lived so far would be on the divine welfare? Think of the cost! How much love would we have to pour on them as they would be so individually isolated and out of their depth for all eternity, a burden on one and all. This would also be an act of cowardice and make us no better than our enemies. It was not a solution and it could bring opposition from our own ranks with detrimental consequences!"

Then she said that to terminate creation would be immoral, and would be the first flaw ever in our divine nature. A new creation without a demon in the works would yield a soft child that could never be an AMGOD. Creation could only successfully occur as an antidote to adversity. She said that the Son and she loved and believed in the current humanity and would be desolated if latter solution were adapted.

Several others said they agreed with Spirinda and the Father said he was glad they had come to that conclusion. Thus the question of cosmic abortion was eliminated. Then they got down to other immediate needs.

Then they agreed to attempt special protection for the Callisto until back in the Universe. Then they reviewed Stephens report on Diva's earlier demands and this included some talk about the proposed Republic. Next they planned to contain Zahtienne's forces but then to open fresh negotiations. The next intention was to offer them psychotherapy assistance and a supply of light and energy like they never had before. Then they decided it might also be possible to arrange host some of them in Purgosia in an effort to find common ground and compromise. The need for vast improvement in security measures was the final item on the agenda.

When that was finished he took grey snow-like crystals of nothingness from the cauldron beside him and rubbed them on the transparent sphere. He gazed into the sphere his face reflecting pixels of light that radiated form its interior. Then he withdrew, looked satisfied and closed the conference.

Chapter 66

The flotilla of Template ships were beginning to arrive for 'Operation Clean Sweep' but their priority was defence of the 'District of Purgosia'. The first to be freed to go to the rescue of the Callisto was commanded by an officer named Johann Baptista. He was one who specialised in spreading the word into the unknown, a true pioneer at heart. Omega communications were able to give him a progress report. In moments he had glided over the blue triangle and got the Callisto in sight. However they were slightly curtailed by Diva and Zahtienne's ships - still two formable obstacles. As soon as he ascertained the latest state of play Baptist reported to .Com/saint,

"This is operation 'Clean Sweep', Baptista reporting. Please connect me with Iesous!"

The Son came on the intercom,

"John, it's a while since I was called that!"

Baptista replied,

"Likewise, it's a while since you called me John!"

Then he laughed and said in a serious voice,

"We are blocked by two black triangles with a kamikaze attitude. The Callisto has done well, but has terrorists on board and is being buzzed by fifty-one blades. As my other ships have not yet arrived I will have to something alone, so I reckon some precise shooting might help."

The Son agreed and said,

"Okay give them some Baptismal fire!"

The Callisto, now under control of the terrorists; hung stationary in the ether. Several blades arrived along side and shot out suction clamps against the side of the ship. The main entrance was then forced open. Amidst a rush of escaping air several black cloaked figures stormed inside led by Commander Fryke and followed by Thormentus.

The crew of the Callisto were gathered in the navigation area and that was quite a lot of people. Some were locked in adjoining quarters and others in sick bay. Rap and Dalia stood with the Excalibur pointing menacingly while Ham had a handgun and ammunition that he found in the armoury. Dalia grabbed Everina by the hair saying that she would kill her if the crew did not do as told. As the gun was inverted Everina notice that it looked very soft in Ham's hand – it probably would not work!

At that moment the intruders burst into the main concourse. They looked so desperate even Rap and Ham were aghast at the sight. There were a dozen of them all about six feet high and wearing black triangular capes. Most of their faces were ash white and their eyes were sunken. Several of them had beards, one was a women and two were dark skinned. Then from their midst, the tallest figure pushed forward and yelped out loud,

"I am Thormentus,"

His piercing eyes were bloodshot yet hypnotizing.

"I am the one who defies what you all stand for. Do not dare obstruct me in any way or you will be destroyed in moments. Obey what I tell you, or you will spend Eternity in captivity. Who is your leader?"

Rap interrupted the flow shouting,

"We are the ones who captured the ship for you, and see here is the Excaliber."

Thormentus glared at them and said 'good work' but who is your leader?

Dave stepped forward and said,

"I'm the skipper."

"Skipper what is that, is it a fish? But no, you look like the Capitan though you are half pink and blue, what an infliction." Then he laughed. And bellowed,

"Now hear this you are all hostages of our state. I want you to accompany us back to Purgosia to collect the Praque that was removed. They will hand it over rather than have their pets keel hauled and killed. They cannot refuse as this is against their modus operandi. Also you are to hand over all tie pins or any Praque material you have."

Then he gave a loud laugh and his cronies joined in. At that very moment, a salvo from Baptista's cruiser burst among the waiting blades. With that Larry leapt across the room and knocked Rap to the floor. He grabbed the Excalibur and swung it at Dalia, who took the flat of it on the face and let Everina go. Everina then turned and flung herself at Dalia and caught her in a vicelike grip.

Dalia screamed and kicked but stopped when she saw Larry now had the sword and was pointing it at Thormentus. Then Thormentus clicked his fingers and three of his troopers came forward drawing swords of their own. Their weapons seemed to be split in two parts and shimmer with fire. Thormentus also produced a sword of his own and shouted,

Burn that infidel, burn him!"

Everina shouted,

"No, Larry, No!"

To late to stop, Larry continued his action.

There was another round of fire from Baptista and more blades were damaged but he also had to contain the other two triangles that were beginning to return fire. Then Richard remembered the fire extinguisher that hurt his head. He grabbed it from its fitting and fired it point blank at the intruders. Several other crew members did the same and some grabbed flares and began to discharge them at the enemy - turning the scene into one of sheer chaos. The head cook bolted from the galley and returned flinging salt from a huge container. At contact with the salt the beetle troopers began to sizzle. Their arms became weak and some dropped their weapons. Lionel though feeling poorly threw his set square like a Frisbee, whacking the face of one of the enemy. Ernst and his team began to work their way back to the engine room to re-start the turbines. The enemy retreated to the exit where one of the villains lunged towards Larry who parried the impact. Then he took a swing at two others knocking them backwards having sliced across both their chests. The sword was well balanced and was easy to wield.

Another salvo arrived from Baptist and Blade evaporated into nothingness. The troopers now quite worried backed off but Thormentus, seeing Larry's defiance, moved closer in the fray swinging his own sword in deadly circles. Larry found himself slashing and thrusting almost out of control. Thormentus realised that this was not an ordinary adversary and no ordinary weapon either. He could not swing his own sword as energetically but he had the advantage of split blades and flaming steel. He was by now at the exit, beaten back by the dexterity and power of Larry's Sword mixed with foam and flare.

So deprived of victory and with a roar of anger Thormentus flung his sword at Larry. The sword hit him in the shoulder pinning him to the wall. One prong was firmly fixed above and the other below his armpit. The flames from the sword scorched his face and arms. There was no pain yet he knew he was burning. He could not move and the painless sensation was terrifying.

Rap, Ham and Delia feverishly followed the demons even to the extent of jumping into a ship despite a voice saying there is no room. Rap who was last, stopped for a moment, turned and looked at Larry's plight laughed and departed. Richard rushed forward and hit the control button closing the door instantly tearing a piece of black material from a trooper's cloak.

Everina and Richard eased the sword from Larry's shoulder and let laid him gently on the floor. A medical team arrived and gave instant treatment. Oddly, his skin was cut but not burned. Another good thing he thought; was that bleeding did not occur in this environment. He was hastily taken to the sick bay, mumbling as he went that he was fine, fit and well, and wanting to continue the fight. With that he passed out. While all this was happening, the Callisto now back under Dave and Ernst's control began to move again, gathered speed and shooting straight towards the opening.

Chapter 67

The intercom clicked on, it was Dave, and he said once again as often before,

"Damage casualty list and report needed?"

An officer sprinted to his side saluted, and said that the ships superstructure was undamaged. The blades are not following but are towing three to safety and it appears two others had disintegrated as a result off direct hits. The sick bay is full but no serious injuries. Lionel was next and reported,

"Triangle still attempting to block us and two others are not in pursuit. The friendly fire came from a template ship 10 km's to aft. I think they are laying down a corridor of fire to allow us escape!"

Larry was soon given permission to leave the infirmary. Everina got leave from her post to assist him. Their first task was this time to lock the precious Excalibur back in the Hybo. With that done and with time to spare they headed towards the stern of the ship. Everina thought how crazy this is. Here I am a simple girl who likes home and family but now travelling on the very edge of eternity with the man of my dreams.

Larry also felt romantic. He wanted to grab Everina and smother her with kisses but he knew given the circumstances that it might spoil their very special relationship. So as it happened, earth etiquette prevailed and he settled for a good heart to heart conversation. She talked with such animation that he squinted his eyes and looked at her through a haze. Through blurred vision she resembled an unfinished Mona Lisa. She looked back and said,

"What are you doing, you're not listening to what I am saying."

Then she laughed and did the same blurting out,

"You look like the Hulk without make up!"

They both giggled and she punched his sore shoulder and said,

"Time's up we better get back."

Up in the highest a traveller was concluding a journey that took him from Purgosia to the zenith of Divinity. It was Jude and he was tired and he was responding to many calls including that of Paulo when he had been under attack. As he hitched a ride towards the Sunhead above the city of Mohammed he said to himself,

"Tar nation Jude, here you are on another daunting quest, probably too late to help all those who trust you, but I must, I must or I'll bust."

With that, the vehicle stopped at the parking lot under the blinding light of the orb. He thanked the group of saints who had given him the ride, and turned towards the Father's abode bowed and said in his thoughts,

"Father almighty, excuse me but here I am again with a list so long."

He held up a golden tablet that contained his requests and continued,

"One extraordinary wish is that the Callisto be saved, just as your friend Paulo had asked."

The orb began to shimmer and two figures emerged. It was the Father and Miriam who was at his right hand side. He responded to Jude by walking down to him and embracing.

"Now Miriam what will we do with this fellow who never gives up? Will we tell him to take his place in the line?"

Jude actually looked frightened.

Miriam stopped the Father,

"Easy now, that's not fair - teasing my good friend."

Jude looked on wide-eyed. The Father then put a friendly arm around Jude's shoulder and said,

"Firstly, I will give priority to Paulo's request though it comes a little late. I will also grant all the others immediately, and on the condition that you join me in Mohammed tonight for some refreshment because I think you need it!"

Jude smiled his first smile in a month and cried out,

"Yes Lord, yes I will, thank you a thousand times and thank you also my good lady. La ora na."

Chapter 68

Now back on board the Reaper Thormentus summoned his squadron leaders Darrell, Lynex and Fryke and then said in a jeering tone,

"We will probably not block their escape at this stage because of cover by that Template Ship so Commander Darrell, to assist you this time I will release the more Hyper Blades. They are so thin they may not be detected and just in case, we will create a lot of fire as a diversion. Your purpose is to follow the Callisto into the umbilical and blast them back before they reach the sanctuary of the rotating arc. Even if they manage to get in the arc, follow them!"

Darrell was not amused and replied,

"Sir may I remind you of your very own warnings to us in the past, when you said that we can only enter the universe psychologically but never in plasma form. We could face annihilation!"

Thormentus did not let him finish, "Darrell if you don't get a move on, I will have you whipped and keel hauled. Face annihilation here and now or scram!"

Darrell spat back,

"I'll go now but if I live I'll tell Old Nick what you said."

Thormentus looked like he would erupt and opened his mouth to speak but obviously thought better.

At last the Callisto was now making good headway. Lionel the navigator alerted the skipper,

"Captain, it looks like we might get to the portal first. There are two entrances we must select the one that flows back into the Universe – not out! Which one do you think?"

Larry joined the group now gathered around the EM/SPEC. It showed that entrance on the right seemed to be receiving the brunt of the outflow. It looked like the way to go?

"Okay Lionel, go for the one on the right."

Suddenly Lionel began to shake, his face was ashen and he could not remain at the controls and staggered back assisted by two crew members.

Dave called out,

"Larry, please take the controls again."

Once again Larry was thrust into the driving seat. It now seemed their choice of entrance was correct as a miraculous swarm of white doves appeared circling the right hand entrance - a good omen indeed. With a mighty roar and with no blades in sight, they plunged into the star-studded tube. Far behind them Baptista was being reinforced by several more Template ships and the triangles were now on permanent retreat.

Now in the tunnel, people watched the black circular canopy close over their heads. Then they felt the enormous lift and drop as the waves came up below them. Then they got a last glimpse of the bright blue world of the giants that they were leaving behind. They were turning their backs once and for all on Aladdin's Cave with all its heavenly riches. That was their last view of the future before they hit the proverbial present.

Now the crest of a mighty wave loomed behind them blocking out the remains of the sacred light. The ship hurled forward and began to free-fall. The crest rolled after them like a billow of dust from a volcano. A bright disk of light appeared up ahead, the Captain said very rapidly,

"Listen up everyone. We are now literally moments from our last barrier, the membrane between our two worlds. Those of you, who wish should pray like heck for a safe delivery of Hiroshi. Both Laura and I wish to say that it has been an honour to share such an enormous experience with you, the finest people I have ever met, and let's keep it that way, God Speed!"

Don Travis was already busy and Nadine Baker was also making offering on Hiroshi's behalf. The EM/SPEC began to hum and click more than usual giving its first physical reading in quite some time.

"Temperature is now registering at infinity. Time is 100/sec to Creation. . There is Evidence of Strong interaction still registering. Electro Magnetic Force is now predominant. W and Z Particles are growing in proportion. Higgs Bossons are evident at 1% Magnitude but reducing rapidly. Velocity, is at the new dimensional crate of C^3 and dropping."

Then it began to show an immense radiation reading. The reading was so high that Quan Chow, one of the physicists, wondered if the ship was about to destructed.

"When we went through the membrane on the way out we were moving with it as it expanded. We exceeded the speed of light just enough to break out and it worked. Now this time we are going the opposite direction. The impact will be far greater as we are travelling in excess of 300,000 k/per/sec and therefore will hit the wall expanding towards us at the same speed. It seems that all light is travelling outwards towards the threshold of the universe. Any alternative light bends and joins the outward trek. Our impact will be like a diver in a pool and will cause light distortion in a major way. Be prepared for the unexpected!"

Dave shouted,

"Thanks Chow for that and this next wave will carry us through – everyone buckle up, all systems go. Maximum Velocity, turn on Automatic Pilot, steady as she goes!"

Larry attached himself to the console prepared for the impact.

Everina equally well strapped in, whispered to herself,

"Good bye, my marsh mallow man."

Chapter 69

Back up in Purgosia, things had returned to normal. Dan, Maria and Jill were driving back to their home in the Sangrias. They were feeling sad and dejected at the departure of Larry and Hiroshi and friends.

Dan said with slow deliberation,

"You know the Callisto left us behind on earth when they left. Then they zipped forward and we all met up here.

Jill piped up impatiently,

"Yeh' Dad carry on!"

"Well then why did they not find themselves here also?

Jill shot back,

"Because, they were maybe saints by then!"

Then she laughed and added,

"But I doubt it."

Dan was unimpressed and continued his line of thought,

"This suggests that there is a flaw in the fabric. Maybe they were never really came and it was just a fantasy! Now they are about to go back in time and the question is that will we also be taken back and wake up back home?"

Maria said quite loudly,

"No Dan. Not this time, you are still a dreamer. This home we have is just right. I'm not giving it up till we move up above!"

Then Jill looked at the sky,

"Look you guys, there is something different about the Arc. As Dan was driving, it was Maria who had the better view and spotted the difference,

"Dan, it's going in reverse – in the out, and out the in!"

Dan just smiled.

Chapter 70

There was a shudder and a familiar high-pitched whine and a bouncing skidding feeling as the Callisto accelerated down the front of the next wave - which in turn had waves. There was a rhythmic, thump, thump, as it made impact with various surfaces.

Mantz who was glued to the EM/SPEC shouted,

"Strange phenomena appearing – time reversal evident – don't follow I repeat time reading minus 6,000 D2 and dropping fast. Now 4,200, 3,400, 3,001, 2,222

The lights went out, there was a flash and a crack and a jolt like they had never felt before. With that the Callisto was hurled back to universal reality. As before people lost consciousness.

Hiroshi shouted,

"Good bye," and then he too fainted.

This was the moment that they broke through the 15+ billion light year perimeter of the universe. Instantaneously a thin bead of brane light, shot up through the ship. It was made of every colour that light can produce and it split into hundreds of shafts that ricochet about the interior. It shattered into particles like snow flakes and seemed to be attempting to make a picture of reality. Then it succeeded as each and every particle belonging to the ship and its human contents became hitched to the brane - which in turn became part of the arc. Then for a fleeting moment there was a freeze; a split moment when everything stood frozen in time. Then the light reversed its direction and flowed.

Larry who was also unconscious dreamt that he was swimming in the lake in the Chasms of Yahweh. This was his last memory of the seventh dimension but then he recalls being hurled back from where he had come. Amazingly Larry was quick to waken perhaps it was the violence of his dream. Slowly people began to come around. Hiroshi's mind was in a whirl. He felt like a rag doll being hurled around in a washing machine. He felt sick and out of control. When eventually he opened his eyes he thought he would be in the Chasms - Grand Central Nation. He looked around for Jill. He looked for the arrival deck of the arc and for the welcoming crowds. For a fleeting moment he thought he could see Jill. Then she was gone, and so were the saints and the scholars. He could see figures, but they were huddled in seats in most drab surroundings. Everything was grainy and flickering, and he felt his body had been packed into a press and squeezed. He felt dejected and disappointed.

Then he realised he should not be sad because he was still on the Callisto! He was alive! He could feel his pulse beat with enormous rapidity, which meant he lived! He was a human once again, but sadly he felt like a trapped mammal in a pool. He felt his stomach rumbling and a pain in his head but suddenly he loved it! Then putting all the discomfort aside he cried out,

"I'm alive, I'm alive. Oh thank you Father- Buddha I'm alive!"

On the outward journey, people had shed their humanity the opposite was more difficult. They missed the sense of freedom that he had enjoyed with disembodiment and now must be contend with incredibly poor vision compared with the clarity of sight that they had enjoyed. This was the restricted world that they had awakened to. Then he remembered the terrible threat from the demon predators.

All around the ship great bubbles of light swirled from the impact of their arrival in terra firma. Some bubbles entered the ship and caused chaos with visibility. Any person in the path of chaotic light had their features distorted and their faces spread all over its surface. It looked so amazing and caused massive distress to the victim. Then as quick as they appeared the bubbles dissolved. Chow who had wakened shouted,

"Those bubbles mercifully slowed our re entry."

Dave shook his head in amazement and submission but then focussed on the EM/SPEC and saw an amazing sight. Blades were following and even at that they were being reformed like objects emerging from a waterfall. He shouted the alarm,

"Bandits closing from the stern, Red alert, resume battle stations. How did those bandits in tin cans get this far?"

Ernst re commenced checking the oxygen pumps they will from now on be crucial to the trip. They appeared to be functioning at about 60% efficiency. Dr Burnette dashed to Hiroshi and gave him a split second examination and pronounced that he was alive. Then the moment of joy was shattered as they were hit with the first shots from the blades. It damaged the navigation fins but the ship just kept going. Larry jammed the control in a spiral twist with a sudden slow down and then acceleration. Two of the crew climbed up to the laser and commenced firing. At that moment there was a sudden chirping sound. Kiki had returned by some very strange means. Laura forgetting about the crisis on hand let her out a cry of delight.

Larry now cranked the Callisto to starboard. The enemy ship now looked enormous and was going to shoot at them at point blank range. For a terrible moment they could see the giant figure of the pilot peering down on them with a look of determination. Inside was Major Fryke, a larger than life patriotic demon intent on self-sacrifice. He did not know where his shattered remains would go, but he believed that he would find eternal glory in his ultimate 'Pitousia' yet if he lived he will try and roast Thormentus!

Larry attempted to change direction but the Blade was too close. It fired a shot that tore a very large gash in the port side. Just like the Omega experience; there was an immediate suction drawing people and everything with it. Sirens went off and because of the enormity of the gash foam began to in pour automatically. Emergency crew ran to assist shore up the area but to everyone's dismay both Everina and Richard had been dragged towards a gaping hole. Richard grabbed Everina's wrist and with the other hand grabbed the leg of some fixed seating. The stabilizing foam now caused them to gasp for air but still gallantly Richard held on. Others set up a chain to reach Richard first. Some threw nets and ropes in his direction. Hiroshi yelled,

"Hold on, stay just like that, hold on."

Benson and he dashed to the lower hold. In moments they were inside the escape and rescue module and with a hiss were ejected out of the ship. Benson was more familiar with the controls and in moments directed the tiny module along in the slip stream of the Callisto. Up above the Callisto red laser fire from the turret was keeping the Blade at bay. He increased propulsion and began to move up the starboard side till they were at the damaged area. They could now see Everina's legs dangling dangerously in the vacuum. The giant blade was looming beside them, they could be wiped out at any moment. Benson yelled,

"Larry hard to port."

The ship swerved and Benson followed. The Blade did not expect the manoeuvre that almost turned then in the opposite direction, and streaked by. Hiroshi manipulated two great claws designed for repairs. He did so in such a way that one closed on Everinas legs and the other her upper body.

Benson then yelled into the intercom,

"Larry, Dave – tell Richard to let her go now!"

Almost immediately Everina came sliding out while still covered in foam. Hiroshi continued to manipulate the claws as gently as possible. There was a look of pain and panic on Everina's face as the hard metal held her fast. She then became unconscious from lack of oxygen but was also in danger of exploding from lack of external pressure in the vacuum. Another salvo landed on the ship and several shots came close to the rescue craft, one fracturing the front window.

Benson roared,

"Open the bay we are coming in fast and backwards"

The module crash landed rear first into the open space while still holding the Everina aloft. The doors slammed closed and air automatically flowed into the area. There was a shudder as another blade shot hit home. A dozen medics and emergency crew poured in and she was laid on stretchers. CPR was given and slowly she began to breath. Hiroshi held Everina's hand and said,

"Larry can't be here as you know he is flying the ship right now."

Everina smiled and rubbed away masses of foam that was still clinging to their faces and uniforms. This was the foam that had inadvertently saved her life. It had kept her from expanding to death. Yet she had received burn marks on her arms and legs where her RP suit was torn. The medics gently carried her away for examination.

The radio squeeked. It was Larry,

"Benson, how is she?" Hiroshi replied,

"A'okay, breathing, covered in scratches but intact and heading to sick bay. Oh did you notice our blue and pink has disappeared!"

Suddenly a mass of black particles streamed past the ship from every direction. In that moment, each blade became covered in seething material obscuring all their vision. The lead ship swerved and hit another further back in the line. Chunks of de-material bounced over the Callisto and a demon was seen spinning away. Richard noticed that a piece of his cloak was missing!

Mantz shouted triumphantly,

"See they are vulnerable to atomic corrosion and anti-matter is also annihilating them!"

Then chaos set in with Blades spinning in every direction as they were systematically crushed out of existence. There was a hideous screech and then silence.

Dave said to Larry,

"Well done, take five, and go to the sick bay. Also see how Lionel is doing!"

Larry headed down and on the way passed Laura already feeding Kiki with bird seed and boiled egg. He met Richard in the corridor and thanked him for being such a friend. Richard had now recovered apart from a few scratches. Larry arrived at the sick bay and found Lionel was under sedation but off the critical list. Finally he got to Everina just as she emerged showered and dressed in a fresh uniform. The medic passed by, winked to Larry and said,

"She will be just fine, just pulled a few gashes and ligaments. Hourly stretching will be needed – plenty of ointments and of course some TLC."

Everina said,

"Well done Larry, your as brown as a sheet once again and is the Callisto still on course?"

Larry nodded and threw his arms around her,

"Well done Eve. You have been in combat at last. Thank God Richard grabbed you. I hope you thanked him and the boys for what they did? "

"Of course Larry I did all that." Larry took a deep breath,

"Yes my little Mexican, now that I am not on duty, may I ask you a personnel question?"

No one was listening so he went ahead.

"Now that you are also back to your old colour, I want to marry you. Will you marry me Lieutenant Everina Spazola?"

Everina smiled and answered teasingly,

"I'll ask my Doctor for advice!"

Larry let out his breath; he was quite used to that treatment by now.

Then she stood up abruptly, took a crutch and said,

"Something more important has occurred to me - what about your Excalibur did it shrink, or will it remain big and destroy us - as we shrink?"

Larry had forgotten about that possibility. His face turned serious. With the thoughts of marriage forgotten, he made his way to the sleeping quarters at high speed while Everina came hobbling behind. Was the ship shrinking around his mighty sword? Would it perforated the structure and cast them into space?

Cautiously he peeped at his cubicle and to his relief the hybo was intact – no damage in evidence. He opened the lock and slowly drew the cover. There was the impression of a sword on the bed, but no sword. Everina arrived. Larry gasped but then slowly slid down his hand feeling the indentation. He felt metallic contours – his sword was there!

"It must have turned invisible at re-version. How do you think it managed to shrink yet remain intact?"

Everina replied after some thought,

"The only bit I can guess is that it shrank because it was within the ship. It obeyed the environment and diminished with us."

Larry muttered,

"God is oh so clever - they knew all this."

Then he smiled and closed the hybo and very carefully turned the lock shut.

An assistant navigator was now covering for Lionel. The EM/SPEC indicated that they had slowed considerably and were travelling at a fraction short of the relative speed of light. Then to everyone's joy, it indicated that the time was exactly the same as at their entry over two weeks ago. There was also a concern that when reach the neck of the umbilical they might get caught in the flow from the other tunnel and pulled out again - to repeat the circle in a state of eternal return. To combat this, Vice Captain Laura suggested again jettisoning any other unnecessary items and applying sharp turn to Starboard. Then using maximum velocity coupled with boosters to travel along the parameter of light threshold till out of harms way. A brave person who shall remain nameless jested,

"There goes Kiki."

All around them, the sky was still curved but seemed to be widening. Up ahead they now could see the familiar interior of the universe. Ernst gave the turbines everything he could and applied the booster rockets as suggested. As the world opened before them and the floating galaxies of their world appeared they turned sharp to Starboard as planned. This proved to be correct judgment and for a short time they enjoyed a spectacular view travelling sideways across the inside of the threshold of expanding light - perhaps the skin of the universe! From the inside it looked like green cellophane paper, full of creases and pulls, irregular and ever changing – quite a sight!

After an hour Dave ordered an alteration of direction which turned the Callisto towards the centre of the Cosmos. As the cooks had their food products irradiated they were soon able to begin producing freshly prepared bacon and eggs. There was consternation when some of the eggs were found to have their yoke on the outside, inversion did not suit them! Then the galley hands turned on music and very soon an irresistible aroma seeped around the ship. Hunger pangs had returned and soon shifts of crew and scientists some wearing bandages and slings began to line up for a good old earth style tuck in.

Don Travis asked if he could speak on the intercom. Laura nodded permission. He delivered the following,

"Let us give thanks to the Lord who is both, Jehovah, Mohammed, Father and the Son, for they have delivered us through the valley of evil. Also to the spirit that was given us, so we might succeed."

Then he quoted from Revelation 1.5-8

"Look! He is coming in the clouds, every eye will see him, even those who pierced him; and on his account all the tribes of earth will lament. So it is to be. Amen.' I am the Alpha and the Omega,' says the Lord God, who is and who was and who is to come, the Almighty."

He concluded with,

"Therefore honour Him and pray for those in Purgosia, they are relying on our support, however, I know I'm preaching to the converted."

Chapter 71

The Captain called a meeting of all senior personnel; RP suits no longer a necessity. It was in their conference room, the room with the cage that now had Kiki in residence. People had also discovered their woollies were had returned. However the meeting proved to be tedious because of the amount of detail that had to be checked. It involved reports by technical services on the fitness of Callisto, damage reports on various parts of the ship, an in-depth study of navigation charts and finally issuing instructions that all people in the ship were to write a report on events. Qualifying notes were later to be prepared where necessary. It was expected that there will be a suspicion that the crew had hallucinated but if their stories coincided there was a chance that the truth would prevail. They had to complete the charting that they had begun originally and could use photo reconnaissance obtained from the EM/SPEC.

Then Mantz asked how soon could they recommence a sky search for Hydrogen based galaxies, but before he could receive a reply the meeting was interrupted by a petty officer that brought in a report as follows;

"Velocity- 225,0000 k per sec, reducing. Now find Completion of Global Symmetry Transfer. Magnitude reduced to pre departure level. Time now altered to Anti Clockwise Arrow direction x c³ brane arc rotation. Temperature- rising from -273 o Kelvin- Phase Transition now finished. Force field now Electromagnetic, (inverse square laws now in effect)

Density - Photon abundance, Purity of inflow -100% clarity, Content Hydrogen and Neutrinos and Muons Alternative effects,- Weak Force W+, W-, Z o and Gravitation, - Gravitons. Background Radiation - 91% active but reducing. Energy - 10/16 1 TeV."

Quang Chow who was beside Dave got to read it first and jubilantly said,

"Radiation 91% and that's down nine points and still dropping, All that liquid in the waves must have protected us. Also the spectrum has recorded enormous background radiation, louder than anything ever encountered. Now let's hope that these records will convince EUSARUS about our discovery."

The word EUSARUS sent a chill down Larry's spine. He realised that this was the authority that could prove to be a legal quagmire into which all the crew would fall. It was good that Hiroshi had not remained in Purgosia, as that would have caused immense problems. There was enough difficulty already created with Ham, Rap and Dalia's disappearance. Then Larry was asked to report on the physics aspect of the events to date. However, he was not in a mood to try and broach such a broad subject in this way. There was just too much knowledge accumulated to be dismissed in one report. Therefore he pointed out,

"There was no hard physics in that alternate dimension except for the Praque examples that we have. Our reports will appear speculative despite being based on strong probabilities and corroborated by eyewitnesses. However in addition to that I would request that Don Travis write a report on the metaphysical aspects to concur with ours."

He then said,

"Furthermore physicists should have to read one another's reports because they are contingent to the story. I am also interested to see what Mantz and Dr Burnette has to say about Hiroshi's fall in and out of death!"

Mantz scowled and said that there is no physical evidence of Hiroshi ever having died in the first place. Therefore it was almost a non event and need never be mentioned.

Dave agreed with Larry's requests and then opened his log. He read transcripts of the last report they sent to EUSARUSS. It had asked for assistance as they were being drawn towards an unknown source. They had in another message asked for a personal profile for Hamish and Raphael and in both cases received no reply though they had visual confirmation that the authorities received the messages. He would like an explanation. To this everyone agreed. He then suggested,

"There is almost no doubt that they will conclude that we had been destroyed by a Black Hole. Therefore the story will probably go along the lines that we managed to survive such an encounter. You see if we say 'Fifth Dimension' they will say 'Black Hole' and if we report 'Omega' they will say 'Singularity' – the same thing! There will be no way that they will either believe or attempt to believe what we report. So what I am saying is just call it a Black Hole experience and I will deal with the loss of the three-crew members. Okay! I am also please to say that Lionel has recovered and ready to resume his duties!"

There was applause and then Dave said,

"Is there any other business?"

Chapter 72

Almost everyone who was not on duty went to rest in his or her Hybos. Larry did the same and slipped into a blissfully slumber. In this state he found that there was a similarity between his dreams and earthly experiences. An example of this was the dream about an incident where someone fired a gun. He saw the flash and ducked, but only then there came the sound which in turn woke him up. To his surprise as he opened his eyes, he heard that same sound but it was a cook dropping a dish in the galley. Very Strange but it almost proves that the fluid in my nervous system moves faster than light relative to ones size!

Soon he was awakened by the beeping of a timer in the hybo. This was followed by gentle music that became louder and quickened in pace. He checked that his sword was still intact and then went to the wash room, shaved and pulled on a pair of shorts and a dark blue T-shirt with east coast surf club written in white. As he made his way to the main concourse he noted that the business as usual attitude had set in. Orange Juice, Coffee and Danish pastries were back on the menu. For Larry it was going to be a busy day. Hiroshi joined and said there had been strange lights in the sky. Larry rolled his eyes up wards and mumbled,

"That's all I need."

Just then the navigator announced that a strange unidentified object was moving in an erratic course up ahead. Hiroshi said,

"There Lar, I told you so!"

A bright disc could now be seen dancing through the stars. As it did so, it seemed to get closer to the ship. Then as if it could see them it closed in at enormous speed. There was no time for evasive action. They were at the mercy of the moment. It looked like a massive UFO was about to ram them. Then the disk covered the ship. The interior became phosphorous white. People felt like they were back in eternity. Everina who had joined them gripped the table, but the expected impact did not occur. There was no explosion or crash; all that happened was the experience of incredible brightness. People once again looked transparent round the edges and everyone gasped as a feeling of lightness overtook them. Everina whispered,

"It's like a return to paradise."

Then the light went out! The disc did not move away it just turned off! They were plunged back to their reality. Then Dave spoke,

"This was not a UFO it's a beam from Omega searching our progress. Evidently the report was satisfactory."

Just then the navigator interrupted,

"Sir, unless I'm wrong, this SPEC shows that we are not where we think we are, we have just been pushed to within sight of our Galaxy!"

Quite excitedly, people gathered around the windows. There in front, lay the great sprawling shape that shone so bright that its light began to penetrate the ship. It was the shape of a traditional fried egg sunny side up. It was pale off white around the edges and hilariously gold or yellow in the central zone. Someone yelled; hip, hip and a cheer came in reply.

Hiroshi grunted,

"I'll cheer when we see the Pacific."

And Larry said,

"It is an Awesome God it is!"

Chapter 73

It took about three months to accomplish entry, starting from the time it first appeared on the horizon to the time the Callisto penetrated its outer limits. During this time Hiroshi did a lot of paintings that depicted every aspect of the trip. He did not have to hide away to perform his artistry; the Captain had no intension of hindering him after all they had gone through. He made copies of his Mandala and of Kuhn's Mural and as a tribute; Travis took one of each for display in the ship's oratory. The physicists were continuously taking photos and recordings of all sorts from every object in their sights.

Once inside their Galaxy, time seemed to pass quickly and soon they were in the solar system. After that they passed several uncharted tiny planets that rotated around each other as they tumbled along. These would be almost the loneliest objects in creation. Then as they came near Uranus contact with earth was re-established.

Jean told the group that it was now time to reset the clocks. On estimating the position of the planets and their movement since departure, they estimated that it was now one and a half years and a few days, since they had departed. Slowly the scene outside became filled with light. Jupiter with its moons winked in the distance, as Io and above all, Callisto came into sight. The Captain arranged for the laser to be fired and all lights out for one minute in recognition of their namesake.

Soon after that it happened, Richard was awake and pouring over physics notes. He was within earshot of the controller and heard his voice receiver suddenly crack into life. There was a sound of static and then the distinct sound of a human voice.

"This is EUSARUSS at Fobos station, zero one seven, please respond and identify yourself?"

Then he began to relay the same message in Arabic, Russian, French and so on. Dave was called, but it was Laura that arrived first. She cut short the broadcast by saying,

"This is Callisto, I repeat this is Callisto C110500/ UM -171. We are returning from extreme mission, code zero, zero, niner, niner, zero, five, one over."

In an instant the main concourse filled with people, it was amazing how quickly they had heard about the contact. Richard awakened Larry and the others and was just in time to hear the reply,

"Well I'll be god' darn, we thought you were goners, now please reconfirm what you said, over!"

The Captain emerged and listened to Laura make the official reply with tears streaming down her cheeks. Everina had her hand over her face and was sitting in a seat with her sides shaking. She was shaking so badly it seemed she was out of control. Larry consoled her but in doing so shed a tear himself. He had forgotten that he had a Mom and a Dad or that there was such a place as home.

From that moment onwards, there was no more peace on board the Callisto. Gone was the delicious boredom, with its long periods of contemplation. There was no time for people to 'Hit the Hybo'. The ship's crew had become celebrities as the S-mail came back on line. The closer they got to earth the more intense it became. At first the Captain had to relate what had happened directly by coded message to the EUSARUSS central command.

He related the bare facts, keeping in mind what could be substantiated by the crews' reports. In fact the crew had included everything down to the last demon. However, he said that the explanation of the events would be down to the scientific team who would make their reports when they get back to base.

Then he had to explain about the missing crew. This was a difficult situation to iterate. He did so by naming the witnesses who saw their self-chosen departure, and that included Larry and Richard who produced the torn piece of the invaders cape that had been caught in the door of the Callisto.

Despite all the secrecy the media got wind of the story and glamorized it about the missing crew and the heroic battles fought in distant places. This side of it took root when the ships scientists and physicists were linked up with national geographic and every science TV show on the planet. Some of the wise one's refused interviews and that way were saved grueling questions. Larry could not refuse because he was instructed to report.

Everina and several of the other female cadets became icons of their gender. Word had it that women's magazines ran stories about them and how their supposedly delicate bodies coped with the massive changes. They were asked if they experienced any romantic feelings while in the next dimension. They surprised each other by admitting they did. However, Hiroshi's experiences were shrouded from the media because his accident was classified information and the matter of Jill was very private.

The last month was filled with photographing planets, making measurements of light refraction and writing up reports. The intercoms became jammed with earth music news flashes and sports reports. The STV also showed all the "razzmatazz" that goes on earth including programs on global catastrophes. When Jules Verne's 'From the Earth to the Moon' was shown it drew a large audience as did a 1960's movie 'The Fantastic Voyage'.

Everina and Larry now began to find time to get to know each other better, because they were in a more relaxed and normal environment. They spent their off time sitting in their favourite rear window seat, gazing at the retreating stars and talking about the future. It was then that Larry leaned over and kissed her ear and whispered,

"Ev, do you remember I asked you to marry me and you have not replied. Do you believe in marriage?"

She turned and looked him with her large brown eyes and replied,

"No, Larry not at all."

"Would you agree then to share our lives?" He asked in dismay.

A broad smile lit up her face,

"Larry whatever we do, it's for ever!"

The Captain said that personal calls to families would now be permitted. This created some real excitement. Finally Larry got to see his parents on a flickering screen and to speak with them,

"Hi Mom it's me Larry, alive and well. How are you and Dad, and Amy and Jill, did you think we were lost for ever?"

"Larry" his mother cried, "Oh! Larry." She said this with tears in her eyes.

"Thank God you are safe and well, we all send our love and look forward to having you. Here is Dan, here Dan say Hello."

"Larry my boy, only for your mom's prayers you would not be back safe, so thank her. Now tell me did you have a great experience. We are looking forward to hearing everything when you get back- a big shin dig will be arranged."

Marie then added

"Amy and Jill sent their love and they will be here to see you on your return. How is Hiroshi, I dreamed he had an accident I hope that's not true."

Larry responded,

"No Mom, Hiroshi is okay there were no accidents. There will be a big delay so I will see you all in about six weeks, Chow!"

With that the name of the next caller came up on the screen and Larry's folks faded from sight. He felt a wave of emotion and thought that his parents looked like they had aged. Perhaps it was because they had thought he was lost forever. He wished he could have got hold of Jill and asked her if she had a 'steady'. He knew poor Hiroshi would not be able to ask the question. Therefore he wrote a letter to Jill on the S Mail. In it he said how much Hiroshi liked her and that she should include him on her "hit list". He received a reply that went like this,

"Dearest Larry, Glad to know you are fit and well, but sorry to hear that you are back giving me big brother advice. However, in view of the fact that Hiroshi is now a celebrity and that you are a pain in the butt, I have written him a message of encouragement. This is secret information, do not divulge. Amy sends her love, me also. Lv Sis."

About ten minutes later, Hiroshi hastened to Larry and said with a broad grin on his face,

"Larry, what do you know I got a letter from Jill, and it turns out she is a free agent? I've made a long distance date with her to occur when I get back, what you think of that!"

Larry clapped him on the back and said,

"You did splendid work brother in law! You are a 'win win' winner. If you pull this one off, you will have Jill both here and in Purgosia."

Then there was no more said about the matter. They both went their ways each one puzzled because now Purgosia sounded so very far off and also quite surreal!

Mantz came to Larry with an idea. He asked

"Larry, can I see you in private for a moment."

When they were out of earshot he spoke,

"I've been doing my home work and I've come up with ten people, as well as you and I, who would be prepared to form committee. I believe there is a strong desire in people to do something as a result of our experiences. We could be named of apostles of a second coming or cosmic Christians or something of that order.

We would be a steering committee for a greater movement that might in time improve world order also as a symbol we might use your Excalibur as our motif. What do you think? Larry was quite taken aback but the idea was not entirely new and had been kicked around earlier in the trip. He reacted positively.

"Yes, Casper, that's one hell of an idea. The implications are huge. Do you think we could co-ordinate such a group?"

Mantz responded,

"Of course, today there is almost instant communications availability. Some of our people are already in influential circles and furthermore to begin with, we are all celebrities!"

Larry questioned,

"Who will be interested in the venture?"

Mantz quoted a dozen names and Larry added a few more that were possible. Shortly after this, with the Captain's permission the group met in the conference room to have a primary discussion. There were suggestions of widening the membership to include almost everyone in the ship, but this was rejected. The idea was that it should be left to a steering committee. To become over zealous would not be a wise course of action. It would be better for people to join when the hype has subsided and when people have faced the hard facts of life back on earth. They established a charter, a set of basic goals. They decided to announce their existence with a paper on the subject and later a book in which each one was to write a chapter. The book might be called 'The Apotheosise of the Human Race' or something about a Republic being in Paradise. To this there was a laugh.

Chapter 74

When the ship docked at the space platform, they got a muted welcome from the crew who did know whether they were heroes or villains. Then they were shuttled to earth in batches, just as they had come up. They were next put into quarantine as was to be expected. Then they were taken daily for questioning and eventually debriefing. The process went on for several weeks, during which time Dave's story was checked and rechecked. The invisible tie pins and broaches were collected for examination. Then Larry surrendered his Excalibur so as to demonstrate that they did have an extra-universal encounter. Dave drew up a document for Larry to have signed by the authorities - that it must be returned after examinations or within twelve months at maximum duration.

Larry therefore surrendered his precious gift. Needless to say it caused a scientific furore but did have the effect of vindicating their reports. The awful consequences of the whole thing were that Ham, Rap and Dalia's families pressed claims for damages because of the loss of their closest. The legal professionals had a difficulty. They had no precedent set law and also there weren't any body's in evidence. It soon became clear that this was a case that would come back, time and time again, to haunt all concerned. However, Dave felt that the administration had enough witness reports to work on and thus got on with his life.

When the interrogations were all but over, there was a civic reception in the luxurious Port Canaveral Hotel that was attended by EUSARUSS representatives, the Governor of Florida the press and famous people from the worlds of science, physics, anthropology and philosophy. Everina looked stunning as she was wearing a delightful midnight blue dress. Larry who was naturally with her, said hesitantly,

"Ev, you look radiant, did I see that lovely dress before?"

She gave him her best Mexicali smile winked and said,

"Yes you did, but no more about that, now let's socialize."

Larry was flabbergasted yet again!

George Kuhn arrived though uninvited causing a small uproar when refused entry. Richard came to his rescue and the old warrior was immediately permitted through. George it seems had gathered more information about what had been happening then anyone so far. He said to Richard and a group of the crew,

"Look fella's. I'll put it this way. The confidential reports remained confidential for a few days, until they were hacked by a kid from Delaware on the Internet. Then the media and the science journals took over, and most have stated that there is enough proof to confirm that the Callisto and crew did move into some other dimension. There is no question of hallucinations or any of that junk. One or two of the reports said that one of the crew died on the way out, but was revived on the way back. This caused a stir but not as much as the missing crew members. Then three subversives were supposed to have been sucked out a door that was not properly locked, true in a sense! In all it seems that scientists see your trip as an affirmation of the Trinity College Simulation!"

Directly after that, Hiroshi went to see his parent in Japan, Richard returned to Clearwater. Everina had a scheduled stop at Pensacola to visit her Cadet College and then she intended flying home to Albuquerque to see her parents. Larry then insisted that he book her on a later flight to Ireland so she could spend Christmas with him and meet his family proper. She was delighted with the offer and agreed. She said he would have to also meet her folks as soon as possible. Then they all said goodbye to one another and of course to Kiki who was now safe and sound in her gilded cage and in the capable hands of Laura her faithful mentor.

Chapter 75

As it was the festive season so her flight Albuquerque, New York, Shannon, Dublin got diverted and she was re routed through London. As they came in to land she saw Big Ben, the house of commons and the ever winding river Themes. From the Airport she phoned Laura Bingley and said a quick hello. Laura told her that she was living near Chelsea where in summer she enjoys their magnificent garden show. Everina said she would make that a must for the not to distant future but then had to go. As she flew into Ireland she really felt she was visiting an Island. Suddenly the world seemed to shrink and things became infinitely simplified.

She thought it was nice to see the word 'Christmas' was alive and well and living in Dublin. She was used to 'Happy Holidays' and was fed up with a world of so called equality and insurance laden bureaucracy where it was unfashionable to be human. She detested the efforts that world systems to pasteurise human input and replace it with machine terminology. She therefore took the opportunity to shout out at every opportunity,

"Merry Christmas, Merry Christmas!"

It was now the fourteenth of December and Larry met her at arrivals. She could not wait for the moment, and so they both embraced blinded by a frenzy of love and affection.

"Larry I cannot believe I am here with you!" she sobbed. Larry who wore a down filled jacket and a trinity college scarf looked quite different from the swaggering space cowboy that he really was. She was also less noticeable in her long black coat and wool hat to match. Larry was carrying a long leather case strung over his shoulder and she knew what it contained.

Everina chirped,

"Hey Larry, that case looks like you'r packin'a shootin' iron. Why you have now become my Mafia Man!"

Larry chuckled.

It was his sword returned earlier than expected. He clutched it so tight that no one would be able to prize it from his possession. He drove into town and left his car on the third floor of a central parkade. It was late afternoon and fashionable Grafton Street was a hive of activity. Being mid winter it was already dark; the Christmas lighting was aglow. People were dressed in all sorts of muffled gear to protect from the chill and this added to the festive atmosphere.

The two space veterans ambled slowly up the street and wandered into the well known Brown Thomas's department store. Then they visited an art shop and then went to Weirs and Sons, intending to buy a wedding ring. They both hoped to be able to show Larry's parents the ring when they meet to celebrate Christmas. Everina was in a happy frame of mind, enchanted with the warm friendliness of all those she had met.

She eventually selected a pink De Beers cut diamond ring, but only just in time before the shop closed. Then out of a sense of gratitude; Larry took her to St Teresa's church in Clarendon Street which lay close by. Inside there was a crib with statues of Joseph and Mary just before the birth of Christ. They both knelt down and tried to concentrate. It was very difficult as it was the first time they had reflected on Paradise since leaving the void. There was a Star of David, painted on the background - something they now both understood from a very different prospective. It was amazing to look at a statue of Mary or Miriam that enchanting woman that they knew so well. No one would ever believe where they had been, and that they knew exactly where their prayers would go and who would do the processing. Though they knew Miriam so very well her face remained intransigent. The features remained wooden and she just stared straight ahead. Larry knew what Everina was thinking and therefore whispered in her ear,

"Don't worry she can, I repeat, she can hear you."

Everina turned, no one was looking and so she stretched out her hand showing the engagement ring for Miriam to see. Then quite sure that the joyous information had been conveyed she withdrew her arm and they both bowed and departed.

They then went into one of the thronging pubs for which Dublin is famous. Larry ordered Irish coffees and they both peered out the window, which was partly obscured with a Christmas decorations. Outside there were florists as usual selling fresh plants form Holand, a Santa Clause collecting for a national charity, and an eastern European emigrant playing the most romantic accordion music Everina had ever heard? She was immensely happy and content she was once again in seventh heaven. Larry was curious, as to her opinion of the city and asked,

"Eve' what do you think of Dublin?" and she replied,

"Larry its arcadia, its 'fab' and I love it, maybe it's this Irish coffee that did the trick!"

She gave him a fetching Mexican smile and took another sip. Larry's cell phone jingled, Meli keliki maca. It was home asking what time they would arrive?

Chapter 76

They took the Luas light rail transport to the suburbs and arrived at Larry's home. His parents and Amy were overjoyed to meet Everina as they thought, for the first time! Maria threw her arms around Everina and congratulated her while admiring her ring. Though Everina had already met the Coughlin's up above and knew them quite well, she kept this to herself, till she found out if Larry was going to broach that subject. Amy was delighted with the load of brightly wrapped gifts that they brought for under the tree when erected. Her first question was had they seen Santa when in space?

Everina took the initiative,

"We were in Santa's city. We discovered there are at least three Santa's with lovely white fur trimmed suits. The first one is clothed in Gold and that is Father Christmas, and the next wears Red and that is the Santa Clause that we already know about. Then there is a magnificent person named Spirinda the one that makes Christmas so crisp and frosty. She wears blue and is covered in a haze and is topped with a crown of silver that sparks. Her smile lifts your spirits no matter how low one feels."

Amy's eyes were wide with interest.

"Lastly there was a little green elf that understands how the children on earth really think and what they love, and it advises the Santa's what toys to make."

Amy's eyes lit up even more, she was flabbergasted. She just gasped and then laughed excitedly and added,

"Oh they must be so beautiful. I would love to meet the Spirinda best of all."

She immediately took her crayons and began to draw pictures inspired by what Everina had described.

Maria took Larry and Everina by the arms and escorted them to the table. She had prepared a welcome dinner over which they stayed talking for hours about all that had happened above and beyond. Now needless to say, Larry did not know how to say that they all had met but as the evening wore on by being pressed for more and more information, he eventually came out with the full story.

As he related what happened in Purgosia, their parent's eyes opened wide. The reports they had got were obviously censored and the story had been quite distorted. They were afraid at first to hear about their own futures, because it seemed to be against nature. However, when they were told that they all would end up united in Purgosia they seemed quite relieved. Jill asked how Hiroshi had managed and did he meet her up there? Larry said that he did but tried to keep the information as scant as possible and he did not tell of the wedding. Larry reframed from telling Dan about his own passing as there was always a random possibility that things might turn out differently. However, he did say,

"Look it will be worth your getting a medical. We want you to die of old age, sitting with a physics book in one hand and a glass of Jameson in the other!

Maria cut in,

"I think it is so reassuring that you saw us in Purgosia, that is that we were together and with friends, and looking forward to something further. I hope it was not just a dream."

Everina spoke,

"Oh no Mrs. Coughlin, I mean Maria. There was no way it could have been a dream. We had all our machinery running and recording and the EUSARUS people have accepted that we did fly into an alternative dimension. The great thing about it is that all of our reports coincided."

Then Maria said as an after thought,

"Did you get to visit White Friars Street Church? You know that is where St Valentine is buried. I bet you met him beyond."

Everina and Larry began to think back. Then Everina remembered,

"Larry it was Valentino one of the pilots."

Maria asked where will they live in future to this Larry said,

"We hope for a house on the north shore of Oahu and the other near work in Florida. As you know we both work on projects that last for a month at a time and then we have long free spells and our travel is free."

Everina was nodding in agreement and Dan was looking forward to visiting in the future. They all agreed to turn in for the night because tomorrow they will go to Traghmahon. Hiroshi should arrive from Japan, Jill will arrive from Germany, Father Pat will be back from Florida and will stop over. Larry reckoned that it would be like old times.

Traghmahon when translated means Mahon's strand. In winter it is not quite so pretty as in summer. Nevertheless, it has a rugged beauty of its own. The bracken on the headland was now quite brown and the bay looked grey, as did the sky. Christmas was a sort of indoor time of the year; hence the dull weather did not matter in the least. Amy and Everina took it on themselves to untie the Christmas tree from the top of the car and to drag it in to the living room. Larry erected it in a wooden barrel. Everina then presented Amy with a Piñata all the way from New Mexico. It was so heavy that it almost unbalanced the tree so they hung it from a wall bracket. It was not long before they had everything in its designated place and settled down to have a nice time.

Chapter 77

The following morning, Dan awoke to the sound of waves rumbling on the shore. He heard a door close, so he got up from bed to see who it was. As he passed Larry's room, the door was open and he saw that Larry was gone surfing. He quickly slipped into his own wet suite and waxed up his seven foot nine inch board and followed Larry to the beach. Larry was poised looking out to sea. He was wearing a full wet suite and helmet and was amazed to see Dan out in the cold. He had begun to think of Dan as having one foot in the grave. This act of self-sacrifice reminded Larry that his Dad was still in the firing line. Together they began to catch wave after wave, paddling and taking off mostly to the left, climbing and dropping and whooping and hollering. Then long shafts of winter sun burst forth. The khaki ocean contrasted with the dazzling light and whiteness of the icy spray. Then the sky became bright blue in patches and what had began as a frosty task was now a warm pleasure. Larry looked out to sea; he wondered if that wave called Gasper would reappear? He hoped not. Then he thought about the world above and his own angel guardian that he still had not met. Amazingly a tear came to his eye, because they were now also his family and he was not with them, and would not be so, for some time to come.

Dan was delighted that the waves were not too large enjoyed every last moment of the experience. He also knew it was a rare occasion and that he might not have another chance to share a wave with Larry again. It was time to go in. Dan's last wave was a well-shaped wall that dictated a ride once again to the left. He whipped across it climbing and dropping in rapid succession, just like he was a new kid on the block.

The following day Hiroshi arrived. He had rented car and was tired from the long journey on twisted West Cork roads. Following his arrival there was much excitement but when things settled down he said to Jill.

"I would like to go to an Irish Pub, will you come with me? It will be just for one drink and back within an hour."

Jill showed lines on her forehead, but slowly nodded and then winked. They drove to the maritime style village of Crookhaven. In the midst of moored sailing boats they entered a neat hostelry called O'Sullivan and ordered two glasses of Murphy's Stout. Hiroshi made sure to seat her out of earshot of others. For some time they both sat in awkward silence listening to the lanyard on the boats clanking on the empty masts and the wail of seagulls in the breeze. Then Jill asked,

"Did you meet me in Purgosia?

Hiroshi was caught off guard. But mustered up a confident,

"Why yes Jill I did."

"Did you like Purgosia Jill?"

Hiroshi could take no more, began his announcement,

"Jill this may be a surprise but I am really crazy about you the same Jill that is right here with me now."

Just then the drinks arrived. Hiroshi paid took up his glass and said,

"Slante" and took a sip. Jill responded with a wide-eyed expression as if she had not known. Then he took another sip leaving a streak of white foam on his lip and blustered,

"Look after what I have been through I realise that you are the only person in this word for me so Jill will you marry me?"

Jill reacted with smooth adjustment to the unexpected development. She did not expect for him to go that far or so quickly. Firstly she smiled and then reached out and took his hand and squeezed it. Then she asked would he be prepared to live with her in Ireland or would he insist that they move to Japan or Saipan or what ever? Like a true cavalier Hiroshi said he would marry her and live anywhere. Jill laughed and said that she was only trying him out because if she married him she would go wherever he wanted, but she will still have to consider!

Hiroshi looked relieved and began to tell her about his experiences but never mentioning their metaphysical wedding. As he told her the rest of the story she was transfixed in amazement. For the whole time he spoke she held one hand to her chin and did not even dare ask a question. However she asked why he did not go to the Omega and Hiroshi said he would answer that question later. Time went quickly and almost an hour later he finished his story and sat back.

"Now Jill after that story will you still consider my marriage offer?"

Jill laughed and nodded, sure it just means I might be marrying a Saint?

Jill went to the wash room and Hiroshi picked up an old newspaper that was clamped on a stick and had been around a long time. His eyes focused on a small two inch report that said,

"Children of Peruvian Ambassador killed in car accident."

The article mentioned their names – Janette and Rico Mendoza five and six years of age."

Hiroshi gaped in horror. He recoiled and could not read any more. Then peace came over him, after all he knew how happily united they were or will be and that made it all acceptable. He thought why is it while we will have a happy ending never the less in the mean time it is so hard to take! He tore out the tiny square of paper and took it with him. Jill returned and said with some concern,

"Hiroshi what happened, you look white?"

Jill my dear it's just me facing up to possibly some new responsibilities."

They both laughed and headed back to the house just in time for the arrival of Father Paddy from Elkton. On Christmas day itself, there were visits to neighbors and in return others who called to see them. It took till about 5pm before they managed to sit down to celebrate. After dinner they opened some remaining gifts, and then they all went for a long walk across the hills and back by the beach. Hiroshi and Jill were straggling behind the others. It was then that Jill declared,

"Yes, Hiroshi, I will!" Hiroshi rapidly responded "You will what?"

"Marry you," she said with conviction.

Hiroshi let out a hoot of delight. It was so shrill that it sent a swarm of birds circling in the air as if a salute to his cause. He picked up Jill and whirled her around several times and they both ran after the others to break the news.

Several nights later; when all the celebrating was done and peace descended on the household a winter storm hit. Everina asked Larry to bring in his sword for all to experience its radiance. Reluctantly he laid the case on the floor in front of the fire and slowly opened it. Jill reached forward and let out a squeak as she felt the invisible texture.

"Ouch this is amazing, what's it worth Larry"?

Larry shot back,

"Not for sale, never will be and anyway it's priceless. I will have to donate it to science!"

By the embers of the fire the sleek outline of the masterpiece could be seen a little more clearly than in any other light. It seemed to emit a glow and to generate a sense of calm and peace that engulfed the audience. Then Larry reverently closed the container and put the Excalibur away.

Hiroshi struck up a conversation. The fire was low and as he gazed into the embers, he looked up at his friends and said,

"I wonder where all this will lead us? Apart from marital bliss I see trouble ahead because we have been endowed with awesome knowledge. What do you all think?" Everyone murmured but no one replied. Then in silence they all stared into the embers each one immersed in thought!

As the embers died a fire sprung up in another part of the world. Somewhere in Eastern Europe, a young man with a passionate heart looked up at the sky and cried out loud,

"I do not care what I must do or who I must walk on or kill, but I must find my Father. I will find him no matter where he is in the great blackness. I detest those who caused his loss, Raphael, I must find you! "

APPENDIX

This is Dan's Theory of Tritivity - a Grand Genealogy of Everything.

This is a coming together of the particle and metaphysical worlds.

ColourDivinity Void Forces in NatureAtomic levelGender
GoldPrime PendulumGravity NeutronNeutrality/Faith
MaroonSecondUpper Triangle Strong Nuclear Proton Masculinity/Hope
BlueThird . Lower TriangleElectromagnetic Electron Feminine/Charity
Green Fourth!Universe Weak Nuclear (Potential)(Potential Gender)

Some Common physics and Scientific Denominators of threes and fours;

*There are **three** parts to an atom-Proton, Neutron and Electron.

*There are **three** quarks in Proton and a Neutron.

*Electricity in a domestic plug has **three** wires, positive, negative and earthed.

*Christian belief in Faith, Hope and Charity – The **Trinity** and **three** wise Kings.

*There are **three** primary paint colours, red, yellow and blue.

*There are **three** light analogies of colour and **three** anti colours.

*There are **four** essences of nature, Earth, Fire, Water and Air.

*There are **three** forces of nature plus the weak nuclear, that's **four.**

*There are **three** dimensions in our universe plus time, that's **four**.

*Mathematics has **four** disciplines, Platonism, Conceptualization, Formalism and Intuitionism.

*There are **four** stages in the fractal generation of a Koch curve.

Time and Time Again;

The theory of Trinitivity states that the universe is in a state of continuous destruction and construction. (Much like the philosophy of Anaximander).

The destruction is the result of deceleration caused by repulsion and chaos in the void. Construction is the result of a rotation extending from the interior of the strong nuclear force. Every (Fermion) particle rotates in and out of existence. It instantly leaves increasing speed accordingly. Then when out it is energized by the strong nuclear triangle and returns at a velocity three times the speed of light (c3.) In effect each particle has returned before it departs creating a ghost like quantum trail. The universe is thus contiguous and unstable while a true continuum is only found within the two higher stratums. A possible equation for this extravaganza might be as follows:

$$T= \frac{MD}{C^3}$$

T = Time. M = Mass. D = Distance. C = Speed of light in a vacuum.
Here Local Time is equal to Mass b Distance over Light Cubed.
If this equation works you might never know because you just end up with reality!
For time travelled in space substitute" G" for " D" (G =The constant of gravitation).

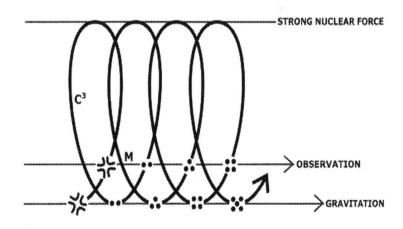

Rotating time propagates mass with every cycle. The explosion marks
indicate where reality becomes observable to an onlooker within that same
system

Printed in the United States
by Baker & Taylor Publisher Services